Bridging the Gap

Bridging the Gap

Raising a Child with Nonverbal Learning Disorder

RONDALYN VARNEY WHITNEY,
MOT, OTR

A Perigee Book

A Perigee Book
Published by The Berkley Publishing Group
A division of Penguin Putnam Inc.
375 Hudson Street
New York, New York 10014

First edition: April 2002

Published simultaneously in Canada.

Visit our website at www.penguinputnam.com

Library of Congress Cataloging-in-Publication Data

Whitney, Rondalyn V.
Bridging the gap : raising a child with
nonverbal learning disorder / Rondalyn V. Whitney.
p.   cm.
Includes index.
ISBN 0-399-52755-9
1. Nonverbal learning disabilities.   2. Parents of handicapped children.
3. Social skills in children.   4. Child psychology.   I. Title.

RJ47 .W48 2002
618.92'85889—dc21   2001036838

PRINTED IN THE UNITED STATES OF AMERICA

10 9 8 7 6 5

All names have been changed to protect identity.

Contents

Introduction   *vii*

1. Zac the Wonder Boy   3

2. What Is Nonverbal Learning Disorder?   14

3. Inside the World of Nonverbal Learning Disorder   33

4. Getting the Diagnosis   52

5. After the Diagnosis   75

6. Implement Your Plan   87

7. Parenting the Child with NLD   97

8. Teaching Moments and Other Parenting Strategies   118

9. Reduce Stress   135

10. Safety   144

11. Social Skills   166

12. Finding the Right School   190

13. The Individual Educational Program (IEP)   208

14. Traveling the Maze of Professional Interventions   223

Epilogue   255

Acknowledgments   259
Appendix A: Resources   261
Appendix B: Sensory Strategies   267
Glossary   271
Bibliography   279
Index   285

Introduction

As the mother of a child with Nonverbal Learning Disorder (NLD), I've experienced firsthand the frustrations and joys of life with these kids. I am also an occupational therapist who has treated many children with NLD and other disorders, and have provided consultation and support to many schools and teachers who want to successfully work with children with NLD. Drawing on both my personal experience and my professional expertise, I wrote this book for parents and educators of children with NLD. I wrote it to share with you what I have learned raising a son with NLD—the difficulties we've faced, the strategies we've developed, our setbacks, and our successes. Parents of children with Asperger's, ADD, ADHD, and other neurocognitive disorders will find this book useful. However, I specifically wanted to address NLD and put forth positive and hopeful information regarding this mysterious disorder as there is currently such a dearth of information to help parents. While some of this book will sound like good parenting for any child, the difference is, those same techniques can be essential for children with NLD.

It's important to me that you know I am not a perfect parent. I have struggled every day to overcome my disorganization, my inner laziness, and irresponsible small self. I was fortunate to have some training and some natural instincts that allowed me to develop strategies that were supportive and helpful. I've figured out some things that worked well for my child and that have transferred nicely to many children with NLD. But I'm not a supermom. I have allowed my son to watch uncensored television while I talked for hours on the phone. While visiting friends, I've yelled and banished him to the cold garage so the rest of the children could sleep, and shut the door in pure exasperation and embarrassment. It's no wonder that when he was six he said to me and my husband, "I want parents with more experience!"

Overall, thanks to many wise friends and an inner voice that told me to listen to them and to my son, we've managed to travel a path of parenting to a home full of love. Our son has become a bright, funny, wonderful boy who inspires hope and a feeling of goodness in others. He is a child with a great spirit radiating from his eyes and his heart, who laughs with deep, soulful belly laughs, and who dances around the kitchen singing, "Oh, yeah, NLD rules, oh yeah, NLD rules!"

Calling a particular neurological profile a disorder or a disability is useful when it makes it possible for children to qualify for services they need to succeed in school and for professionals who need a shorthand way of communicating with one another. Unfortunately, the terms *learning disorder* and *learning disability* imply that something is wrong with the child. I don't believe that.

I believe NLD is a difference, not a flaw. Kids with NLD are wired differently from most people. Unfortunately, in our culture the only way we can talk about that difference is to call it a neurological deficit. Our society tends to assume all brains are alike (despite massive evidence to the contrary), and our language, culture, and schools tend to be set up for one kind of brain. That is why in order for these kids to succeed in our society, we need to accommodate their differences.

My son thinks his unique learning style "rules," and I agree with him. He and other children with NLD have some different ways of being in this world. If we could honor their ways of being, we could transform our world into a more honest, loving, and gentler place. When you see children with NLD in this way, you'll know that they are truly a gift.

The message these kids bring is, "If you tell me exactly what you mean, if you are honest with me and kind to me, I'll be the most amazing kid you've ever met. And if you're not, I'll be your worst nightmare. Not because I'm trying to punish you, but because I don't know how else to be. So you can use me as measure of your clarity, your honesty, and your kindness. Here I am."

What benefits children with NLD benefits all children. NLD children need kindness, understanding, and a strong sense of community. While other children seem to have a greater ability to rebound when faced with indifference, children with NLD require support to succeed and their needs teach us how to change our society for the better. I deeply believe this is the gift of NLD.

Once thought to be rare, Nonverbal Learning Disorder is now thought to be as prevalent as dyslexia. Estimates place NLD occurrence between 1 in 1,000 to 1 in 100. Unlike other learning disorders, NLD appears to equally affect males and females. Nonverbal Learning Disorder is a syndrome that creates poor visual-spatial-organizational skills, poor motor performance, and marked deficits in social arenas. In addition to these weaknesses, NLD is a syndrome of specific strengths including precocious language use, advanced reading skills, profound rote memory skills, and average to superior intelligence.

Why all of a sudden are there so many cases of NLD? Have children with NLD always been around without anyone understanding their learning style or giving it a name? Or is this "explosion" of cases of NLD a new thing?

Most clinicians believe there is a genetic component to NLD. Many children with NLD have parents with some of the NLD syndrome criteria. More research is needed to quantify the genetic component, but many clinicians report anecdotally that the parents and children in their waiting rooms are easily matched.

Theorists link the rise in incidence of NLD to a variety of causes: environmental toxins, prolonged low-level exposure to radiation from computers, later-life pregnancies, and our stressed lifestyles. My work as an occupational therapist has lead me to believe the increased incidence of NLD arises from the changes in lifestyle, education, and family life of the past half century. I believe that just as many children were born with NLD fifty years ago, but NLD did not manifest as severely because the roles of children in those days provided sufficient opportunities and challenges for children with NLD to develop their areas of performance that they were lacking, specifically motor skills, social skills, and visual-spatial-organizational performance.

Fifty years ago, most children ran, rode bikes, explored in the woods, and climbed trees for hours. They skipped rope and played hopscotch, jacks, and softball after school and on the weekends. They played with a small circle of friends who lived within walking or biking distance from their homes. Peer circles remained fairly stable over many years. Extended families were the norm. Neighbors felt free to intervene with rowdy children, and many caregivers were around to coach children on appropriate ways of behaving. In schools, academic demands were concrete and expectations were pretty clear. Recesses were 20 to 30 minutes twice a day, and lunch was an extended period. Playground play was unstructured. Children climbed trees and monkey bars, and played on teeter-totters and swings. Homework was infrequent and reasonable.

Because of the proximity of friends, neighbors, and caregivers, opportunities for social-skill development were everywhere as well. Unlike today, the opportunity to devour information, as children with NLD love to do, was low. A family might have driven to the local library on Saturdays, but they didn't have access to vast informational input at the click of a mouse or a remote.

Today's children have far fewer opportunities to engage in casual social interactions or motor-skill development than their counterparts fifty years ago. We now keep our children inside because it is not safe to let them roam the neighborhood. Play dates are arranged weeks in advance to accommodate busy schedules. We celebrate when kids begin to read at age three. We put pencils in the hands of four-year-olds and encourage them to write their ABCs. It's not enough to learn the alphabet; we expect preschoolers to respond to a two-dimensional visual prompt on a computer when Grover from *Sesame Street* holds up a number. We have children who are able to increase their rote knowledge daily. They can surf the Internet and acquire vast amounts of factual information, becoming experts in bats, or trains, or *Pokémon*. They have access to a vast array of technology, books, magazines, and television aimed at children. Thus, the gap between motor skills and verbal skills widens. By the time a child with NLD enters school, he has vast knowledge but deficient ability to coordinate his hands together to perform simple tasks. She probably never played jacks or jumped rope, he likely cannot ride a bike and fatigues after walking more than three blocks. A child with a 50 percent deficit in motor skills before attending school may now have regressed to 40 percent, while his verbal skills have increased to 99 percent. This gap, indicative of NLD, becomes disabling. Additionally, the lack of foundational development at the lower levels of the nervous system (connections between movement, vision, and attention) are not able to develop and the downward cycle of disability begins.

When children are not allowed free play and are forced into structured education situations too early, before they are neurologically prepared, breakdowns in learning can occur.

Fifty years ago, the child with 50 percent motor skills would likely have developed them to 70 or 80 percent (enough to be fully functional) due to the everyday demands of her world. Research demonstrates that play is the foundation of creative thinking, socialization, sensorimotor-skill development, and role acquisition. Play is how a child learns to learn. Play enables the child to understand and find meaning in her world, to develop ways to cope with life's tasks, to develop mastery in certain skills.

During play and as a result of play, changes occur in the nervous system. Play provides essential sensory stimuli that helps it grow additional neural connections, resulting in both functional and structural changes to the brain. This enhanced capacity of the nervous system allows the child to interact with the environment in more complex ways and to develop more sophisticated strategies to deal with new challenges.

Play is the work of childhood, and yet it has been devalued in most academic settings. Recesses have been shortened or discontinued and are often removed as punishment when a child can't sit still and listen. Lunch hours are staggered in many elementary schools to deal with overcrowding. By the time the children eat (no socializing, no sharing), they have time to go to the bathroom and then maybe time to play for five or ten minutes before returning to the classroom for an afternoon without recess. Movement and heavy work are the very things a wiggling child with NLD needs to organize himself and get ready for more learning. Is it any surprise that children are struggling to develop social and motor skills?

I know, personally and professionally, that interventions for NLD in the areas of movement, social relationships, and visual-perceptual development are the areas that provide the most success. I hope that this book will give you the information you need to understand your child's Nonverbal Learning Disorder, to work more efficiently with teachers and the school system to get him the help he needs and ultimately to discover the wonderful child who may have been hiding behind the label of NLD.

From the Mouths of Babes

Zac was in kindergarten when I was in my final semester of my Master's program in occupational therapy. I had chosen to attend a very rigorous graduate program that required me to commute at least four hours each day. If I left class at 4:05 instead of 4 (the minute class let out), this delay often added 45 minutes to the commute because of California traffic. I had a child who was miserable at school, and unsafe, and any number of horrific events could have transpired on any given day, and I was two hours away at any given moment.

I said good-bye to Zac each morning at 7 A.M., Bill dropped him off at school at 8:30, and I picked him up again from the after-care program at 6 P.M. When my husband was traveling for his job, I dropped Zac off for morning care at 7 with his McDonald's meal packed. What could I do? Class was at 9, and the commute was at least two hours by the time I dropped Zac, drove to the carpool site, drove to school, parked, and walked to class. Yes, I, too, would strongly advocate against this schedule for children with NLD, but our lives at the time demanded imposed demands upon us. And, I consoled myself, I had a child who would love the extra enrichment of the after-school curriculum.

At that time I carpooled with three classmates who quizzed me on class work, shared their notes, and endured my frantic hyperventilation over being a minute or two late for Zac's pickup. One day, one of them, a soft, sweet-voiced woman, said, "I think you should ask Zac how he feels if you're late. I'll bet it doesn't bother him and he's just playing away, never giving it a thought." That sounded so rational and calming. When I arrived at his after-care, I did just that, I asked Zac how he felt when Mom was late. He said: "It's horrible. I feel like I can't breathe and I think I must fall to the floor and never rise again." I'm not sure if he was yanking my chain or not, but that's what our lives are like when we live with a verbal, articulate, and precocious child.

One

Zac the Wonder Boy

As many parents do, I thought my child was exceptional. By the time Zac was six he was reading at a twelfth-grade level. His vocabulary was better than mine, and he had an amazing memory. I was convinced he was a little genius. However, there were aspects of Zac's development that weren't up to the level of his verbal skills; for example, he frequently fell out of chairs and had difficulty writing. But if you had suggested to me that my golden child had a neurological dysfunction, I would have thought you were crazy.

When Zac started kindergarten, we were thrilled to have him enter a charter school. He was in an open classroom, in an unstructured setting, working not just with his teacher but with the parent volunteers who staffed the classroom. The school's philosophy, "We nurture the individual," seemed to promise that Zac's intelligence would flourish. Zac was much younger than his classmates, but he was so gifted academically we were sure he'd keep up. It was all supposed to be perfect. For quite a while it was.

Toward the end of kindergarten, he began to have difficulties. When the class sang songs, he would hold his ears and rock as if the noise were painful to him. At assemblies, he did the same or "got himself excused by his behavior," as Susan said. When he signed in (a tradition in the classroom) he signed his name "Z-1" instead of Zachary. He later short-ened his name to Zac so he wouldn't have to write so much.

Zac began to have "meltdowns," fits of anger and crying that seemed out of proportion with their ostensible causes. The meltdowns started out infrequently, so my husband, Bill, and I thought they were just nor-mal kid behavior. We'd rationalize Zac's meltdowns by telling ourselves, "He's just hungry or tired."

We had not yet gotten a diagnosis for Zac's NLD and while we didn't know what to call it at the time, Zac was already having many interpre-tive problems and sensory processing difficulties. What we considered a clear message about behavior was meaningless, random, and confusing, and he couldn't make his body do what he wanted it to do. In parent training, the protocol is to ignore the meltdown, and if the meltdown escalates you say, "go to your room." If it escalates some more, you shut the door. Typical children learn very quickly to end the meltdown, but Zac's would escalate. If we put him in his room and closed the door, he was in danger of hurting himself. He would bang things and pull stuff off his walls, turn things over, and fall. Some behavioral experts sug-gested removing items from his room until it was bare except for a mat-tress. This not only felt too harsh, but intuitively I knew it was the wrong strategy. I had seen that if I approached Zac and hugged him tightly and rocked him or read to him or talked soothingly and logically, he began to calm down.

It took some time before my husband and I realized the seriousness of Zac's problems at school. A law was passed in California mandating that kindergarten classrooms have no more than twenty kids. Zac's classroom had thirty, so the school broke up his class and hired a new teacher, Erica. She believed very strictly in behavior modification, which we would later learn is disastrous for kids with Zac's disorder.

Zac began spending more time in the corner of the classroom with lots of pillows and books. The theory was that if a child was misbehav-ing, he could take a break there and come back into the group when he was ready. But because this was a nonverbal intervention, it made no sense to Zac. He had no idea what the adults meant by "come back when you can behave," because he had no concept of what he had "done" in the first place. Erica told us, "Zac gets himself removed inten-tionally. He's just spoiled, a mommy's boy."

As the year progressed, we could see Zac becoming depressed. He was sent to the office nearly every day, and he never understood why. Eventually his level of confusion and frustration grew so much that he acted out in class by kicking or pushing tables or chairs, or by running out of the classroom.

I now understand that when Zac left the classroom, he was doing what he needed to do for his own survival. In the classroom he could not read the nonverbal codes that everyone else understood. He saw children excel at tasks he knew he should be able to do easily, given how smart he was, yet he would struggle with them. He knew everyone considered him the "bad kid," and that's how he began to see himself. Under this unbearable stress, flight was a natural reaction.

One day he ran away from his classroom and would not come back. I was called to come and get him. Up until this point the principal had been extremely considerate and kind to us. But when I arrived to get Zac, I could tell by her face that she'd had it. Even though it was the first opportunity I had to see that running away was Zac's pattern, I could see that the principal had already given up on him. It was clear she thought he was a little jerk.

That was a scary, awful day. I took Zac home, we sat on the couch and cried and held each other for two hours. I said, "I'm sorry, I don't know what to do. I'm sad and can see that you're sad." I told him, "I love you, we'll figure this out, the whole thing."

Zac's meltdowns at home became more frequent. We could see that he was depressed. He would say "I suck" about a hundred times a day. His physical health began to deteriorate as he began getting chronic sinus infections. I was studying to get my Master's degree in occupational therapy, and, ironically, I was writing a thesis on how stressors affect the immune system. It was obvious to me that Zac was stressed and that his stress was affecting his health, but I couldn't identify its source. We were a loving family, blessed by great friends, secure lifestyles, and great families. Our son was in one of the top schools in the nation. Where was the stress coming from? Zac was wilting and I had no idea what was causing his pain.

I began to hear from other parents at Zac's school that he was "defiant." Erica insisted that Zac could "be good when he wanted to." That's when I began offering him behavioral rewards—bribes: "If you stay out of the office, I'll buy you a Nintendo." We instituted an elaborate scheme of rewards, gold stars, and incentives, but every day when I picked Zac up from school he'd sit next to me in the car, his little shoulders slumped, and say, defeated, "I was sent to the office again." I began to see him shrinking, withdrawing more and more, apologizing each time he got in trouble. I escalated the bribes, and he failed over and over again. Nothing he could do seemed to make a difference. He was never able to tell me what he'd done to get sent to the office. Once he said it was because he'd scratched his foot. He was confused. I was confused. Punishment seemed random and inconsistent to us. In lab rats, when punishment is random and inconsistent, they stand in the corner cowering and trembling, they lose hair in patches, and they die prematurely.

Zac began to beg us not to send him to school. We'd have a wonderful weekend. He'd be so *happy*. Then Sunday night as we tucked him in, we'd say, "Okay honey, tomorrow's a school day," and like the flip of a switch, he'd turn into a depressed, sad child. He'd cry and complain of stomachaches and leg pains. He'd grab our necks and beg, plead, and cry. "Don't make me go to that torture chamber! Please!"

I didn't understand what was happening. I had always loved school. Initially, Zac had loved school. I began to search for medical explanations for Zac's behavior. I had him tested for allergies, but the tests showed nothing. I took him to a homeopathic doctor, and though her treatments seemed to work dramatically for a short while, there was no long-lasting change in Zac's behavior or his state of mind.

Meanwhile Zac's teacher, Erica, was trying to solve Zac's behavior problems by looking for their psychological basis. In a meeting with the principal she suggested that my husband and I were having problems at home. The team assumed Zac's behavior problems were emotionally based. That's what they were trained to look for, as are most teachers in this country, and every piece of evidence they gathered was skewed by their misperceptions. Their intentions were good, but their particular frame of reference narrowed their focus and limited their field of vision. Like us, they were unaware of Zac's Nonverbal Learning Disorder (NLD).

Erica viewed Zac as a "mommy's boy" because he was fine if I was in the classroom. What she did not understand, and which I myself could only barely articulate at that point, was that Zac was fine because I was interpreting the nonverbal cues for him. She believed that if we would just let her do the behavior modification she was trained to do and ignore Zac's negative behavior, then everything would get better. She believed we were rewarding his negative behavior with attention. She defiantly refused to implement any of the strategies we asked for.

The teacher suggested, "Let's keep a journal to see if things like this occur during the times your husband's traveling," and "Let's really tell the truth about whether or not you and your husband are having problems." I diligently kept the journal. We sent it back and forth, trying to piece together what was causing his behaviors. I called five or six of our good friends and said, "You know us well, are you aware of problems Bill and I are having that we're somehow oblivious to?" They all responded, "No, no you guys are doing great. You're really good parents." Bill and I were baffled and frustrated, Zac was depressed and angry, and we couldn't seem to solve anything.

Zac began to say things like, "Why don't you just kill me?" One night when I tucked him in, he said, "You know, Mom, I saw a big cliff yesterday, and I was thinking if I just stepped off it your life would be all better again." Few six-year-olds can even conceive of suicide, but here was my son telling me he had envisioned a specific plan for killing himself. I knew from my training in psychology and occupational therapy that I had to take Zac seriously. I was so frightened I could hardly breathe.

That night I called my mother, a retired elementary school teacher and counselor, and asked her to come and help me. "Mom," I said, "you've got to come and help me keep Zac safe." I was two months from finishing my Master's degree. Getting my Master's meant a lot to me. In my family, when you got your graduate degree, you were somebody: it was considered the sign of adulthood. If my mother could not help me, I would have to give up my work and stay at school with Zac all day. At first she tried to put me off, offering other approaches I could take. Finally I burst into tears and begged her, "You have to come help me. I don't know who else to ask. You *have* to come help me. Can you come tomorrow?"

I'm sure she thought that I was overreacting. She knew Zac, and she thought he was an intelligent, well behaved boy, a "teacher's delight." But she did fly from West Virginia to California to go to school with Zac and observe. I thank God she did because the next morning, a Friday,

Zac walked out of his school building and started walking home across a six-lane highway. My mother ran and caught up with him, and they walked home together. She spent the day with him analyzing the contents of all of the things on the pantry shelf. She took copious notes on their day together, charting his intellectual and emotional abilities. When my husband and I got home that evening, she said to us, "I know you love that school, but it is not a good fit for your child. He is intelligent, competent, and happy at home, but at that school, he just doesn't fit in." I did not want to hear that. We had chosen that school and it was supposed to be perfect. The school had a waiting list to get into kindergarten, and *we'd* gotten in!

One thing about the school was not perfect. No one ever called from the school to find out if Zac had made it safely home. Although it was the school's responsibility to inform us that he was missing, no one ever called. When I took Zac back to his classroom the following Tuesday, Erica said, "I was so worried all weekend." Yet no one had bothered to notify me that Zac had left.

With eight weeks left in the school year, Bill and I decided to have Zac tested. At this point my interpretation of Zac's situation was that he was so gifted his teachers didn't know what to do with him. I knew the school system could provide gifted testing, but not until the third grade. So I thought, "We'll just pay for it ourselves—how much could it be?" I asked my friends where we could take Zac, and they steered us toward the Children's Health Council at Stanford University Hospital in Palo Alto, where people from all over the world go for testing when they have children with undefined problems or issues.

At the Children's Health Council, an educational therapist and a psychologist gave Zac a battery of tests. Afterward, they told Bill and me that Zac had a Nonverbal Learning Disorder. I was shocked. Although I have a Bachelor's in psychology, I had studied learning disorders in my graduate work, and had worked with children for over 15 years, but I had never heard of it.

They said that Zac was reading at a twelfth-grade level, his math was at a fifth-grade level, and his motor skills were those of a four- to five-year-old. For the verbal test he had no ceiling; he got almost every question right. But he couldn't do any problems requiring him to use his pencil. He ranked in the first percentile on fine motor skills and 99.9th percentile on verbal skills. His IQ scores were in the 99.9th percentile for verbal and overall in the superior range, but performance skills were average. The educational therapist explained, "This means it's really hard for him to demonstrate his intelligence. It's very frustrating to be that smart and yet feel stupid because he sees other children doing things that he feels should be easy for him, given his understanding, but they are in fact really hard for him." We came to understand that part of Zac's brain (the left hemisphere) was so overly developed that it was suppressing the development of other parts. He overrelied on his verbal skills at the expense of his social- and motor-skill development.

They explained that Zac's poor coordination, including his frequent falls from chairs, were part of the neurological deficits of his right brain. They explained that he was unable to recognize the nonverbal cues that make up more than 50 percent of communication. That was why he had such difficulty understanding what was expected of him in his class-room. Then the psychologist told us, "I don't see emotional problems. What I see are educationally-based frustrations."

This was the first time I understood what a huge gap Zac was experiencing between his intelligence and his ability to understand, communicate, and execute his intentions. "Oh no," I thought, "my kid is lost in a gap."

A few nights later, I was looking at Zachary at the kitchen table. I saw him spill his milk and fall out of his chair, and I suddenly realized he could not *not* spill and not *not* fall. That was the first moment I understood what Zac had to face every day. In that moment I felt a warm flood of compassion for Zac come into my being, and it has never left me.

When I could recognize Zac's experience for what it was, I knew what to do. I knew how to care for a child who was hurting. I knew how to care for a child who was lost, frustrated, and afraid of life. A whole new set of rules came into my head. I understood that when a child falls because he *can't not* fall, we must be compassionate. It was obvious to me what to do. What Zac needed was the opposite of the behavior-modification method. When he would run to his room, I would run after him. I'd hold and squeeze him and talk to him until he calmed down. I developed a whole new set of interventions. Although previously I had ignored them, now I completely trusted my instincts.

But even though I had a new attitude toward Zac, I was anything but relieved by the NLD diagnosis. Both Bill and I were devastated. We were frightened, and we were grieving the loss of the child we'd thought we had.

At first I assumed I could fix everything. I thought, "I'll just ask my friends in occupational therapy and get the information we need, and it will all be okay." But it turned out there was very little information on NLD. Eventually I found a book, *Nonverbal Learning Disabilities: The Syndrome and the Model*, by neurologist Byron Rourke, the expert who had identified and studied the disorder.

Rourke's book told me that children with Nonverbal Learning Disorder have a grim prognosis—they will have a lifetime of withdrawal, or the life of a total recluse, with suicide to be expected. Reading this book plunged me into depression. I'd go into Zac's bedroom while he was sleeping and look at my beautiful boy. I'd try to picture him as a miserable, wretched, depressed adult, or worse. When I tucked him in at night, I'd think, "This is what it will be like when I tuck him in the night before he commits suicide."

After that initial grieving period, I reread Rourke's chapter on prognosis. Finally, I realized Rourke had given me information about the *diagnosis* (from the Greek, "to know") but not about *our child,* Zac and certainly not about the *prognosis* (from the Greek, "to know before"). I realized that none of the children in Rourke's study had early intervention. The children he studied had suffered years of misdiagnosis and misunderstanding, and all of the people he wrote about had been studied *after* they had been institutionalized or mistreated. I realized that the researchers can give us information about NLD, but that they could not predict my child's future based on his disability. The truth is, no one can predict the future. I told myself, "They don't know what we're willing to do for our child—not *my* child!" Every place Rourke wrote, "and the child will have a life of withdrawal," I'd pencil in "without intervention." Where he wrote "outlook is grim," I wrote "without intervention." It wasn't enough for me to think it. I had to write it. I was claiming my son's future for him. I was claiming our right to hope. With that act of writing, the energy poured into me: *this will not happen, as God is my witness!*

Through good luck, persistent digging through the library, and networking with friends, I eventually found a book that helped me make my hope more concrete. *The Source for Nonverbal Learning Disorders*, by Sue Thompson, began to change our world. We began a series of interventions, starting with finding a school that would better serve Zac's needs. We hired a tutor who specialized in helping children regain a love of learning. Zac began speech and occupational therapy. He saw a psychology intern to make sure he wasn't too traumatized and could move forward safely with our plan. He started karate and attended a camp that was full of warm, caring counselors.

Zac began to bloom. The child we knew as a sweet, loving, fun boy began to be seen in that way by others. He began to tolerate frustration. He began to express his feelings. He began to see himself as competent, and he began to smile. The new school went well. The teachers were supportive, kind, and competent. After about a year, he developed dimples, deep, lovely dimples. We had thought they had disappeared with babyhood, but they were back. Sue Thompson's book had, in my opinion, saved our son's life.

Our story is testament to an important fact: If children with NLD are not diagnosed or are misdiagnosed, then they are treated for behavior problems or problems of motivation. This leads to a downward spiral. Labeling these children "behavior problems," "discipline problems," "bad," or "lazy," does nothing to help them. Children develop rigid compensatory activities or obsessive thoughts in an attempt to cope with their confusion. Parents and professionals need to think through the cause of the anxiety and behaviors and get down to the cause and effect before they can develop interventions that prevent disability. Well-meaning parents or teachers who try to modify these childrens' behavior through punishments or rewards make their lives increasingly difficult and their secondary problems, such as anxiety and depression, more severe. If a child experiences the classroom as extremely stressful because the nonverbal cues governing behavior there are unintelligible to him or her, then that child will grow anxious when approaching the classroom. Anxiety drains energy, and this means he or she will not have enough energy to use learned coping skills. The child will often regress, which appears to others as "acting out." The stress increases when an adult tells the child, "I know you can behave more maturely," or makes judgments like, "It's not neurological, it's spoiled behavior." This response inevitably affects the child's self-esteem and creates feelings of hopelessness, depression, anxiety, or obsessive-compulsive behaviors. Early diagnosis and the proper therapeutic and medical intervention are crucial. We need to treat children with NLD for their neurological deficits before they develop other behavior patterns or feelings of failure. If we don't intervene, we risk losing the child altogether—to depression, withdrawal, and even suicide. (If you are the parent or teacher of an older child with NLD, that child can certainly still be helped. The child will need extra care and probably extra services, however, to help him or her cope with the wounds and protective behaviors he or she has developed because of being misunderstood.)

Children with NLD are not suffering from "behavior problems." They have a neurological deficit that leaves them at a loss for understanding the codes of behavior that most of us take for granted. Properly identifying the child's mode of learning and teaching the child accordingly are the only ways to help a child learn the functional skills he desperately needs. I must emphasize that the correct diagnosis, as early in the child's life as possible, followed by the appropriate interventions, is the only hope these children have of becoming the happy, productive people they are capable of being. As parents and teachers, we owe these children this hope—and more.

I am certain that if we had not learned of Zac's NLD when we did, he would have ended up on medication, or have become withdrawn, or a social misfit or, God forbid, dead. In many ways, our family was very fortunate. Because of my network of friends and colleagues, I was able to get Zac diagnosed properly and locate the appropriate interventions. We were also fortunate to have supportive family and access to sufficient financial resources to put these interventions into place. We borrowed from our parents, held yard sales, and bartered for services. I returned to work, and we made many, many sacrifices to support the interventions Zac needed.

We're still on the journey, but for the most part, Zac is a kid who likes himself, feels happy, and plays with friends. He dreams again about being an inventor, president of the United States, a rich and famous author, and a video-game tester. We feel the world knows the child we've always known and that our child finally sees himself as we see him: our beautiful wonder boy.

Grief

When Bill and I were told about Zac's diagnosis at the Children's Health Council, what I expected to hear was "Your son is a genius!" They did say that, and the team also told us about Zachary's NLD. I remember working very hard to stay present and to listen, to just hear what they were saying and not go away.

I thought I was fine. I thought, "I understand this. I'll just do some research, and we'll figure out what to do." But what I really was feeling was as if someone had died. I was totally lost in my grief. I was lost in that numbness. It was a very surreal, lonely world. My life was going on, my body was there, traveling into the spaces it was expected to be, but no other part of me was present.

I was still in school working on my Master's degree when all this was going on. I really understood what I was feeling when I got back a paper from a professor with, "B-, not up to your usual level of work," written across the top. It wasn't the grade that shocked me, it was that I had no memory of this paper. None. I knew it was mine by the font and the other ways I uniquely marked my pages, but I had no memory of it, the subject, having written it, or having turned it in. It looked like a rough draft, just some notes on paper that I'd turned in.

I remember sitting in that class, getting that paper back, and thinking, "Oh my God, I haven't been here. I haven't been here. Where have I been?" I wondered if I could ever get back and, if so, back to what. . . .

Two

What Is Nonverbal Learning Disorder?

WHAT is Nonverbal Learning Disorder?

For professionals who have been trained to treat learning disorders, a label like Nonverbal Learning Disorder (NLD) can be helpful when establishing a treatment plan or in communicating with other professionals. But most of us need to know the nature of NLD and not just its name. The term *learning disorder* describes a situation in which a child does not learn the way we typically expect him to. When a child has a learning disorder, he does not take in, process, and respond to information or sensory input the way the majority of people do. A learning disability is a gap between a child's ability to perform in the world—to move a pencil across the paper, to summarize paragraphs—and his measured intelligence. It's a gap between potential and performance. If a six-year-old is performing at a four-year-old's level, and his intelligence is also at a four-year-old's level, this would not be called a learning disability. Instead, it's called "mental retardation" or "developmental delay."

Every disorder is defined by its own specific criteria, a set of markers or symptoms, that have been identified by researchers in the field. Nonverbal Learning Disorder is often characterized as a syndrome to reflect that a person who has NLD does not need to have every one of the markers of NLD to be diagnosed. Sometimes a child will be said to have "NLD-like symptoms," meaning many of the criteria fit, but not enough to meet the threshold for a diagnosis of NLD.

Nonverbal Learning Disorder can coexist with other disorders such as Attention Deficit–Hyperactivity Disorder, Attention Deficit Disorder, Tourette's, Obsessive Compulsive Disorder, dysfunction in sensory integration, and even mental retardation. It can also be a secondary problem after a child sustains a head injury or other brain trauma such as hydro-encephalitis. But it is not the same as these other disorders.

Neurologist Bryon Rourke has explained the elements and dynamics of the NLD syndrome through parallel tracks of assets and deficits—strengths and weaknesses—in the neurological processing of thoughts and movements. In order to have the NLD diagnosis, a person has to have a significant number of both the strengths and weaknesses of the disorder.

I would say the most disabling aspect of NLD is that the person has difficulty interpreting and understanding nonverbal cues in the environment. Most researchers estimate somewhere between 65 to 90 percent of all communication is nonverbal. Studies have shown that 55 percent of the emotional meaning of a message is expressed in nonverbal cues such as facial expression, posture, and gesture, and another 38 percent is transmitted through voice tone. That leaves only 7 percent of the emotional meaning that is actually expressed in the words that we speak. Therefore, a person with NLD who attends to words and not inferred meaning between words can miss as much as 93 percent of the emotional meaning of communication. Without intervention, that will result in a significant handicap. Children with NLD miss out on many of the areas of social development that more typical children are picking up as part of their natural, daily lives, compounding the disability.

There is more to NLD, however, than failing to comprehend nonverbal communication. According to Rourke, the primary neuropsychological assets of NLD include strengths in auditory perception, strong simple-motor skills, and good use of routine or already memorized information. Children with NLD have good attention to auditory and verbal stimuli (a secondary asset that comes from the primary ones), which in turn promotes the tertiary assets of advanced auditory and verbal memory. This means that children with NLD typically have large vocabularies at a very young age; their use of language is advanced for their age; they can accurately repeat back what they hear; and they remember an extraordinary number of facts, so that they appear to be "little geniuses."

Although children with NLD speak and read early, and almost always meet developmental motor milestones on target, NLD is a problem of language and sensorimotor dysfunction. These children have strong rote-language skills, and they often score far above grade level on standardized tests and assessments administered in a one-on-one situation. However, they have great difficulty with the functional use of language in everyday conversation. Children with NLD tend to speak in a pedantic, overly formal manner, relying on parrotlike phrases, which are often used out of social context. For example, a child with NLD might inadvertently learn to begin all conversations with, "Hello, who would you like to speak with?" This phrase may be appropriate when answering the phone, but inappropriate when greeting someone at the front door or when attempting to join a ball game at the park. Because of their problems with language, children with NLD often lack competence in the social arena. They lack smooth, integrated movement, have poor spatial orientation, and poor rhythm, which ultimately affects their ability to perform in social interactions, conversations, and abstract academic endeavors.

NLD: A Technical Definition

Rourke has studied the syndrome of NLD for many years and has contributed a great deal to our understanding of the disorder. He defined the NLD syndrome in technical terms. Technical language has the advantage of being precise and deliberate, but to the average reader it can seem like a secret code. I'll "decode" Rourke's criteria, but it is important to remember that he identified NLD in people who had had little or no interventions. With appropriate interventions, many of these symptoms can be minimized or reduced to such a level that they no longer stand out.

Rourke's Criteria for NLD

1. *Bilateral tactile-perceptual deficits, usually more marked on the left side of the body.* The child has difficulty understanding or perceiving information through the skin of both hands (tactile), but the left hand has even more difficulty than the right.

2. *Bilateral psychomotor coordination deficiencies and complex psychomotor skills, especially required within a novel framework, tend to worsen relative to age-based norms.* People with NLD are clumsy. Their movements aren't smooth or fluid. These children don't "outgrow" their clumsiness or awkwardness in a natural manner as we might expect from most children. As the motor challenge increases in difficulty, the awkwardness worsens.

3. *Outstanding deficiencies in visual-spatial-organizational abilities.* People with NLD have *tremendous* trouble organizing materials, clothes, and other objects. If they need to take notes in school, they find it difficult to organize the notes on paper. This is one of the contributors to problems with handwriting, turning in homework, and finding assignments on the board and writing them down under a tight time deadline.

4. *Extreme difficulty in adapting to novel and otherwise complex situations with an overreliance on prosaic, rote behaviors.* People with NLD have problems when they encounter new information, new situations, or a break in their routine. They have difficulty interpreting the cues in the environment, so they don't know how to react.

5. *Marked deficits in nonverbal problem solving, concept-formation, hypothesis testing, etc.* A person who has trouble figuring out how to break down the meaning of nonverbal information can be quite funny, but others aren't necessarily laughing with him.

6. *Concept-formation deficits in hypothesis testing and the inability to benefit from positive and negative informational feedback in novel and otherwise complex situations.* It's hard to know what is expected of you when you don't see the big picture in a situation, when you only get some of the information, and the larger themes are beyond you.

Someone once told Zac that he'd probably win a Pulitzer Prize some day because he's such a good writer. No one thought anything of that, in fact, it seemed to us to be a compliment. Zac just shrugged it off, but he certainly didn't appear to feel complimented. We forgot about it until days later, Zac heard on television the winners of the 1999 Pulitzer Prizes. The television had a written headline posted "Pulitzer Prize Winner." Zac bolted out of his chair and said, "PUL-itzer prize! I thought it was BULLET surprise, that they got a bullet in their head if they wrote the wrong thing." That's a concept-formation deficit.

The disability begins with one level of impairment, but that creates other problems, and those problems lead to more problems, and the cycle spirals downward, compounding itself as it goes and creating a great deal of confusion and pain. For example, problems with visual-spatial perception creates problems with being able to write down assignments correctly. Then the assignments are not turned in on time or are done incorrectly. Then the child gets behind and has mountains of homework and feelings of frustration and inadequacy. The child begins to feel dumb and classmates make fun of him and on it goes in a downward cycle.

7. *Extremely distorted sense of time.* Time is abstract and nonlinear and is difficult for children to grasp if they don't have a handle on abstract concepts. A quarter till the hour is fifteen minutes, but a quarter of a dollar is twenty-five cents. That's pretty abstract. What's a quarter of something that doesn't exist in a material way?

8. *Well-developed, rote, verbal capacities.* Children with NLD have big vocabularies, use words in a precocious way, and they memorize words with ease. This strength is a particular mark of NLD.

9. *Much verbosity of a repetitive, straightforward, rote nature, etc.* People with NLD talk a lot. They have long, circumlocutious sentences that use lots of words but make few points. There is little content to their language. When they speak, it sounds more like reporting or a verbatim telling of a story than like a summary, and they often leave out the main point. It's hard for them to begin again when they're interrupted, and they are quite likely to restart to finish their tale.

10. *Children with NLD have difficulty with the fluid use of connectors, segues, and dialogue.* NLD talk is often a monologue. Children with NLD overuse language, talking nonstop when other children are trying to play soccer or Legos. There is little or no speech prosody, which means turn-taking in conversation, or being aware of the pauses and rhythms of speech. Their misspellings are almost exclusively of the

phonetic variety, which means that the way the child spells a word makes sense even when it's incorrect, often leaving out vowels.

11. *Outstanding relative deficiencies in mechanical arithmetic as compared with reading and spelling, etc.* There's a big gap between reading and math skills, and most kids with NLD struggle with math as it becomes more complex. While their rote reading skills are strong, their *comprehension of complex text is poor* because comprehension requires reading between the lines and making guesses about how characters feel and think. Although they can tell you the names of all the characters in *Tom Sawyer* and repeat the story almost verbatim, when you ask why the boys in the story helped Tom whitewash Aunt Polly's fence, they're likely to say, "How should I know? That's not written down anywhere." Children with NLD often miss the overall pattern and instead concentrate on the details, missing the meaning of text, pictures, social events, and conversations.

Sensory Integration

Although Rourke's definition of NLD is very detailed, he does not address a key aspect of these children's impairment in his published work (although he applauds it in his presentation). The atypical neurological functioning we see in children with NLD results in atypical processing of sensory information or perhaps even is due to atypical sensory processing. Children need to process sensory information effectively so they can respond to their environment. This is known as sensorimotor integration and poor sensorimotor integration in children with NLD manifests in different ways: poor registration, sensitivity to stimuli, sensation seeking or sensory avoiding. Sensory integration is a technique supported with years of continuing research. It can be very helpful to know your child's sensory profile so that you can modify her environment appropriately while she is working in therapy on sensory integration.

Children with NLD may have either a high or low sensory threshold. A child with a low sensory threshold has a nervous system that responds too readily to stimuli. It does not take much input to register and trigger a response. When a child has a high sensory threshold, it takes so much input to reach the threshold that his nervous system does not respond to stimuli; therefore his sensory system is dormant much of the time.

A child with poor sensory registration has a high neurological threshold and a tendency to act consistently with those thresholds. She is underresponsive to sensation. A child with poor registration can appear uninterested in her environment, can have a flat or dull affect (meaning her face muscles are slack and emotionless), and does not seem to notice some or all of the sensory stimuli in the environment. She will have low energy levels and appear fatigued. Her brain is not getting enough sensory input to generate a response and as a result, the child becomes apathetic and self-absorbed.

A child who is sensitive to stimuli has a low neurological threshold and a tendency to act consistently with those thresholds. He will tend to be distractible and may display hyperactivity. He will direct his attention to the latest stimulus, drawing his attention away from whatever he is trying to accomplish. A child who is oversensitive to stimuli will have difficulty distinguishing between relevant and irrelevant information. He does not have the ability to habituate to stimuli, meaning he can't shut a sensation (a scratchy waistband or the ticking of a clock) out of his consciousness; it continually nags at him, demanding his attention.

A child who is sensation seeking has high neurological thresholds with a tendency to act to counter that threshold. These children are constantly active and engaged. They add sensory input to each aspect of their daily lives. They make noise while working, fidget, jiggle their feet, chew on their skin, rub or slap their body parts, bounce, jump, and crash into objects in an enjoyable manner. They may appear excitable or seem to lack consideration for safety when playing. These children have brains that underregister sensory input, but they are driven to meet their thresholds by creating opportunities for themselves to increase input and meet their sensory needs.

Children who are sensory avoiding have low sensory thresholds with a tendency to act in ways to counter these thresholds. Their sensory thresholds are met too frequently with stimuli of too great intensity. Their sensory systems are quickly overwhelmed with too much input. As a coping strategy, these children engage in disruptive behavior, either withdrawing as a method of protecting themselves from the noxious stimuli they perceive in their environment, or by creating dramatic outbursts in an attempt to communicate the level of their distress. They may create elaborate rituals and appear stubborn and controlling. However, from a sensory perspective, the child is creating a situation to limit sensory input to those events that are familiar and therefore easy for his nervous system to interpret. Children who avoid sensation are resistant to change because change means being bombarded with unfamiliar stimuli, which they perceive as noxious.

Children with NLD: A Functional Description

Children with NLD are sweet and vulnerable because they're trusting. They are not cynical. They tend to be attractive, having the innocence and features of a delicate spirit. I've heard many parents refer to their child with NLD as "holy." Many of them are funny (sometimes not when they mean to be) and tend to be fun to be around, especially when they feel accepted and understood.

They have unusual perspectives that if channeled, give us creative writing, art, and other inventions. Most children with NLD are talented writers if someone will allow them to dictate their expansive ideas and help them learn to organize their thoughts. They're persistent. They are very logical and, in fact, they can understand and integrate explanations about proper behavior (learning them like a rule that should not be broken) when the rules and explanations are presented in a logical, practical manner. They can be very compliant once they understand the expectations of a situation. Often sounding like lawyers or judges, they have a keen sense of fairness and are deeply affected by unfair treatment of themselves and others.

They tend to be accurate reporters, especially when reporting on verbal information. If they say a poisonous snake can strike with a lethal bite on its day of birth, believe them. Children with NLD may not recognize when they sound sarcastic themselves, nor will they necessarily recognize sarcasm in others. *In* fact, they wilt around sarcasm. For example, if a teacher sarcastically asks a student with NLD if he plans to work on a particular assignment all day, he may respond with a "Yes." Although the message the teacher is sending is "Stop what you are working on," the child comprehends the literal words spoken. His innocent answer will probably be interpreted as disrespect or defiance. Similarly, despite their precocious vocabularies, these children have great difficulty interpreting nonliteral language such as metaphors and idioms (e.g., "I put my foot in my mouth"). Because they take everything literally, they can be very gullible. They won't recognize when another child is lying to them or teasing, and thus they are often the target of bullies.

When I was working in stroke rehab, one of my patients was a woman who had had a right hemisphere stroke. Some of the deficits of injuring the right side of the brain include disorganization, problems with time, and lack of understanding of inferential language, deficits which are very similar to NLD. This woman took forever to get dressed each morning because she couldn't keep her concentration, and my job was to help her learn strategies so that she would be more efficient and stay on task. One morning, I said to her, "I'm going to help your roommate get dressed, and while I help her, you get ready, and we'll have a race." After five minutes she still just sat there holding her shirt, so I said, "Hurry up or we'll beat you!" She looked very frightened and asked, "You're going to beat me?" After I reassured her, I alerted my supervisor about the misperception this patient had, so if she began to talk about an OT who threatened to "beat her," we could all understand what had transpired. Kids with NLD are like that, too. We are often unaware when we've said something that has frightened them or led them to create odd thoughts.

Children with NLD typically have high intelligence, extraordinary verbal memory, and advanced verbal skills. Their high auditory skills allow them to be good at foreign languages, speech, and accurate pronunciation. These children typically begin to speak very young, often before age one. With their strong letter and number recognition skills, they learn to read early, often as young as three. They have extremely advanced vocabularies and speak like adults at age two or three. Their memories for facts are so good they often give the impression of being "little professors" at an early age. When Zac was three, he looked up into the garage and saw a bag from Toys"Я"Us, hidden away for Christmas. He said, "I want the toys in that bag." When he was five, we said, "Let's go get a p-i-z-z-a," spelling it out so Zac wouldn't know. Not even looking up from his book, he said, "That code won't work anymore. I broke it. Let's get the pizza from Pizza Hut this time."

These characteristics yield specific academic strengths. A child who pays attention to verbal and auditory input, has strong rote auditory memory skills, and the ability for simple motor acts will develop strengths and include strong verbal skills, written expression (when not using a pencil), word decoding, rote spelling (applied spelling is harder), and verbatim auditory memory.

However, in fourth or fifth grade, when additional demands are placed upon them, children with NLD are likely to experience difficulties in problem solving, reading comprehension, reasoning, and written expression. They have difficulty imagining relationships such as cause and effect, comparing and contrasting, and anticipating results of behaviors. Parents are often shocked that their little genius is struggling. While children with NLD typically score in the normal range for mathematics at this age, they frequently have difficulty with rapid retrieval of math facts, particularly the multiplication tables. They tend to overrely on left hemisphere strategies (rote learning) and will often employ "self-talk" as a way to organize motor and cognitive tasks. They tend to have poor ability in mechanical arithmetic, mathematics, and science often due to misaligning numbers in columns, sequencing, and problems forming abstract concepts from concrete facts.

Math-based survival skills such as time, money, and measurement are problematic. Children with NLD are often confused by systems and units of measurement, and make outrageous estimates regarding size, distance, or quantity. Doubling and halving the size of a recipe are particularly difficult. It is important to note, however, that many children with NLD are gifted with math and, with appropriate interventions, continue to perform mathematics at or above grade level, but their math skill is always relatively lower than their verbal skills, or it's not NLD.

Children with NLD generally don't recognize or interpret one or more of the following areas of nonverbal communication: facial expressions, postures, gestures, the meaning of tone, intensity, and loudness of voice, the appropriate distance between people, the rhythm and timing of conversation, or appropriate grooming and hygiene. Social interactions usually depend on these subtle elements of nonverbal communication. As a result of these nonverbal language deficits, children with NLD typically have poor social perception, poor social judgment, and poor, basic social interaction skills. Children with NLD also have difficulty with the prosody of speech—the ability to understand when to take one's turn in talking in social situations. For example, they often do not know when it's appropriate to share their thoughts or how to hold their thoughts in their head. As a result, they often blurt out ideas that are off topic and irrelevant to classroom discussions. They have difficulties interpreting the nonverbal cues (such as rolling eyes, fidgeting, or walking away) that others use to convey boredom. They may have annoying habits such as butting into conversations with irrelevant, weird information.

Children with NLD have difficulty adjusting to novel situations and difficulty processing original material. Children with NLD often withdraw from new, potentially threatening experiences. This creates another area of developmental delay. Children who won't touch glue or Play-Doh begin to lag in the development of hand skills. If the child doesn't experience joy from drawing a picture of Mom or Dad with a crayon, he is not going to draw pictures of Mom and Dad, and while his peers develop prewriting skills, he doesn't. Thus children with NLD tend to get further and further behind. They may avoid sports and social interactions with peers. It's difficult to learn about interacting with preschool peers if the child is afraid to venture into the unknown, unexplored classroom environment. This can lead to lack of friendships, loss of learning opportunities, and rigid adherence to rituals as a way to control the novel aspects of a school experience. They also have difficulty making transitions and need a clear structure to help them move from task to task. This symptom also overlaps with dysfunction in sensory processing and is not unique to NLD. It does, however, contribute to the unique expression of NLD.

Children with NLD typically lack the ability to use past experiences to understand new or unique information. They are usually unable to generalize from one situation to another. Even if they know the social rule for one situation, they may not realize it applies in another situation. They may know not to eat with their fingers at home, but not realize this also applies at Grandma's house.

Children with NLD tend to be lethargic, tire easily, and require frequent breaks when studying. They tend to get overwhelmed and need "down time" rather than an overly ambitious schedule of therapies, sports, and after-school events. Because their sensory integration impairment and social incompetence typically means they live with constant stress, they are subject to frequent stress-related illnesses such as upper-respiratory infections.

In the course of normal childhood development, infants, and pre-schoolers learn about the world around them through physical exploration. They pick things up, drop them, pick them up again. They taste, smell, bang, and throw. Through crawling and walking they learn to negotiate their way through space and around objects. These activities are key to developing both their motor skills and their visual-spatial perceptions.

However, as infants and preschoolers, children with NLD are relatively inactive. Rather than investigate objects in the environment through a variety of different sensory inputs (tactile, visual, and kinesthetic) they are content to ask questions and rely on verbal inputs for description. With low registration, they don't receive a satisfying level of input from touching the nubby ball, so they don't explore it like other toddlers. Instead, they receive and perceive understanding and enjoyment from learning the word *nubby*. This lack of satisfaction and therefore motivation to explore results in a depressed production of tactile, visual-spatial, and other neuro-sensory pathways. Consequently, children with NLD don't make the connections (neurological) and associations (behavioral) between objects in the environment and the social-emotional responses most children learn automatically as they go through their day-to-day lives. This deficit in exploration can create deficits in occupational performance. They don't learn the weight of a vase, they don't learn that if you pick something up that is too heavy it drops and breaks on the floor. Their brains lack cause and effect wiring.

Children with NLD are prone to self-deprivation. They deprive themselves by not joining in groups after failing at social relationships too often. They withdraw and, as a result, continue to miss the development of social skills such as turn-taking, developing friendships, talking on the phone, running in the park, playing hide-and-seek, and so on. The withdrawal has pervasive, lasting consequences as it promotes a spiral into more withdrawal and less and less success in social relationships.

Children with NLD have some degree of tactile imperceptions (finger agnosia), meaning they do not receive adequate information from the tactile sensory system. They lack the ability to understand or profit from information gathered through the sense of touch. When the child with

NLD reaches into the kitchen drawer to find a fork, her fingers do not tell her when she's touching it. Most people can put their hands into their purses or pockets or drawers and retrieve their keys or other objects without using their eyes. They know by the information received through their fingers that this shape and texture must be a key or a pencil or a wallet or a packet of tissues. But the child with tactile imperceptions does not get the information that tells her "that's my pencil" or "that's a fork." They often will have to take everything out of their pockets and backpacks to find what they are looking for, making a mess and creating additional chaos. As a result of deficits in the tactile system, children with the NLD syndrome often demonstrate poor early writing (graphomotor) skills such as drawing shapes, coloring within the lines, and writing their names.

The problems with motor skills associated with NLD appears to result from a decreased awareness of the body. Children with NLD don't receive adequate information from the sensory system to respond quickly to being off-center, or they fail to anticipate the consequences of an action; therefore, they frequently lose their balance. They tend to have delayed responses to movement because their bodies don't experience that they've moved for an interval after the movement happens. Because their bodies don't properly register where they are in space, children with NLD tend to bump into people or objects, especially on their left side, and frequently fall out of chairs, usually falling to the left. Until Zachary reached fifth grade, he had a purple bruise on the left side of his head for practically every single school picture.

In general, these kids are clumsy. They turn to walk through the door and hit the door frame. Because of their poor motor planning, when they walk through a room to get a ball, they don't think, "I need to walk around the chair and step over the jacket in order to get my ball," so they walk across the room, crash into the chair, trip over the jacket, and end up flat on the floor. This is a daily, hourly experience for these kids. Even when they are being really good and minding their own business, all of a sudden they are on the floor, taking their dinner plates with them.

Children with NLD generally have poor safety awareness because they don't anticipate the consequences of their actions. They are prone to frequent injuries. In an example from our lives, Zac was watching television when a kissing scene came on the screen. Being a nine-year-old boy, he hates kissing scenes, so he snapped his head away and whacked it against the wooden arm of his chair. He had a black eye for two weeks. If he'd hit half an inch higher, he could have lost the eye. Most people would register that they couldn't turn like that within one inch of a chair arm, but Zac did not have any perception that the arm was there. Our lives are riddled with that kind of accident. As parents, we are hypervigilant because we know a potential head injury is a moment away.

Children with NLD have low tone, which means that their muscles tend to be soft and spongy rather than hard and defined. This muscular weakness in turn limits their physical strength and endurance. Because of the limited endurance, children with NLD have a tendency to develop a sedentary lifestyle. They avoid activities that will overwhelm their balance reactions, such as moving rapidly through space with a ball, and thus they miss out on many social interactions and opportunities. Their lack of tone and endurance contributes to difficulty in transitions. Moving from one position to another requires a great deal of energy, and for someone who has lower reserves than is typical this start/stop change of position can be quite taxing. Low tone makes a comfortable couch and a remote controlled TV or video game system very attractive.

Children with NLD also have impaired complex psychomotor skills. They are the children who still have elastic-waist pants and Velcro-closing shoes when they are twelve. They have difficulty with buttons, zippers, and laces. They have trouble opening packages or getting a paper into or out of their notebooks, or a wallet out of a back pocket or money out of a wallet. They typically also have impaired handwriting (graphomotor) skills. Imagine performing your daily tasks with gloves on. That degree of clumsiness and imperceptions that you would experience is typical for children with NLD. These children repeatedly experience failure and frustration when confronted with ordinary motor tasks such as handwriting, dressing independently, eating without spills, or staying in a chair without falling when reaching for a glass of milk. As a consequence, they often avoid or reject simple motor challenges, responding with very stubborn refusals or tantrums, or using verbal armor to deflect or distract in an attempt to control their environment. It can become very frustrating to have a child engage in verbal fencing matches with you when you just want her to put on her shoes. You are trying to get the family out the door on time, so you just give up and tie her shoes, again. The distraction of the argument saves the child from having to perform a task she knows she can't do.

When this type of avoidance becomes a long-term pattern of behavior, the child misses important motor and social experiences such as playing games with peers. Children don't want to look incompetent while playing the game, so they don't play, and they don't develop the skills needed to play. When a child is at this point, we start to see the onset of "controlling" behaviors, when children negotiate endlessly, or act out to avoid trying to do something they know they can't do. However, I am convinced that these behaviors are not innate to NLD. Rather, they are both a means of avoidance and an expression of the deep frustration these children experience being in an environment that never understands.

Visual perception is another area of deficit. Spatial thinking develops in infancy from the information gained from exploration. Moving through the world, we learn to relate the sizes of objects to our own bodies to allow us to better understand our world. We use this information to know location, shape, quantity, direction, time and movement. We form visual memories of our environments. We make mental notes regarding the effort needed to move a ball or lift a glass successfully to our mouths or walk through a room of furniture. But children with NLD often lack this ability to gather, interpret, and understand information taken in through the sense of sight. This leads to the secondary deficit of poor visual attention. If a child is not perceiving visual information correctly, then she begins to rely on other means to gain meaning about her world and therefore begins to pay less attention to the visual input.

Problems in visual-spatial organization result in poor visual recall, faulty spatial perceptions, and difficulties with spatial relations. Children with NLD have impaired ability to imagine a shape in their minds. They have trouble holding an image—like a letter or a number—in their minds and then creating it on paper. This causes great difficulty in following directions. Most people remember directions by forming mental pictures of the required steps. This is a very difficult task for the child with NLD. Developing visual memories of size, distance, shape, and weight helps us to develop ways of solving problems. We imagine relationships between items, and anticipate the consequences of our actions. For example, we judge the weight of a bag of groceries and problem solve how to lift it from the car trunk. When we don't plan ahead, we tear or spill the bag. We make plans for retrieving the milk from the top shelf as we anticipate the relationships between the milk and the orange juice carton, and when we don't, we knock over one reaching for the other. A student may visualize her class assignment and anticipate what books to take home to be able to complete the homework for the evening, and when she doesn't, she arrives home unprepared to complete the assignment. These tasks are extremely challenging for children with NLD because their bodies and senses haven't been trained with experience as others' have.

When children have a decreased sense of self, a poor sense of where their bodies are in space, and a poor understanding of how to safely move and navigate in their environment, they tend to invent coping strategies that serve to control their environment. They often choose to adhere strictly to routines, because eliminating novel experiences helps them feel more confident and comfortable. They find that decreasing the number of changes decreases the number of new demands placed upon them. With this control in place, they have greater opportunity to succeed using their routines, their rote learning, and their past successful performances.

However, play with others is full of challenges, changes, and unexpected events. This can be stressful and difficult for children who crave sameness as a way of coping. They can easily become anxious about play and try to avoid it. While they long for friends, they may be working so hard on trying to control play to ensure their success and limit their failures, and to limit the levels of anxiety they are experiencing, that the child they're attempting to play with feels controlled and considers the other child bossy. Of course, this breeds a cycle. Avoiding opportunities decreases the chances for learning new play skills, learning to negotiate, share, and be with others in relaxing ways. As these kids grow older and experience increasing difficulty and frustration in academic and social situations, they are prone to anxiety and poor self-esteem. Children with NLD are very trusting. They believe what they are told, and if they are told they are lazy or bad, that's what they'll believe. Thus the misdiagnosed child is prone to depression. If they are not diagnosed and properly treated, they are at a high risk for depression and even suicide.

A Personal Definition of NLD

I consider NLD a disorder of invisible gaps: gaps between performance and potential, gaps between rules that are visible and rules that are invisible. Children with NLD are lost in the gap between what we expect of people who are extremely articulate and what they can actually do. These children get lost in the gaps we perpetuate by expecting them to be like us, to be the way we believe they *should* be. We need to acknowledge, name, and honor the gaps in their lives and bridge the gaps each time we can see them forming.

Our kids are terrified by the chasms no one else seems to see. Imagine screaming at a child for not jumping into a raging river and swimming across. We wouldn't dare. We need to remember that what we perceive as a trickle, they perceive as a raging river, and we're telling them to hurry up!

I think each time we explain an invisible gap to our son, we jump the chasm and carry with us an invisible thread, a strand of a spider's web. After going back and forth over a gap a number of times, each time carrying the thread, we build a bridge. We need to help these kids by filling the gaps with bridges that become obvious, sturdy, and trustworthy in their minds. They won't realize they are expected to say, "excuse me" at Grandma's table just because they've learned to say it at the table at home. We need to help them build it through practice. "We're going to Gram Linda and Granddad John's. At their house, the rule for leaving the table is to say, 'May I be excused?' Let's practice," and the family pretends to be at different people's houses. With enough practice, the child will have enough experiences in traversing that gap that he can find a thread of an example for a new situation that will most likely work.

When I studied brain anatomy in my training, I learned that memory exists in tracks going from one location in the brain to another. Neuroscience tells us that our brains actually build new tracks or "bridges" with new experience. Children with NLD need those tracks built to enough areas of their brains so that they can access information from wherever they are at a given time. We can't ask them to build a new bridge at any moment to get them to a familiar track. We need to have enough bridges so that all the tracks connect.

Monkey Bars

I never let Zachary climb off the ground without my being close enough to catch him if he falls. This has been my instinct since he was born. I never found a pattern to predict Zachary's falls except that he seems a bit fragile emotionally for a day or two, and then he falls again or gets a cold or a sinus infection.

When Zac falls, one minute he's fine, the next he's on the floor. He has a large scar on his chin from when he jumped off a chair and somehow—I was right there and saw it and still can't say how—somehow he hit his chin on the edge of a table five feet away. I thought he'd fractured his jaw, but he was fine, except for the cut. I have seen him sitting in his chair and without moving, POOF! he's on the floor, often hitting some part of his head on the way down. I swear the kid has a magnet in his head and Mother Earth pulls him to her at odd times.

One day Zac's teacher intercepted me as I entered the playground to pick him up after school. She had that look I'd come to know, the look of a teacher telling me my child has been injured. I looked past her, looking for my son. I couldn't see him. "He fell from the top of the monkey bars . . ." I didn't hear anymore. I was scanning the playground for Zac. "Lost his breath . . ." *Where was he?* "Inside . . ." "Ice . . ." Her eyes told me that this time it was serious.

I found him inside, alone, with red-rimmed eyes, little fist marks around his eyebrows where he'd tried to stop the tears and hide them from his friends. He was more scared than I'd ever seen him.

"Mom, I couldn't breathe." Except for his look of rattled shock he seemed okay, though his back ached, and he had deep skid marks and bleeding scratches on his arm.

I reviewed his fall in my head, saw him tumbling to the ground, felt the guilt of not having been there to catch him. I told him I did not want him on top of the monkey bars anymore.

Zac was devastated. "But that's where the big kids sit!" A broken arm was the worst that could happen if he used the equipment correctly, but, I insisted, he was never *ever* to sit on top of the bars again, because a fall from that height was too dangerous. He agreed, but I knew sitting on the top of those bars was where the big kids sat, and he would never understand how to be safe and play.

I couldn't be at school all day. I had to make him understand. Zachary is very logical. If I appealed to his logic, he would never forget what he'd learned. That's one of his greatest strengths.

When I got out the eggs to make some cookies the following Monday, the answer came to me.

We took the eggs outside to the front porch. "Zachary, your head is as fragile as an egg. This is what could happen if you fell from the top of the monkey bars." I held an egg up as far as I could stretch my arm and dropped it from that height onto the porch. The egg splattered on the concrete. Zachary's eyes were huge. "Now, this is what happens when your head falls the distance the architects who built the monkey bars meant for you to fall," and I dropped the egg from about five inches off the concrete. It got a small crack. Zachary looked at the eggs, then me, then the eggs, and laughed. "Now, watch what happens when I drop it onto padding more appropriate for the fall." I doubled the rubber doormat on top of the padded, kitchen mat and dropped another egg from six feet. It didn't even crack.

I pointed to the shattered egg dripping across the porch. "Can you pick that egg up and fix it for me?" Zac laughed again. "A head is just like that. We can't fix a head that's been injured that badly. No amount of occupational or physical or speech therapy can make it okay again, and no surgery, and no doctor, and no medicine. But this one that's a bit cracked we can work with, just like we can fix a broken arm with a cast."

It took two more eggs to see what an egg looks like with the momentum of an arm toss behind it, like a head with no seat belt in a car crash. We hurled another one so we could see it smeared on the grass to know what it would look like to crack a head in a flying slide. Then the point was made. Zachary doesn't sit on top of the monkey bars. He did ask if he could have two eggs to take for show-and-tell, to demonstrate head injury. I told him I could spare a few more eggs for the advancement of science.

Three

Inside the World of Nonverbal Learning Disorder

As parents, we need to understand how our child with NLD experiences daily life—what it feels like to him—in order to understand why they have meltdowns, why they are stressed and anxious, why they have difficulty in school and making friends. The more we are able to put ourselves in their place, the greater our compassion and the more effective our care for them will be.

For children with NLD, life in our world is a lot like life on an alien planet. On a minute-by-minute basis, they are trying to figure out the unspoken rules, and are trying their hardest to figure out what other people expect of them. They are bewildered. They want desperately to please, so they make wild guesses that are wrong more often than not. When their attempts to fit in and function fail again and again, they get frustrated, angry, sad, and exhausted, and often end up in screaming meltdowns.

When Zac was in kindergarten, he was frequently sent to the principal's office for "bad behavior." He rarely knew what he'd done wrong. One day he thought he was being punished for scratching his foot. He was just convinced. "Mom, I guess the rule is, you're not supposed to scratch your foot. So I think if I don't do that tomorrow, maybe I won't have to go to the office." He was trying so hard to make sense of a situation that made no sense to him at all. We never knew the real reason.

Often when we interpret a situation for Zachary and explain the non-verbal rule he didn't see for himself, he'll say, "You're kidding! *That's* what that was?" There are times when I just want to drop to my knees and hug him for his courage, because he is trying so hard.

NLD touches all aspects of life.

If a child has dyslexia, she leaves her learning disorder behind when she leaves the classroom and goes out to play. If a child has NLD, however, every minute of her life is affected. That's why they are in a constant state of stress. Because they lack strong muscles and good endurance, they fatigue very easily. Put this together with continual social stressors, and it's clear why they are always exhausted and frequently over-whelmed. One child with NLD said: "I feel every day the way other people feel in a crowded shopping mall just before Christmas."

A Day in the Life of a Child with NLD

You wake up still tired. You know that some mornings you can sleep late, and some mornings you can't, but you don't know which it is today. Your mom comes in and tells you to get up and get ready for school. You feel angry and frustrated, why does today have to be one of the school days? Your mom reminds you to brush your hair. You brush your hair the way it feels good, straight forward, but then your mom says, "Back in the bathroom, we need to fix your hair."

"But I brushed it! I did what you said!" You don't understand why she is being unfair and mean.

A lot of children with NLD are very perfunctory in their dress and grooming. Because these kids don't pick up visual cues, they don't think it's inappropriate to wear a bathing suit to school with a wool sweater, or to match stripes with checks. From their point of view, it's clean, so what's the problem? They don't perceive subtle distinctions in grooming. Zachary used to comb his hair all the way forward and from his point of view, he'd combed his hair, and it was clean, so what was the big deal? When I tried to fix it, he would get furious and throw the comb. He'd combed it as I had asked him to, and from his point of view, my objections on the basis of style were arbitrary and unfair.

Of course, I could say, "Stop it. Just let me comb your hair." But what we've chosen to do is say, "It's just a rule in our community that people wear their hair a certain way. If you wear your hair the way you have it, you're basically telling people that you're goofy." Or I'll say, "If people look at your teeth and if you haven't brushed them, they immediately think you're a dumb person."

Zac will say, "What? You're kidding."

"I know, it doesn't make a lot of sense, but that really is how people think. I think the impression began back in our history when only educated people could afford toothbrushes and dental care." Once it's explained to him as a rule, he'll usually accept it.

In the kitchen you try hard to be careful but you spill your cereal. There's food all over your clothes and you have to change again. You're staring at your dresser drawer, and your mom comes in and says, "I told you to hurry and change your clothes. What are you doing?" You're frustrated and angry, because you're trying to hurry, and you don't know how to start. Hurry how? Is it a shorts day or a pants day? Finally your mom pulls out some clothes and gives them to you, and you put them on. You go back to the kitchen and start to walk out to the driveway, and your mom says, "Where's your backpack? Go back to your room and get your backpack." She's so mad again and you feel like crying but you can't because kids tease you when your eyes are red.

Children with NLD will feel the stress of the situation, but they often can't connect it to words. It's like a strange feeling in the air that affects them without their really understanding why. It's another example of the gap between what we expect our children to be able to do and what they are actually able to do, a gap between what we think we are saying to them and what they are hearing us say. The child gets lost in the gap. By the time school starts, the child is a stressed-out wreck, in no way prepared for the bombardments of the school environment, much less for learning.

When your mom drops you off at school, you're supposed to get in line and wait for the teachers to call everybody in. Every day, you get in line behind Billy, and every day Billy insults you. If you move to the back of the line, he moves back there and insults you. No matter what you do, he insults you. The teacher doesn't care. So you figure that must just be the way it works: He gets to insult you, he can call you names. You know the rule is you can't hit him, but it's not fair. Billy is also at your table in class. There's nothing you can do about his bullying there either, because the teacher knows Billy's mean to you, and she put him at your table.

Children with NLD are frequently the target of bullies. Because they take things literally, because they are so trusting, and because they rarely tattle, they are the perfect victims. Often they can't tell the difference between bullying and friendly banter or dangerous intentions. Unfortunately, bullies know exactly how to mistreat others without letting grown-ups see them. A child with NLD won't be able to read the subtle cues that tell the bully the teacher isn't paying attention, so he is likely to assume the teacher sees the bully's behavior and condones it. Frequently, the teacher *hasn't* seen the bully's behavior and the teacher only sees when the child with NLD *reacts* to the bully's taunts. A child with NLD will react whether the adult is around or not.

Children with NLD are easy victims because they won't recognize when they're being taken advantage of. When Zac was in first grade, I would give him fifty cents a day to buy a Popsicle during his after-school program. Later, I'd ask him what kind he'd gotten that day, and he'd always tell me he'd gotten one that I knew wasn't his favorite. Then he'd say, "I bought Johnny a Popsicle," or "Today I bought Kenny one." I'd say, "Oh, that was nice of you." Then I found out he wasn't buying their Popsicles out of generosity, but because they were telling him he had to. Children with NLD are extremely compliant. So when Kenny said to him, "You're supposed to buy me a Popsicle," Zac just assumed it was a rule he had to follow. He never questioned it and never thought to come home and ask, "Is it a rule that I have to buy a Popsicle for Kenny?"

Now that Zac has had intervention through language therapy, it's rarer that kids will take advantage of him. When it does happen, he'll ask us about it because now it's confusing to him instead of just something he assumes he has to accept. He also internalized that it is possible to get help to figure out social rules. Some kids do not develop the internal sense that help is available to them when they need it.

When you get to the classroom, you discover that the teacher has rearranged all the cubbies and tables. You can't figure out where you're supposed to put your coat. All the other kids are rushing past you and the teacher tells you to hurry up and take your seat. You still can't find it. You can feel she's angry at you again. She says, "Right there is your seat, can't you see your name?" The other kids are laughing at you when you finally find your seat and sit down.

Children with NLD have great difficulty with novel experiences and change in their routines. When Zac was in kindergarten, his school day was relatively unstructured. While he was reading or working on an art project, one of the parent helpers would come to tell him it was his turn to come and play with Play-Doh or whatever that day's activity was. He would get extremely frustrated at having to shift gears. When he got to school and found out that the place to put his coat or lunch box had been changed again, and he had to figure out where his things were, he would have a meltdown. At recess, it took him a long time to find his snack, then to plan his movements and find a place where no one would annoy him with their chatter (Zac was auditorially hypersensitive). By the time he got out his snack, it was time to pack up and "go play." He would get so upset! It's no wonder that when recess was finally over, he felt like he hadn't had a break and would refuse to come inside.

Class begins. You're trying to take the spelling test, but your hands feel as if you're wearing rubber gloves. Of course, you make a mistake in your first word. You reach into your desk to pull out an eraser, but with those gloves on you can't feel it. You have to physically crook yourself around and look into the desk. You have to take everything out, and it's awkward with those gloves on. Meanwhile, the spelling test drones on. You become more flustered, and your body and chair are in odd positions, so you fall. Your teacher gets angry with you for your "intentional disruption." All you're trying to do is find your eraser.

In science class, you still have those gloves on. You're supposed to investigate owl pellets. You've got the probe to manipulate and the pencil to record your findings. You try to pull the pellet apart carefully and not destroy it with the probe. But with those gloves on, you don't get the feedback to guide your hands. Your owl pellet looks like a smear now.

You're supposed to be working with peers, but you get so frustrated the teacher tells you to work on your own at a back table.

Because of their tactile imperceptions and awkward or inefficient movements, children with NLD have a very difficult time with ordinary classroom tasks. Writing, manipulating tools, and sitting in a chair without falling can all be very difficult for them. Unfortunately, their clumsiness and falls can be interpreted by others as deliberate misbehavior—clowning or intentional disruption. But kids with NLD are usually embarrassed by their clumsiness. They don't want to fall or to spend fifteen minutes looking for an eraser, and they feel that humiliation and failure deeply.

At recess, you want to play on the monkey bars like the other kids do. One minute you're holding on, the next you're flat on the ground, and the other kids are laughing at you. "Who wants to play with you? You're such a klutz you trip when you're standing still!" You walk around the edges of the playground, looking at your shoes.

Back in class, sentences are on the chalkboard. You're supposed to copy them with all the mistakes the teacher put in, then write them again correctly. It takes forever! You remember words by sight, but these words don't make sense to you. When your teacher collects the papers, she stops at your desk, looks at your almost blank paper, and says, "I couldn't possibly make it any easier for you."

Finally, it's time for reading. You read faster and better than anyone in the room, but when your teacher asks you why Pippy Longstocking thinks her dad is going to return someday, you have no idea. You try repeating what you read, but that doesn't seem to be the answer, even though you know you said the words exactly the way they were in the book.

When it's time for math, you know how to add, and you know most of your multiplication tables when you have a little extra time, but the bell will signal time for science in just 10 minutes. You can't seem to make the numbers stay in a line on your paper. You know in your head that the ones go in the ones column and so on, but writing your numbers and putting them into columns is just impossible!

Each time you look from your book to your paper, you need a few seconds to make your eyes focus again. You have to ask yourself over and over, "Now, where was I?" Your teacher, again, asks you to do neater work. You get less than half the worksheet done, so you take it home along with your other homework.

When you get home, you get out your homework and the two assignments you didn't complete at school. It's 3:30. By the time you finish, it will be 8:30 at least. You wonder how come other kids can be outside riding their skateboards while you're stuck at the kitchen table every night. It's not fair.

For kids with NLD, homework is an arena filled with challenges and conflicts. Many of their deficits, such as difficulties with sequencing, completion, interpretation, and handwriting, come to the fore when they're doing homework. In addition, homework comes at the end of the day when they are tired and stressed, so they make frequent mistakes. Their frustration often manifests in negative self-talk: "I'm so stupid. I'm never going to get it. I suck. Why don't I just quit school." They'll hit themselves in the head and make negative sounds. It's not unusual for the child to have a meltdown over homework. Most districts have homework guidelines, suggestions for reasonable amounts of time for homework. Parents need to say "enough" when homework takes an unreasonable amount of time for their child.

Most kids could copy twenty addition problems out of a book and solve them in about fifteen or twenty minutes, but it would take Zac about two hours. First he would sit down and then he'd have to get a drink. Then he'd sit down again and he'd have to go to the bathroom. This was not so much procrastination as trying to increase his level of alertness. When he finally got started, copying twenty problems out of the book would take him an hour. His paper would have erasures all over it and barely be legible. Then he'd begin to solve the problems. The work seemed to go on forever.

Another problem that shows up in homework is how these kids misinterpret their assignments. When Zac was in second grade, one of his assignments was to write three sentences about his dad's car. You might expect this to be an easy task for a child with language strengths. But children with NLD have difficulties with written expression. They don't have a good sense of closure, so their thinking tends to go on and on. Zac had been working on this assignment for an hour. He had completed one sentence and he had to do two more. He had his head down on the table in sheer exhaustion.

Eventually I realized that this was an interpretation problem. Zachary thought an assignment to write three sentences meant the equivalent of three pages. The teacher was expecting something like "My dad's car is yellow," and Zac was writing a sentence that was half a page long. I took what he'd written and with a red pencil I marked all the sentences in his long paragraph.

I explained, "Now, this is like a high school sentence. But what the teacher is asking for is three second-grade sentences." I explained to him that all he needed to write was a noun, a verb, maybe one descriptive word, and a period, what I called a "stopping dot." Zachary was *thrilled*. He said, "You're kidding! That's all? Why didn't she just say that?"

Homework also highlights the difficulties children with NLD have following something through to completion. Completing homework is actually a complicated series of steps, and there are many places where the sequence breaks down. Either the child doesn't write down the assignment correctly, or she writes it correctly but it's too time consuming or too difficult, or she doesn't understand what she wrote down, or, once the homework is complete, she fails to turn it in to the teacher.

I have often run into conflict with Zac because I am able to infer what the teacher meant, but Zac will insist, "She didn't say that, Mom, so I'm done." He's right; she didn't say that, but he'll still get in trouble for not doing the assignment that was implied.

"Well, you're supposed to be working on it for an entire month, so I think your teacher is looking for more than stick figures in the illustration."

"No, Mom, that's all I was supposed to do. I'm done."

For a few years I would try hard to convince Zac to do the implied assignment, but now I have realized that sometimes I have to go to the teacher with Zachary and get clarification. Once Zac hears his teacher be more specific, then he'll dutifully complete the assignment.

Sometimes I'll know that he did the assignment, and then I'll get a note from the teacher saying he didn't. I'll open up his notebook and say, "Zachary, it's right here, why didn't you give it to Mr. Jones?"

"He didn't ask for it."

"Did he collect homework?"

"Yes, but I think it was just math."

If the teacher asks for an assignment using a slightly different name for it, these children will not know what the teacher intended, and will fail to turn their homework in. Every child with NLD that I have worked with struggles to turn in homework after its completed.

> *Your homework still isn't done, but it's bedtime. You're exhausted. Your mom says, "Go put on your pajamas and brush your teeth." It takes you forever to put your pajamas on because you're so tired. You go into the bathroom and brush your teeth, and then your mom comes in and says, "You missed half your mouth! No bedtime story for you, young man." You completely lose it. You just can't handle one more thing. All you can do is scream and cry.*

Getting ready for bed involves organization and sequencing, things that are hard for these kids, especially when they're tired. People consider these activities of daily living (ADLs) to be invisible and automatic, but they are neither. They are very complex and difficult to describe all the steps.

When I was training for my Master's in occupational therapy, we had to do an activity analysis of brushing your teeth. An activity analysis breaks down all the things that the brain and body have to do to accomplish a task. Most of us wrote about six pages on teeth brushing before we said, "I quit. Just give me a C." We discovered that brushing your teeth is a very complicated task. You have to open the lid of the toothpaste, you have to squeeze the tube perfectly, not too hard and not too soft, you have to coordinate the two sides of the body together, you have to have good eye-hand coordination to get the tube to the toothbrush, then you have to put the paste on with the right force and direction— otherwise it falls into the sink—and then you have to navigate the toothbrush around your teeth. This is an extremely high motor-planning skill. For children with NLD it is a major challenge, and they will often miss half their mouths.

> *Your mom takes your toothbrush and jams it into your mouth. Then she drags you off to your room. You're still crying, and your pajamas are scratching you, and your room is too hot, and it's all too much. Then your dad's there, too, and he dumps you into the top bunk and he turns*

off the light and says, "That's enough. Be quiet and go to sleep." But you
can't be quiet. You want to, but all you can do is cry louder and harder.

A child with NLD may be neurologically incapable of crying herself
to sleep. (It certainly never happened in my home.) Her ability to calm
herself is minimal at best, and when her sensory system is so overloaded,
she won't be able to access whatever she may have learned about calming down. Instead, her meltdown will escalate, and it can get very ugly
for both the child and the parents, who are, of course, tired themselves
and probably at the end of their patience.

A lot of kids with NLD are very uncomfortable sleeping in a bed
that's elevated from the floor. If their sense of balance is not in place,
they can fall out of bed, and so they feel a lot of anxiety being there. A
bed may not make them feel safe, no matter how much we try to make it
a beautiful, safe environment for them. Many kids with NLD sleep on
the floor in a sleeping bag (and a lot of them sleep in their clothes so they
don't have to deal with pajamas).

Fortunately, bedtime doesn't have to be so awful. Even if the rest of
the day has been misery for your child, you can make bedtime a relaxing, soothing time, and the bed and bedroom a sanctuary for your child.
Yes, some nights your child will have meltdowns, but if you know the
triggers, such as brushing teeth and putting on pajamas, you can have
your child brush her teeth after dinner before she's too tired, and make
allowances for pajamas. If you know your child's sensory needs, there
are choices you can make to make bedtime simpler.

These children have a tough time pulling themselves together and
winding down, and you can help them do that. Because they are so
word-driven, so focused on books and stories, a bedtime story can be
their salvation. Sometimes reminding them of the choices they're making
with their actions can be helpful such as "If you hurry, we'll have time
for a longer story." If they *can* hurry, that is, it will be helpful. If you're
setting up just one more thing for them to fail at, then it will contribute
to their inability and anxiety.

If you get your child tucked in nice and tight, giving her that external
security, or she gets to sit and cuddle with Mom or Dad, or whatever
works for her, you've created a space where she can relax and end the
day with some peace and pleasure. No matter how old these children

are, being read to is a great joy for them. Bedtime can be a very nice time if you understand the value and importance of words to your child and make the time to read to her even if you're exhausted. (Or even when you have work of your own you need to do. I've tucked Zachary in many a night reading him my anatomy book or a case study. Obviously, the richer the words, the lovelier it is for your child.)

Bedtime is also a nice time for bringing the sensory strategies together, like deep pressure (the sensation from swaddled blankets, cuddling, and firm massage) and letting your child dictate her needs—that particular blanket arranged this particular way. Let bedtime be a place of comfort.

To increase our compassion for our children, some other aspects of the world of a child with NLD bear examination. Some of their traits can cause a lot of conflict in a family. However, if you understand how the mind of a child with NLD works, you will discover that the child you thought was willful, disobedient, defiant, and rude is actually compliant, eager to please you, and painstakingly honest.

Literal Speech

One area of conflict for children with NLD and the adults in their lives centers around literal interpretation of speech. They do not hear the implied meaning of our words. They hear what we say, no more and no less, and they will do exactly what we tell them to, no less, and no more.

One Saturday I gave Zachary the chore of washing my car. He got started, and later I went out to check on him. He'd washed the car, but he hadn't used any soap. I said, "What are you doing? There's no soap on this car."

Zachary looked at me and said in a most obnoxious tone, "You didn't ask for soap, now did you?" (He doesn't always know what his tone of voice sounds like to others.)

I was just about ready to kill him, but I took a deep breath and said, "Okay, Zachary, I need you to wash my car, and I need you to use soap."

"Oh, okay, fine. Why didn't you say so?"

When Zachary came inside a while later, I said, "Did you wash my car?"

"Yes."

"Did you put the bucket away?"

"Yes."

"Okay, you can go play now."

Then I looked out and I saw there were dried soap bubbles all over my car.

I marched into the living room and said "Zachary! You didn't rinse the car!"

Zachary stood up. He was so mad that he just stood there and shrieked at me, *"You didn't say that!"*

This time I had to take ten deep breaths before I could bring myself to say, "I'm sorry. You're right. I didn't say that. Now let's go rinse the car."

It would be very easy to interpret this behavior as deliberate defiance. That's why these kids often get labeled with Oppositional Defiance Disorder (ODD) and why adults think they are rude and bratty. But there is a simple way to distinguish their literal interpretation of speech from defiance. We discovered that once we were clear with Zachary, once we made sure he knew what we expected of him, he was completely compliant and often more than compliant—usually cheerful.

When he was old enough, we gave him the chore of taking out the trash. In the beginning, I'd say, "Zachary, you need to take the trash out now." He'd grumble a little, then he'd get the trash and take it out. Later I'd open the door and I'd find the trash bag on the front porch. I'd say, "Zachary, you need to take the trash out."

"But I did!"

"No, it's on the porch. You're supposed to take it to the curb."

"You didn't tell me that. Why didn't you say so?" Eventually I understood I needed to explain about putting the trash bag in the outdoor trash can, putting the lid back on it, and wheeling the can to the curb for the garbage truck to pick up. Now that Zachary knows what we mean by "take out the trash," he does it the way we want him to. Before I did that, "out" to Zachary meant just out of the house. We had to be clearer. We've discovered that the more we are clear and precise in talking to Zachary, the less we have this type of conflict.

Another conflict that results from their literal interpretations comes up around time. If I tell Zachary to go to bed at 9:00, and at 8:57 I'm trying to hustle him to his room, he'll insist I leave him alone for those three minutes. It is more helpful if we say to Zac, "It's 8:15 and we need to leave by 8:30 so you need to stop reading, brush your teeth, get your backpack ready, and get in the car for school."

One situation that makes adults crazy occurs because children with NLD do not understand that we use polite requests to soften a command. The parents who volunteered in Zachary's kindergarten found him annoying when they would say to him, "Would you like to take your turn now?" and he'd say, "No." If they had followed that up with, "Will you do it anyway?" he would have said, "Of course," but they didn't know that. They just thought he was being obnoxious.

This happens in our home, too. I'll tell Zac, "At the commercial, would you like to pick up your clothes in the living room?"

"No."

After a lot of speech therapy and explaining to him that this is a polite way to talk that really means, "Pick up your clothes in the living room," now he'll say, "Is this one of those that's really a command that you're pretending is a question?"

"Yes, it's really one of those."

"So I don't really have any choice. I have to pick up my clothes at the commercial?"

"Yes, you do."

We have that type of conversation all the time.

As parents we expect our kids to grasp this idea when they're very small. We "know" everyone picks it up by the time they're six or seven, so if they don't get off the sofa and pick up their clothes, we "know" they're being defiant. But that's a false assumption. Kids with NLD might interpret language so literally that they really believe you were just asking about their preferences. When you get angry, they are likely to be confused and hurt and wonder why are you yelling when you gave them a choice.

Correcting Adults

Another area of conflict is the habit children with NLD have of correcting adults' language. Sometimes reading a bedtime story to Zachary is not a very enjoyable experience *for me* because he corrects me on every sentence. Or if I ask him a question about something he knows a lot about, like a video game, and I don't phrase something exactly right, he *has* to correct me, even if my mistake is irrelevant to the question. When Zac was in kindergarten, one of the parent helpers told me they had been instructed by the teacher not to engage in a verbal argument with my son because "he would win." While this protected the adults from losing face to a kid, it left Zac without a way of learning what to expect and what was expected of him.

An insistence on correcting makes children with NLD very good editors. Many of them will use this skill in some professional capacity when they're older. Even now, I'll give Zachary things of mine to edit because he's great at it. But when it's my mother-in-law who's being corrected, it's not great. When it's a teacher, it's not great. Children with NLD will correct their teachers or grandparents because they correct everybody. It can often look like arrogance, even though these children don't intend to be arrogant. It can make some teachers crazy. Because, of course, the adults want to stop everything and teach this insolent child to behave with respect. Then the "insolent" child is confused: They wonder "Why are you mad at me? I just told you a fact. I just told you a rule. I don't know why you're mad."

Because they're so tenacious about it, you may have to come up with an outlet for them: they can only correct once a day, or they can only correct at recess, or you can give them "correction chips" that they can cash in, three a day.

Monologues

Living with children with NLD typically means having to endure long monologues. These kids can talk and talk, but there's not a lot of content to their speech. They stop for long pauses to look at their toes while you have to wait for them to finish. It's hard to find enough ways to be kind to these kids when you interrupt. To them, it's an issue of fairness: You're teaching them to not interrupt, to listen to others, and then you interrupt them. It can be very tempting to just say, "Okay, now be quiet," or "Get a grip," or "Pay attention." But those responses aren't very helpful. What we've learned to say is something like, "Look at me. Look at me when you talk," because if Zac's looking at me, he's not looking at something else in the room, he's likely to get distracted. Then we'll say, "Okay, two more sentences." Or "You know what, I'm having a hard time listening here. I'm getting lost. Tell me one more thing about this." We try to make our responses very concrete and to give him specific instructions to follow.

Compliance

Children with NLD follow the rules. They are compliant and dutiful even in situations when we wouldn't want them to be. The good side of that is, I know that when Zac uses a public rest room, he will wash his hands for one minute, using soap, turn off the water using a paper towel (so he doesn't recontaminate himself), and throw the towel in the trash can, but the bad side is he takes a long time in the rest room and sometimes I have to open the door to the men's room and say "Zachary, are you okay in there?" I've startled more than a few men. I know that if he is at a movie with a friend, he will not leave his seat to go buy candy unless his friend or the grown-up in charge goes with him, and he will not ask the grown-up to buy him popcorn. The bad side is, even if he had to go to the bathroom or there was an earthquake, he would stay in his seat if no one was available to accompany him.

One rainy day, my husband drove Zachary to kindergarten, dropped him off at the curb, and left. Around ten I got a call from the school: "Zac's here, and there's no school today."

It turns out that it was a teacher-learning day. After his dad had dropped him off, Zac went over and stood outside the classroom under a two-foot eave. It was pouring rain. He just stood there for nearly two hours before a teacher happened to see him.

"Zachary, honey, what are you doing?"

"Well, my dad dropped me off."

"Didn't your dad know there's no school today?"

"I guess so."

"What are you going to do?"

"I think I'm just supposed to stand here and wait till they come and get me."

He would have stood there for four hours. It never occurred to him to knock on a door, and say "How come the door isn't open?" or to go to the office and say, "My dad completely messed up, so please call him." He was just going to obediently stand there in the rain for four hours.

There are so many times we discover him dutifully doing what no one else would do.

Integrity

Children with NLD have rock-solid integrity and a keen sense of fairness. They are not deceitful. Other kids try to get by with mischief or outright wrongdoing. Zac doesn't. Neither do the other children with NLD I know. If you ask if they touched the ball on the soccer field, they'll tell the truth. In fact, many parents of children with NLD celebrate their child's first lie because it indicates a leap in their understanding of language.

Being able to trust your child is a wonderful gift. We know we can trust Zac. If I ask if he's brushed his teeth, he'll tell me the truth. If I say, "Did you eat your carrots at lunch?" he'll say, "No, I ate my candy bar first, ran out of time, and gave my carrots away." Even though he doesn't like his helmet, we know he always wears it when skateboarding because it is a rule in our family.

Of course, Zac's impeccable honesty works both ways. Once, Zac and I decided to play hooky and not go to speech therapy. I was exhausted, and Zac was perfectly willing to skip his appointment. I called and said we didn't feel well, which wasn't a complete lie. When we went to the next session, the therapist asked, "Are you feeling better? You were sick last week."

Zac said, "No, we weren't sick. We just decided to play hooky and called in and said we were sick."

Sense of Humor

While many researchers suggest the opposite, parents and therapists know children with NLD often develop a sense of humor that can be quite sophisticated. Bill likes to read the *Dilbert Newsletter* to Zac and to pore over the Sunday comics with him. If Zac doesn't understand something in *Dilbert*, he wants very much to get it, and he'll stick to his questioning until he understands. Bill is endlessly patient with Zac and breaks down each joke until Zac understands. As a result, Zac has developed a wicked sense of humor.

Zac often catches us off guard with his humor. One of his recent jokes was "Why is child abuse illegal?" We went into a long explanation, and then he said, "Well, I think a child should be able to use his abs [meaning abdominal muscles], so what's up with making child ab-use illegal?"

The Pleasures of NLD

Without intervention, life for children with NLD can be overwhelming and miserable. But it doesn't have to be that way. A lot of pleasure and satisfaction is available for these kids when the right supports are in place.

Zac takes great pride and satisfaction in his ability to remember everything. He's a fast reader. When he read the latest *Harry Potter* faster than any of his friends, he thought he was just so cool. He's not just skimming either. His teacher tells me that when his class is doing book reports, Zac is the only one who will open up the book, find what he's looking for, and read it to the class. He hasn't marked the pages. He just remembers the story that well. He's one of the students the other kids model because he's determined and works quietly at his assignments and gets good grades.

Reading and books are a real pleasure for these kids. Language is an area of pleasure for them as is the accumulation of factual knowledge. They love discovering how language works. Because they have such amazing memories, they take pleasure in gobbling up information. They get pleasure out of being the kid who knows a lot of facts. Being able to use the facts for conversations and relationships is important but often one of their challenges.

I think of children with NLD as little aliens on our planet, wonderful aliens who have come here because they have something important to teach us. They arrive in our world with a beautiful innocence, and they hold on to it for a long time. We need to help them adapt to our world, but we must also be very respectful of their innocence, or they get hurt. Sadly, human beings can be quite mean to each other when they do not take the time to understand. As parents, I believe we have a sacred responsibility to treat our children with compassion, to honor their differences, and to cherish all they bring us.

Zac's Essay on Being Clumsy

I always end up hitting people if they stand too close to me. I'm a disaster area! I can't see them so I don't know they're there. I might put my elbow up and out to the side by my ear, maybe I'm scratching, or I might hit them in the chin when I'm stretching.

In general, I'm very clumsy. I hate being clumsy—it's annoying Sometimes I accidentally hit people I like. Or I fall on them. Sometimes I drop plates—Oh my GOSH is that ever embarrassing!!!

The morale of the story is—while they say three feet is a good space to keep between normal people, five feet is more like it for us clumsy kids. You'd think people would remember I'd done all those clumsy things and stay back but they don't. Maybe I'll wear a shirt that says, "Go away! I'm gonna blow and I don't mean in anger I mean in energy! My body will fly all over the place and eventually hit someone and that someone could be YOU!" or maybe, instead, of "E=MC²" I could write on my shirts, "E=ME² — so *WATCH OUT!*"

It gets pretty funny at my house. One night my mom was putting me to bed and she said "Good night" and bent down to give me a good-night kiss. I stuck my hand up to hug her back but I accidentally punched her in the head. I reached out to say I was sorry and I poked her in the eye. We were laughing so hard and would you believe it that I head-butted her in the nose! We laughed really hard then. I sometimes think there should be an announcer that follows me around saying "Embarrassing Funny Moments will be right back after a word from our sponsors."

Another time I dropped a bowl of berries all over the kitchen floor within minutes of my mom finishing mopping it. If you look in our family's photo album, you'll see me standing there looking at a floor covered with berries and berry juice. I'm standing in the pictures with my hands on my head, my mouth dropped open, probably screaming, and looking down at the mess. I have the look on my face like food aliens have invaded my house. I know that at some people's houses the mom screams "GO TO YOUR ROOM YOU LITTLE BRAT!" but in my house the mom goes and gets the camera—just taking a record of my childhood.

Being a disaster isn't always funny. At the time, it's actually very embarrassing. But later, when I think about it, it's hilarious and I can laugh. Hee hee hee hee Heh heh heh.

By Zac, age 8

Four

Getting the Diagnosis

THE earlier a child's NLD is diagnosed, the better the chances for effective intervention and the lower the risk of secondary problems like anxiety, obsessive-compulsive behavior, or depression. Unfortunately, early identification of these children can be difficult for a number of reasons. Schools may not recognize the child's symptoms for what they are, but may instead label them "bad behavior." The child might be misdiagnosed with ADD and inappropriately medicated. Or the child's deficits might not seem significant to teachers or parents at first. Because these children are able to rely on their strengths until about the fourth grade, it's very easy and common for them to slip through unidentified. In the meantime, their clumsiness, disorganization, and social difficulties get worse and worse because they miss all the other things other kids pick up on as they go through the day. My hope is that as NLD becomes more widely understood, early diagnosis will become the rule rather than the exception.

"I always knew there was something different about my child, but no one believed me."

"Her teachers said not to worry because she was so smart."

"The teacher insisted it was ADD and that we get him on medication, but I just didn't see that the medication made any difference."

"Our pediatrician said he'd grow out of his clumsiness."

"No one would listen to my concerns because there wasn't anything specific."

These comments are typical of parents whose children have ultimately been diagnosed with NLD. Although parents often don't have the language to describe what they've intuitively sensed, their perceptions were accurate. It is important to keep in mind that your knowledge of your child and your intuition about your child's needs and capacities are a critical part of the diagnostic process. "Experts" have training that allows them to make an official diagnosis—a label that helps you get the services your child needs—but *you* are the only one who is an expert on *your* child.

Jennifer's Story

At their parent-teacher conference halfway through her daughter's first grade, Gina expected Miss Norman to tell her what she'd heard so often: how smart Jennifer was. Jennifer had spoken and read early, and her vocabulary was better than Gina's or her husband's. She loved to read and had an amazing memory for facts. Lots of Gina's friends called her "the little professor." Though Miss Norman spoke gently and non-judgmentally, what she said shocked Gina.

"Jennifer seems to be struggling. She is having more difficulty with handwriting than the other children, and when I give directions to the class, she doesn't get started on her work. I don't think that she's purposely or deliberately trying to avoid the work. My guess is she doesn't understand. When she's on the playground, she's often alone at the very edge instead of playing with other children. She doesn't seem able to find a place for herself when we do small-group activities. She is often clumsy. On the playground or in PE class, or when we do classroom activities, she often bumps into things or falls, and she frequently spills or drops things. I'm concerned there's something going on that keeps her from being as successful as we think she could be."

"But she's so smart!" Gina said. "She's a brilliant little girl."

"Yes, she is," agreed Miss Norman, "in some areas. Her verbal skills really are exceptional. But if we look at the expected social and motor skills for her age, Jennifer seems to have trouble. So what I would like to do, with your permission," Miss Norman continued, "is to start by having our occupational therapist take a look to see if there may be underlying problems getting in her way."

As Gina drove home, she was so infuriated at the teacher's suggestion that she could hardly think. Yes, she acknowledged that Jennifer was a little clumsy, and it was true she didn't have real friends. But that was because she was so much smarter than other kids. There couldn't possibly be anything wrong with her precocious little genius. Gina decided to disregard the conversation.

When Jennifer began the second half of the year, she still found handwriting very difficult, even writing her own name. She used Gina's computer instead. Her grades began to go down, and she started to resist going to school. "The other kids don't like me," she'd say. "And I always get in trouble." Gina went for another conference with Miss Norman, who taught the first- and second-grade cluster. Miss Norman repeated most of what she'd said a year before. This time, Gina listened. She could see that Jennifer was not growing out of her clumsiness, and she still had no friends. Jennifer seemed to be sad a lot of the time. She had never been invited to a birthday party, and worse, no one came to hers. Gina agreed to an evaluation by an occupational therapist and the school psychologist.

After the testing was complete, Gina came to a meeting with the school psychologist, the occupational therapist, Miss Norman, and the school's resource teacher. The psychologist talked about a lot of numbers, talked about verbal IQ and performance IQ and none of it meant anything to Gina.

The occupational therapist reported, "Jennifer is a lovely child," she began, "just a delight to be around. But I think it's really frustrating for her when she can't keep up with the written work. Her body doesn't process movement efficiently, and she has trouble making her body do what she wants it to do." When Gina looked confused, the therapist explained. "I asked Jennifer to follow simple three-step directions, like jump, stop, clap your hands, and she couldn't do that. Every time she would mess up she would turn and say, 'Well, that's extraordinarily difficult for a child my age, wouldn't you think?' Then I tested her visual memory by drawing letters on her back with my finger. I drew an A on her back and asked, 'What's that letter?' She said, 'Z?' Even if I drew the letters from her own name, she was guessing. So it's pretty clear that one of the reasons she's having trouble with handwriting and letter formation is because she has problems with visual memory and poor sensation in her hands. She has a lot of strengths, but they're insufficient to compensate for her weaknesses. She has strategies for coping and compensating, but those strategies are not as successful for her as others could be. She isolates herself on the playground and avoids small-group activities."

The team told Gina that all these tests indicated that Jennifer had Nonverbal Learning Disorder. Gina was in shock. How could her intelligent child have a learning disorder? Her head was still spinning from all their strange words and numbers, so that she could hardly take in the information they gave her. All she grasped at the moment was that they were saying something was wrong with Jennifer. Gina was scared and angry, and she didn't want to believe what they were telling her. Fortunately, she realized she was too confused and upset to make any decisions. When the team asked her to sign some papers, she took a deep breath and said, "Can I take all this home with me and look at it? It's just too much to take in right now." The others nodded sympathetically.

At home that night, Gina told Rick, her husband, about the meeting. As they slowly began to comprehend the difficulties their daughter had been struggling with, they cried together. They looked over the reports Gina had brought home and decided to get on the Internet and find out all they could about NLD. A week later, Gina went back to Miss Norman. "Now I see what you were trying to tell me," she said. She pointed to the criteria for NLD. "This is exactly what Jennifer's like. I just never knew it had a name. And I guess I didn't really understand how much it could get in her way. I assumed she would outgrow it." Once Gina and Rick were educated about Jennifer's learning style, they were eager to do whatever it took to help her.

The educational team at Jennifer's school put an IEP (Individualized Educational Program, the federal document that outlines a plan for intervention) into effect. The psychologist monitored her case, and the resource teacher worked with her in the classroom every day. The occupational therapist trained Gina to provide Jennifer's therapy at home and gave her very specific homework in addition to working with Jennifer at school twice a week. After six months of therapy, Jennifer had made great progress. Her handwriting improved, and she could write a whole sentence, sometimes two. She was almost always able to keep her focus on her work long enough to complete it, she wasn't falling out of her chair, she was able to participate in PE, and she was starting to make friends. Her first invitation to a birthday party was one of her most prized possessions.

Daniel's Story

Daniel, a second grader, was always getting sent to the principal's office for being rude to his teacher, for hitting other children, or for creating disturbances in the classroom. But Ted was sure that the problem lay with Daniel's teacher, not with his child. It seemed to Ted that ever since kindergarten, Daniel's teachers had been determined to misunderstand his child and blame him for their own incompetence. Daniel was brilliant. Why couldn't they see that? They had to be idiots not to see how brilliant he was. Why, Daniel's test scores showed he read at a twelfth grade level.

Ted believed that everyone at the school was envious of Daniel's intelligence and that they purposely set up situations to get Daniel into trouble. He was sure he was the only one looking out for Daniel. Many nights he was so consumed with rage at the school that he couldn't sleep, and many days he thought the endless battles he fought for his son would give him an ulcer. He must have been to 20 meetings about Daniel in the past year.

The school professionals had told him Daniel needed to be in a special classroom. They told him Daniel had Attention Deficit Hyperactivity Disorder (ADHD). They told him he had Oppositional Defiant Disorder (ODD). They told him Daniel needed Ritalin and antianxiety medication, and they'd recently started saying, "Maybe Daniel isn't appropriate for our school," and talking about special education class.

Not his Daniel. No way!

Ted was convinced not one of these people knew what they were talking about. He was so busy fighting with them that Daniel got overlooked.

Ted got another phone call from Daniel's school saying his child was in the principal's office, out of control. Ted left work early to pick up

Daniel. When he arrived at the principal's office, Daniel had exhausted himself and was sitting slumped in a chair. His face was red and splotchy, as if he'd been in a fight.

"Hey big guy," Ted said. "What happened this time?"

"Mrs. Tasini said I had to come here, but I don't know why," Daniel mumbled. Daniel hit himself in the head with his fist. "Why don't you just kill me?"

"That idiot," Ted said. "Can't she even bother to tell you which of their stupid rules you're supposed to have broken?" The principal's door was opening, and Ted spoke louder. "What kind of lousy teachers do they have at this school?" The school psychologist came out with the principal.

"Mr. Royce," the psychologist said, "we're hoping you can come to a meeting next Monday."

"Another one? Just because Mrs. Tasini can't teach smart kids? What's the matter with you people?" Ted put the meeting on his pocket calendar, but he fumed all the way home while Daniel curled up in a little heap on the seat of the car. "I don't understand that school. Why can't they just see how smart you are? I mean, we know you're brilliant, Daniel. Mrs. Tasini is just incompetent. If they'd just hire teachers who knew something, everything would be okay."

The next morning Ted decided that since everyone at the school was against him, he needed to get a professional who would be on his side. He called an educational consultant he'd heard about and asked her to meet with Daniel. Then he called the school and asked them to forward Daniel's file to her and to delay the meeting till the therapist had a chance to make a report. He wasn't sure this was the right move, but at this point he was worn out with fighting and he wanted some help. He thought the consultant might be able to finally prove to them how smart Daniel really was.

A few days later the educational consultant called Ted and said, "I spent a lot of time going over Daniel's file." No kidding, Ted thought, it's four inches thick. "What I discovered is, when Daniel was evaluated by a neuropsychologist two years ago, he was actually diagnosed with Nonverbal Learning Disorder. I think that's very likely the correct diagnosis, but to be sure, I think we may want to have him further evaluated by our occupational therapist and speech and language pathologist."

Great, Ted thought, another diagnosis, another therapist, another evaluation. Why does Daniel have to keep going through this? "What's Nonverbal Learning Disorder?" Ted asked. "I never heard of it."

The consultant explained, "A shorthand way of describing NLD is a child who does not comprehend the nonverbal aspects of communication. In Daniel's case, when people say that he is being defiant, I don't think that's the whole story. He either truly does not understand the rules, or he's incapable of complying because of a neurological deficit, or maybe both." The therapist gave Ted the occupational therapist's phone number. When Ted called for an appointment, he asked her about the educational therapist's explanation of NLD. The occupational therapist agreed. "When a child who has NLD doesn't obey the rules, it's not always because they're defiant. Sometimes it's because they are unable. Let's check out Daniel and see if he fits the criteria for NLD from a sensorimotor perspective. I can also review the reports and synthesize them so they make sense to you, and help you come up with a plan for things that will help Daniel."

A few weeks later, Ted was at another meeting. This time the occupational therapist and the educational consultant joined the crowded room. The OT explained to the team what she had already told Ted. "Daniel does meet the criteria for NLD. What that means is the behavior modification plan in place for him is inappropriate, and maybe medication is premature. We don't want to rule it out, but we can start with other strategies first."

The psychologist spoke up. "But we know already that Daniel has ADHD. If Mr. Royce would only consent to giving him Ritalin, I'm sure we'd see improvement."

The occupational therapist said, "Possibly there is an element of impulsivity in Daniel's case, but when he falls out of his seat, he is not clowning. He is not trying to disrupt the class. He falls because he has a neurological deficit, which means he can't keep himself from falling. When he doesn't copy down the assignment from the chalkboard, it's not because he's being defiant, it's because it's very difficult for him to move from a vertical visual plane to a horizontal one. It's not that he's attending to everything as is the case with ADHD, it's that he's paying attention to too little in his environment. If he doesn't put down his pencil when you flash the lights, it's because he doesn't recognize the visual cue. So if we can teach Daniel how to do those things, he'll have a lot more success than if we punish him for not doing the things he doesn't know how to do. I think if we give him the benefit of the doubt and try some strategies to improve his understanding of nonverbal cues, improve his postural and motor control, and give him strategies to control his arousal, we can then make a better plan as a team to support his learning."

The room was quiet for a minute as everyone took this in. Ted felt he almost wanted to weep. Was this really what his son was experiencing? He spoke up. "I think we should put her plan into place," he said. "It makes sense to me." To his surprise, for the first time he found other people in the room agreeing with him.

Daniel's IEP was revised. He began occupational and speech therapy. As Daniel improved, Ted started to relax. He began to realize he'd spent so much energy fighting for his son that he'd had no time left over to just enjoy him. He made it a policy to spend some time with Daniel every evening. Ted took some of the assignments the occupational therapist gave Daniel and made them into games they could play together.

However, Ted's battles and Daniel's troubles were not so easily solved. Despite the NLD diagnosis, Daniel's teacher and the school psychologist continued to insist Daniel's behavior was purposeful, that he needed Ritalin or he should be kicked out of the school and moved to a classroom for social-emotional disturbed children. Daniel was frequently deprived of recess for not completing his schoolwork, and he continued to be sent to the principal's office and not know why. After countless meetings spent arguing that behavior modification plan wasn't working, Ted is now looking for a new school for Daniel.

Adam's Story

Helen was desperate. She was at a meeting she hoped would finally change things for her son, Adam, who was in seventh grade. Tina, an educational therapist, asked her to describe Adam and explain why Helen had come to her for help.

Helen began talking tentatively, but as she spoke she found herself rushing as if she couldn't get the words out fast enough.

"Adam has been having difficulties with his teachers. He has two teachers who really love him, and he's making As in their classes, but all the rest of his teachers say he's uncooperative and that he just won't try to do the work. Homework takes him forever. Every night I spend two or three hours with him begging and fighting, and it's still not done. He gets an F and doesn't seem to care. But he's written some wonderful stories, and I know when he wants to do it he can do great work. It just seems like sometimes he won't or doesn't or can't. It's such a struggle and we spend many nights in tears. It'll be ten o'clock and we're still not done. I'm exhausted; he's exhausted, and this has been going on for years.

"I'm also worried because I think Adam is a little bit immature. He plays well with younger children, and he gets along great with my friends, but he doesn't have any friends of his own. Birthday parties come and he's never invited. When his birthday comes we have no one to invite. We've tried Boy Scouts and sports, but it seems like he always gets in trouble, so he's dropped out of all those things. We have a lot of fights over how much computer he can play because he would prefer to play computer games all day and do nothing else. And—" Helen hesitated. It was such a relief to finally give words to all these things, but now she felt she might break down in tears. "And it just doesn't seem like he's as happy as other kids. It seems like it's getting worse. I'm worried about what's going to happen to him."

Tina listened sympathetically as Helen spoke. When Helen finished, she asked, "How does Adam's school address these issues?"

Helen sighed. "They keep saying it's a motivation problem. I just can't believe that can be the whole picture, but they don't believe me. They think he's lazy, that he's a smart kid who just won't do his work. Adam scores above average on all the standardized tests, so they won't even consider testing him for anything. They keep telling me it's my fault he's not motivated. They say I'm inconsistent in my discipline. That I'm too easy on him. The last time I talked to one of his teachers, she said, 'You're saying to me over and over that Adam won't do his homework unless you help him and sit with him for three hours. So just don't sit with him. Let him not turn it in. Let him fail. We'll hold him back a year and that will teach him a lesson.' And then she outright told me I should hit him. She said, 'Why don't you just try swatting him one?' The awful thing is, I did that once, one night when I completely lost it. It just made everything even worse. He was on the floor sobbing—miserable—and I couldn't bear it. He's already so anxious. I don't know what will work for Adam, but I do know my son, and I know he isn't being bad on purpose. I just wish I could figure out a way to help him, because I'm exhausted and scared and I don't know where to turn."

Helen dabbed at her eyes with a tissue and cleared her throat. "I heard you were a really amazing tutor. Maybe there's a way you can show him how to do his homework or something. . . ."

Following this meeting, Tina met with Adam and did a battery of tests that indicated many of the markers for NLD. Helen took Tina's report to a neuropsychologist, who corroborated her work and gave Adam an official diagnosis of Nonverbal Learning Disorder. Although Helen was angry that she had had to pay for all these services herself when the school could have tested Adam, she was grateful that she and her husband made enough money for them to afford an independent diagnosis for their son. Mostly, though, she was enormously relieved to finally understand Adam's difficulties.

When Helen returned to Adam's school with the neuropsychologist's report, her relief dwindled and her frustration returned. When she pointed out that both the neuropsychologist and the educational therapist recommended occupational therapy for Adam, the school professionals insisted that the district could not pay for special services for him because he was performing at grade level. "If you want Adam to get therapy, you'll have to pay for it yourself," they told Helen bluntly.

That night Helen and her husband took a hard look at their budget and decided they would have to make the sacrifices necessary to get their son the help he needed. They found an occupational therapist who began to work with Adam on a strengthening program so he had more endurance and on a visual-motor program so his eyes didn't fatigue so quickly. The therapist included Helen in each session and taught her many activities, exercises, and strategies. Helen felt like a cotherapist and began to feel more confident. Mostly, she felt hopeful as she watched Adam relax and do better. He was happier.

After working with Adam for a few weeks, the therapist met with Helen and suggested that she go back to the school and ask for a 504 Plan to put some accommodations in place. "What's a 504?" Helen asked. "I've heard of IEP's, but never that."

"Well," the OT explained, "a 504 Plan is an agreement between the

school and the parent. When a school agrees to an IEP, that's a legal contract they have to abide by, but a 504 is more like a gentleman's agreement. You might get them to abide by it, or you might not, but it's
certainly worth trying and following up on. It will put some of the
strategies we've found helpful for Adam in place at school."

Helen scheduled a meeting with the school psychologist and Adam's
teachers. She asked them to give Adam extra time in class to complete
his work. As the occupational therapist had recommended, she asked for
him to have movement breaks throughout the day, to have something
sour to chew on, to have a sports water bottle on his desk, and for a regular recess even if his work had not been finished, because he really
needed movement breaks. When Adam did twenty minutes of really
good work on his homework, Helen asked that she could sign his paper
verifying he'd put in that time, and that would be enough. She also
asked that when his work was graded, that he be judged on the quality,
not the quantity of the work. Helen made a clear presentation to the
educational team, and they agreed to her plan. Later she commented
wryly to her husband, "They won't spend a penny on Adam, but at least
they're willing to do things that don't cost them any money."

With these interventions and accommodations in place, Adam started
getting his homework in and improving his grades. He was less anxious,
less tired, and for the first time in years he began to feel more competent.
After six months of therapy, the OT discharged him with the understanding that he would put the skills he'd learned to work in the school
drama club he had joined. Tina joined a support group run by the Nonverbal Learning Disorder Association (NLDA) that met once a month.

For Jennifer, Daniel and Adam, identifying their NLD was relatively
easy. Unfortunately, for many parents of children with NLD, getting an
accurate diagnosis can be very difficult.

School-Based Diagnosis

For most children with NLD, the path to diagnosis begins in school. Your
child's teacher might have alerted you to some difficulty your child is having—problems with handwriting or "bad" behavior in the classroom. Or
you may have concerns about your child that the teacher discounts. The

teacher might attribute your child's problems to laziness, willful misbehavior, or to your parenting style. By federal law, schools are mandated to assess the learning difficulties of any child over three, but you might have to be assertive to make an effective case that your child qualifies for this right. (If your child is younger than three, you would go to your pediatrician, but most of the time NLD won't show up that early.)

When you approach your child's teacher with your concerns, reporting the problems and symptoms you've observed in your child, the school may set up a Student Study Team. All schools are mandated to do this, and usually they do it effectively. (If not, there are legal consequences that parents can pursue through their state educational office.) This team is called different things throughout the country, but essentially it means that the school professionals—the resource teacher, psychologist, and the classroom teacher—sit down with the parents, discuss the child's strengths and weaknesses, and devise some strategies to help the child. If your child really has NLD, those solutions or strategies may prove to be insufficient if they don't accurately address the underlying deficits.

Although one major problem typically alerts the parent or teacher, when a Student Study Team meets they will often realize that the child's difficulties go beyond that single problem—"At first we were just thinking it was handwriting, but he never finishes his homework and he can never stay in his seat and he doesn't seem to have any friends"—and the team realizes the problem is more serious.

At this point, the parents and kids start traveling the maze of professional help. I think of it as a maze because it's so often hit or miss whether a child gets the right diagnosis and interventions. Let's say your child has trouble with handwriting. The teacher refers him to the school's occupational therapist.

If things do not improve for the child, you may need to request that the school do some further assessments. Again, schools are required to perform these, but you may have to do some nudging to get them to. A resource teacher can do academic testing, and the school psychologist involved can do psycho-educational testing. They will then look at their results together. Often these are not evaluations, but an assessment to indicate that there is enough evidence of a problem to go to the next step of completing a more comprehensive evaluation. By law, the school has to have access to a full team of professional therapists so if special testing is needed, the school has a means of providing it. Schools have some leeway in how they arrange that—they may have therapists on staff, or they may have contracts with independent therapists—but there has to be some kind of professional relationship in place.

Get Started

1. Approach the school psychologist and request a Weschler's intelligence test (WISC) for your child. You might find it easier to pay for a private psychologist to administer this test. On the WISC test, not only is the total score helpful in the diagnosis of NLD, but there are various sub-tests that quantify classic signs of NLD. In fact, of the ten things delineated to diagnose NLD, four of them are based on the WISC. If your child's verbal score on the WISC is significantly higher than her performance score, that gap could be an indicator of NLD. This result would alert the school professionals to potential problems, so with a WISC test in hand, it may be easier to persuade the school to continue with other necessary testing.

2. Have the school's occupational therapist assess your child's gross and fine motor performance and visual motor performance. An occupational therapist would be asked to look at your child's deficits and to assess his strengths. If you ask your child's teacher for an assessment of visual motor and gross and fine motor performance, that assessment can provide information that addresses three or four points on the diagnostic criteria list.

3. Assess your child's social performance. How does the child get along with her peers? Does she have friends? Does she play at recess? If you ask your child's teacher what you might typically expect kids to do at her age in play or in groups, and if your child is not doing those things, that can help you make a case for an evaluation. Speech therapists, occupational therapists, or psychologists who are trained in assessing the social role of the child can make observations and bring in some concrete data showing that she is not meeting developmental markers in the social environment.

Assuming you get your school's cooperation, the evaluation process typically follows these stages: Your child's teacher says, "I think Chris is struggling. I've asked for some testing to be done. Here's who is going to test Chris, and here are the tests they are going to perform. If that's okay, then sign this form." The form will tell you the psychologist is going to administer certain tests, the speech therapist is going to administer other tests, and the occupational therapist is going to perform her own tests.

After testing your child, a meeting will be scheduled to go over the results. Because it will be incredibly difficult for you to understand all the information they will present to you in that setting, before you sign the form giving permission to test your child, I urge you to add to it, "All test reports will be mailed to me prior to the meeting." It is a reasonable request and if someone says, "I can't get my report to you before the meeting," postpone the meeting so you have time to review the reports. You may also want to ask for an agenda and purpose for the meeting ahead of time so you can be prepared.

Understanding the Reports

Once you have the reports, you can read them, make notes on them and come up with your questions for the meeting or call each expert individually to ask specific questions prior to the meeting.

The reports you get will have several sections, and it's important for you to know what you are looking at in each section. Most reports start out with a section called "Relevant History," which presents the history of your child that you provided, but sometimes mistakes are made, so you will want to make sure it's accurate. If it says, "Child spoke at eighteen months," but your child spoke at eight months, that's an important distinction you need to point out to the therapist.

The next section will explain what the test measures. You don't necessarily need to understand this section in detail. It's just to give you an overview of the purpose of each test. Next will come a set of numbers from the tests. There will be numbers for raw score, standard score, standard deviation, and percentile or age-equivalent. Those numbers are really there for the next therapist who reads the report. They probably won't make any sense to you, and they are not intended for you, so set that section aside.

Anyone can read a test manual and administer a test. What makes a test valuable is the interpretation, where the therapist explains what the numbers mean for the individual child. The interpretation will say something like, "Given that Chris scored in the first percentile in the part of the test requiring use of a pencil, and he scored in the ninetieth percentile in the part of the test not requiring a pencil, Chris knows much more than he can demonstrate with a pencil." Or, "The results suggest Chris has a lot of trouble when he has to look at the chalkboard and then refocuses on his paper." Or, "This score indicates Chris may have trouble moving through the classroom." Or, "It means he'll have trouble reaching for a glass of milk and not spilling it."

After reading these reports, you can go to the meeting as prepared as possible. Ask specific questions that will help you understand your child's learning needs. Find out what classroom accommodations are being suggested and how those accommodations will be implemented, when, and by whom. If they say, "no services are indicated," and you have the report ahead of time, you'll be in a position to respond more effectively. Being prepared for the meeting ahead of time gives you a lot of power and helps you be a strong participant of the IEP team, not just an observer.

After the meeting, the school professionals will give you some documents to sign. The documents may list skills and goals the school will now work toward with your child. Alternatively, they will ask you to sign a form reading, "I understand no services will be offered to my child." Because you may be overwhelmed and possibly distraught, it can be hard to resist the pressure to sign the forms then and there. Despite the pressure, I urge you wait, take the papers home and read them carefully, then mail them back. You need to understand that *you are signing a contract* when you sign those forms and you should give them the same attention you would give to any binding agreement. If you agree with what the team offered, go ahead and sign that contract. But if you don't agree or don't understand, you have the right to ask for some time to read it before signing. If you believe the school's plan is not an adequate response to your child's situation, you have the right to negotiate for a different plan.

Independent Diagnosis

Sometimes the school will insist there is nothing wrong with a child, even if the parent knows, or suspects, there is a problem. In this situation, the parent may have to go outside the school to have the child evaluated. It is expensive, but not treating your child's NLD is more expensive. Sometimes health insurance will pay for this testing. If outside testing indicates services are needed, the school will often reimburse you for the cost. It's worth asking.

Start with a good, child neuropsychologist. You can find names on the Internet, from the school, from your physician, or by calling any psychologist in the phone book and asking for a referral to a neuropsychologist who can do testing for a learning disability. That assessment is key. Ask at your school if a Parents Helping Parents or similar support group is in your community. Its members may be able to help you.

Making It Official

The official diagnosis of Nonverbal Learning Disorder can be given only by an MD, the psychologist in the school, or a neuropsychologist with a PhD. The therapists' role in the diagnostic process is to observe and report. Speech and occupational therapists have a critical role in providing important information that helps MDs tease apart the behaviors necessary for an accurate diagnosis. Then the psychologist or physician will assess those observations and reports and make the diagnosis. If, as sometimes happens, you get a private evaluation of your child that indicates NLD, but your school psychologist refuses to accept that diagnosis, you can take the evaluation to your pediatrician. Show him or her the criteria for NLD and say, "You may have never heard of NLD, but take a look at this information. What I need is an official diagnosis in order to encourage the school to provide services to my child or to seek insurance reimbursement."

According to the IDEA (Individuals with Disabilities Education Act), a diagnosis of Nonverbal Learning Disorder and your child's inability to access the general curriculum means your child's school must, by law, provide free, special services, such as therapy and accommodations in the classroom. You must be able to demonstrate that your child cannot access the curriculum. Most schools have a list of diagnoses for which they will provide services. NLD is not on that list, yet, although the Nonverbal Learning Disorder Association (NLDA) is making an effort to change that. Schools usually use their discretion and place NLD under LD NOS (Learning Disorder Not Otherwise Specified), disorder of written expression, developmental coordination disorder, or other health impaired. You can ask what criteria the school uses for Asperger's, too, that can be helpful to know and NLD would qualify in the same manner. You may have to be assertive to persuade the school to take this route. Remember, school officials are "gatekeepers," and part of their job is to keep people from getting services indiscriminately.

If NLD is not a diagnosis the school has provided services for, as is often the case, these labels give schools a legal way to provide school-based services. If your child's school feels unable to qualify services to a child with NLD, you can suggest that they classify him according to the following definitions from the *Diagnostic and Statistical Manual IV* (DSM-IV): Sometimes schools will use the diagnostic labels Disorder of Written Expression, Mathematics Disorder, or Developmental Coordination Disorder for children with NLD. These labels describe the functional performance deficits that children with NLD experience.

Regardless of the label professionals assign to your child, it's important to remember that *you do not need the diagnosis to get therapeutic interventions for your child outside of the school.* Therapists treat symptoms of disorders, not diagnoses.

However, beyond the issue of negotiating with the school, I think it's psychologically important for you to know your child's diagnosis. The diagnosis helps you know your child better. It can be a comfort to know the name of your child's disorder because then you can let go of your fears of all the other things you worried might be wrong with him. Finally, the diagnosis gives you access to a body of knowledge and a group of people with experiences similar to your own.

Misdiagnosis

All too often, children with NLD are misdiagnosed and are either not treated at all, or are provided with inappropriate, counterproductive treatment. This occurs for several reasons:

1. NLD is not as widely known as other disorders, and therefore diagnosticians do not necessarily recognize its signs and symptoms.

2. The coping strategies used by children with NLD can be misinterpreted as defiance or willful behavior. Because most children would rather look bad than incompetent, adults often assume that they are being purposely difficult and label the child's coping strategies as behavior problems.

3. NLD can coexist with many other disorders such as ADHD, ADD, Tourette's, Obsessive Compulsive Disorder (OCD), dysfunction in sensory integration (DSI), and even mental retardation. It can also be a secondary condition after a child sustains a head injury or other brain trauma such as hydroencephalitis. Diagnosticians who are more familiar with these other disorders may not recognize the underlying NLD deficits.

4. Some professionals mistakenly believe that when an impairment is not severely debilitating, it does not merit a diagnosis for which services can be provided by the school.

You can determine if your child has been misdiagnosed by assessing if your child is making progress with intervention. If the interventions are not working—your child is not improving—then the interventions are probably inappropriate to your child's disorder.

The following is a brief summary of common misdiagnoses. It is not a comprehensive discussion of these diagnoses, but will give you a sense of what can happen with your child.

Attention Deficit Disorder (ADD) and Attention Deficit–Hyperactivity Disorder (ADHD) ADD and ADHD are marked by failing to give close attention to details in work, problems sustaining attention in tasks or play, and failing to follow through on assignments. Children with NLD exhibit similar behaviors because they are paying attention to too few things, whereas AD/HD is marked by a person paying attention to too many things. Another difference is the cause of the behaviors and therefore the interventions that will be effective. Children with NLD need more input, more explanation and more guidance to understand the rules of expected behavior, while children with ADD/ADHD need us to minimize the amount of explanation and sensory input.

Stimulants frequently prescribed for ADD have been shown to be counterproductive for NLD as they further perpetuate their tendency toward sedentary lives, further hampering their ability to engage in social interactions. The fidgeting seen in children with NLD is often due to low tone and is an attempt to gain increased stimulation. Children with NLD aggressively avoid novel experiences while children with ADD/ADHD seek novel input. Children with AD/HD are impulsive and fail to stop to consider the consequences while children with NLD are unable to anticipate consequences. Finally, children with NLD benefit from logical explanations whereas children with ADD/ADHD benefit from minimizing verbal input when offering feedback.

Obsessive-Compulsive Disorder (OCD) is a real disorder, but sometimes children with NLD are diagnosed with OCD-like behaviors, which have developed as a coping strategy used to relieve anxiety. Children with NLD are at risk for developing OCD tendencies as a secondary disorder, but its underlying cause is NLD.

Oppositional Defiance Disorder (ODD) is a pattern of persistent, deliberate violation of the rights of others and opposition to authority figures. Children with NLD are not intentionally oppositional. Rather, they are usually very compliant. However, over time, as frustration builds, their coping mechanisms can become more and more similar to deliberate opposition.

Tourette's syndrome is defined as multiple vocal and motor tics (any stereotyped movement or vocalization that is sudden, nonrhythmic, rapid, and repeated) occurring frequently throughout the day. It can be as simple as rapid blinking, can resemble a stutter, or can be as severe as having the uncontrollable desire to touch others or to shout out profanity. Tourette's symptoms are exacerbated by anxiety and stress. Some children with NLD also have Tourette's.

Anxiety Disorders There is a difference between normal anxiety (worry that inspires a person to act, such as the feeling that causes us to check to see if we turned off the stove) and clinical anxiety (worry that disrupts function and causes us to check to see if we turned off the stove over and over and prevents us from leaving the house). Anxiety is a normal part of life and is a protective mechanism against threats. It becomes abnormal when it prevents rather than helps successful daily function and when it persists without causing the person to act in a way to remove the stressor.

Although a diagnosis of anxiety disorder can be a misdiagnosis, many children with NLD do experience severe anxiety and antidepressant medication is frequently prescribed to manage anxiety in children. More and more, I see children with NLD benefiting from antianxiety medication. Medication can be very helpful in easing the anxiety brought on by social imperceptions and thereby decreasing the symptoms listed above. This in turn allows the child to be more able to learn, allows greater opportunity to engage in social interactions, and allows possibly greater success in their environments. However, while medications can be enormously helpful, I believe that decreasing stress and relieving anxiety for children with NLD through lifestyle changes may be the more appropriate first step.

Asperger syndrome (AS) Asperger's syndrome is usually diagnosed in childhood. Asperger's is a lifelong social disorder characterized by a lack of empathy, little ability to form friendships, one-sided conversations, clumsy movements, and intense absorption in special interests (Klin, et. al, 2000).

Many symptoms of Asperger's and NLD overlap, but there are differences as well. They are similar in that they are both disabilities of the nonverbal type; both children with NLD and children with AS are verbal, often verbose, but they miss out on the nonverbal cues in their environment and, as a result, they have social deficits. Two key differences between NLD and Asperger's include the visual-spatial-organizational area (a strength in AS and a weakness in NLD) and command of verbal language, which tends to be higher in NLD than in AS.

Both children with NLD and children with AS have difficulty understanding the perspective of another person, but when taught that perspective, children with NLD seem to recall what they've learned and apply it more often and more effectively. Children with AS seem to need more repetition of the social concepts and more practice in the application of those concepts. Children with NLD more commonly want to be in relationship with peers so badly that they have a tendency to be annoying and overbearing in their overtures. People with AS, however, tend to be more aloof, more content with one or two friends, and have a greater tendency toward social withdrawal or isolation.

One of the diagnostic criteria for NLD is tactile imperceptions. Children with NLD have trouble recognizing objects placed in their hands when their eyes are closed. They also have difficulty identifying letters drawn on their fingers (called finger agnosia) when their eyes are closed. In my clinical experience, I have not found this to be true with the children with AS, but it is always true in the children with NLD.

Both children with NLD and those with AS are prone to sensorimotor dysfunction, depression, and anxiety. Both have problems organizing their supplies. Children with NLD have difficulty organizing their thoughts, supplies, and time. Children with AS do, too, but they have perseverations, or rituals, where they *require* some objects—those they care about—to be placed in a certain order or sequence, or they get upset. Children with NLD don't do this. Both have difficulty demonstrating their knowledge with a pencil. They both benefit from speech/language therapy that helps them organize their thoughts and understand the nonverbal elements of communication. They both benefit from a good sensory diet that allows them to regulate their levels of alertness, arousal, frustration, and motor-skill development.

Distinguishing NLD from Other Diagnoses

Part of the difficulty many parents and clinicians have in distinguishing among NLD, AS, and other diagnoses is the classification scheme in the DSM-IV. The DSM-IV uses the term Pervasive Developmental Disorder (PDD) as an umbrella term, which includes autism, Asperger's, and a few others. Many of us in the field of NLD and AS believe that in the next DSM, Asperger's will not be listed under the subheading of autism, but will be in a separate category of social disability or some other umbrella heading, perhaps along with social anxiety.

NLD is not in the DSM-IV, though it probably will be included in the DSM when it is revised and reprinted as the DSM-V. As of this writing, NLD is diagnosed using criteria from an educational psychological perspective. It is important to keep in mind that the DSM is always a work in progress, and as our understanding of learning and psychological problems expands, the DSM changes to reflect our new understanding as well.

It's safe to say NLD is not autism, it's not HFA, and it's not PDD. It is a separate entity. Autism does not evolve into Asperger's, HFA doesn't evolve into AS, and AS doesn't evolve into NLD. If a child has delayed language and meets the criteria for autism, then at age nine she starts to look less impaired and begins to appear more like Asperger's, it is technically incorrect to say she has outgrown autism and developed Asperger's. Autism cannot be outgrown, although, with intervention, the impairment can be made less severe. In the same vein, a child with Asperger's cannot become a child with NLD because children with NLD have marked deficits in the visual-spatial-organizational realms, while children with Asperger's have this as a marked strength.

As long as diagnoses are given incorrectly, our understanding of the disorders will be incorrect. For example, I think it is a grave disservice to parents to say a diagnosis of autism has changed to Asperger's. It is both accurate and more empowering to tell parents that there is hope with autism and other problems of social cognition, that symptoms can be treated successfully and the resulting disability greatly lessened.

When diagnosticians fudge the labels to help children gain services, or to help ease a parent's reception of the diagnosis, it makes intervention, research, and prognosis very difficult. Even though I understand why parents choose to accept a misdiagnosis of AS for their child with NLD, because sometimes that's the only way they can get the school to provide services, I think a more helpful, proactive approach is to lobby school districts to accept NLD as a diagnosis for which services will be provided.

It's essential that our children be accurately diagnosed and that we acknowledge the labels our children have. By doing so, we provide hope for others and demonstrate the truth that interventions work for these kids. Because my son appears so typical now and blends in so well with his peers, I have had moments when I felt like denying that he has a learning difference. However, I truly believe it's empowering to him to know he has unique ways of experiencing this world, to know that his family and community supported him, and to know that he has worked hard to keep his uniqueness *and* fit into the society into which he was born. I think that is an urgent and essential message to send out, and I am inspired by the parents who had the courage to do this before me.

Humor and NLD: The Controversy

At one of the NLDA symposia, Dr. Herb Schreier was presenting on the distinctions between NLD and Asperger's syndrome. Dr. Schreier has a low, soothing voice that practically lullabies one to sleep, not out of boredom, but by calm rhythm. His hair rivals Einstein for odd formations. As is his custom, he was using videos to make his point, showing children with both NLD and Asperger's, presenting research and cracking dry jokes. Zac sat in the front of the room listening carefully, directly in front of the podium, on the floor with several other participants. Zac laughed at each joke Dr. Schreier cracked, sometimes the only audience participant who realized a joke had been made. After 45 minutes of lecture, Schreier reported on a recent study he'd conducted using a specific joke. When Schreier told the joke, Zac laughed so loud I could hear him from where I was sitting and could distinguish his laugh from the others in the room.

Schreier went on to explain that children with NLD and Asperger's do not get humor, that their brains have insufficient executive function to cognitate the subtle meanings behind humor and that in his study, children with these disorders failed to laugh.

Zac looked to me, his eye asking permission for something. I trusted him and nodded my head, encouragingly. Zac raised his hand and when Dr. Schreier called on him, he said, "I have NLD and I got your joke." Dr. Schreier laughed and said, "Good for you, Zac, prove the experts wrong. Next time we need to have you and kids like you in the study."

Five

After the Diagnosis

PARENTS always want to know what caused their child's learning disorder. Moms will ask if it was the glass of wine they drank during pregnancy or the length of delivery. But those questions come from a frame of reference in which the brain is a machine, a lump of material that is fixed in place, with predetermined genetic instruction hardwiring a life of disability. In fact, the brain is complex and plastic, and it is impossible to predict how any one factor will influence a person. In a developing brain, each component initially develops on its own. But after a certain level of maturation is reached, the environment begins to exert its influence, connections are made, and the brain evolves in a unique and multimodal, many-layered way.

The brain is like a set of muscles. It responds to use and lack of use with either growth or atrophy. Neuroscientists agree that mental weaknesses, whether a learning disability or an inability to recall names, are like physical systems in need of training and practice. If we want to support a child to succeed, we need to understand how the brain learns and what supports and impedes learning, and then to embark on a course that enhances those systems.

The brain is resilient and wired to learn. Thoughts, actions, and emotions are all known to change the structure of our brains. In his new book, *The User's Guide to the Brain,* John Ratey describes the brain as less like a machine than an ecosystem, with many of its systems in competition with one another. Any event has the potential to upset the balance of power of each subsequent event. The predisposition of genetics and injury has influence, but is not determinative. Ratey says, "Debates as to which genetic, cultural, or environmental factor is the true cause of a phenomenon are often a waste of time; the brain is the binding principle behind it all."

The Prognosis

Taking in the fact that your child has a learning disorder can be a wrenching experience. Unfortunately, upon receiving the diagnosis, parents are typically given little guidance about understanding what they have learned. If they are given any information at all, it is usually a couple of pages from Byron Rourke's published work that suggests dire outcomes— a lifetime of withdrawal and depression, and early suicide. Most parents are not given adequate information about the interventions available for NLD. They might receive some generic recommendations, like a social skills group, but nothing tangible or useful. It's not unusual to become depressed and mourn for the loss of hopes and dreams for your child's future. Too many parents encounter the insensitivity of diagnosticians who present a dire prognosis and do not present any coping information.

Before you fall into the trap of hopelessness, remember that Rourke's published research is based on observations of children with NLD who had had no interventions and who had been institutionalized, usually because of secondary issues arising from lack of intervention, and that he now acknowledges in his lectures the increased positive outcomes that have come out of good interventions being offered earlier and earlier.

We now know that interventions do work for children with NLD, and there is a long list of things you can do for your child. With appropriate treatment, children with NLD can thrive. These children can grow up to live healthy, productive lives. There is much to be hopeful for.

Your Response to the Diagnosis

When a child is diagnosed with NLD, we experience some strong, complicated emotions. You might feel tremendous guilt. You might feel relieved to finally have an explanation for your kid's difficulties. You might be tempted to retreat into denial, insisting, "She doesn't have a learning disorder, she's too bright!" I see many parents in denial, and I too went through that when Zac was diagnosed. Denial is a natural response. But, don't let it prevent you from moving forward into a plan of action.

You will probably also feel grief, which is normal and valid. After all, you've just been told that you don't have the child you thought you had. Because you've lived for years with a child whom you know to be brilliant—a genius!—and because everyone has told you how precocious and bright he is, it's natural that you would become very attached to this image of your child. For parents of children with NLD, this can be a very high ledge to fall from. It is important to take time to feel your grief and acknowledge it as real.

Caring for Yourself

If you had just found out that your child had a devastating illness, you would want to spend every second helping him, but what he really needs is for you to take care of yourself. When you're on an airplane and the flight attendants explain the emergency procedures, they always tell you to put on your oxygen mask first, and then put your child's mask on her, because if you can't breathe, you're no help to anybody. The same is true of daily life. If you don't take care of yourself physically and emotionally, in the short term you'll be functioning at less than full capacity and therefore giving your kids and your spouse less than you'd like to. In the long term, you'll fall apart and get sick or depressed.

Grief and depression are normal responses to a child's diagnosis. To counter those feelings, I recommend that you get up and get active. Take a shower. Get dressed as if you were starting your day, and make sure your children do, too. We feel better when we are clean and well groomed. Even though we may be going through the motions, those motions have value to the nervous system and to the chemicals in the body. A shower produces endorphins. Those are the body's "happy" chemicals. Grooming increases endorphins, and when we are depressed or grieving, we need every one of the endorphins we can get into our systems. Other countermeasures against depression can be to get outside, engage in some physical activity, resume your normal social events, and make contact with your friends.

This is also the time to call in your support system, call your family and your friends. Though you may feel isolated, make the effort not to isolate yourself. It is essential to connect with your support structure.

Give yourself permission to grieve, but tell yourself, "I will be depressed for one month. I'm not going to do a thing. I'm not going to clean. I'm not going to cook. I am really going to be depressed for one month. And on May 1, I'm going to get up, take a shower, clean the house, and then I'm going to move on." That's a linear, logical approach that works for some people.

Another plan might be, "Everyday I'm going to do just one thing. Once I do that one thing, I am done. I'm off for the day, I'm not working on this NLD thing anymore. And the one thing is, I'm going to drive my kid to OT, or the one thing is, I'm going to help my kid with homework." Then you check it off your list everyday and know you've done a good job. With this plan, you are not beating yourself up for not doing everything you think you should be doing. You give yourself permission to do just one thing and you celebrate your accomplishments.

Whatever strategy, you have to *give up the right* to beat yourself up. You have to forgive yourself when you don't accomplish all that you had planned. A friend of mine calls it "shrinking the lag time." How long did it take you between beating yourself up and catching yourself and saying "I'm not going to do that again." Two weeks? Good. Celebrate when it's ten days. Work on shrinking that lag time between when you did something you didn't want to and when you discovered you did it and made a new choice. I have another friend who used to say to me all the time, "Rondalyn, you need to stop 'shoulding' all over yourself." I think of that when I get mad at myself over all the things I think I "should" do.

Getting into the action is important. This may be easier said than done, but hard as it is, it's essential to your well-being and to your child's.

Educate Your Spouse

Sometimes when a child receives the NLD diagnosis, one parent will better understand and be able to move into action while the other parent is either not helpful or actually obstructive. It can be hard if one parent is still in denial: "No, our child does not have this." Or "I don't have time for this, you deal with it." Or "I'm not spending any money on this." If this happens to you, you may need to educate your spouse so that he or she can become a partner in the work you need to do to help your child.

A safe approach can be to buy a book on NLD and give it to your spouse. You can say, "Please read this. You're my partner and I need you to read it or I will read the book, and every night you're going to listen to me tell you what I read, that's the least you can do. Or every night when you come home, I want you to spend one hour reading this book. I'll have your dinner ready, and I'll take the kids for a walk for an hour so you can have this quiet time. I want you to use it to read this book because it's that important to me."

When you are educating your spouse about NLD and your child's needs, remember you have to give him or her time to go through the learning process you've gone through. Often it's the mom who has read a book or looked NLD up on the Internet. Then she may go to the dad and say, "This fits our child exactly. Let's do something about it," and the dad says "No way, I'm not doing it." It's easy for the mom to forget that she has spent fifteen hours online researching NLD, and she's given the dad a ten minute summary. He may need time to assimilate the information.

Those of us who are the first in a marriage to understand our child's diagnosis are often people who have some training or some kind of background that allows us to understand. In my own marriage, Bill kept saying, "You understand because you have more background." He was right. I had a BA in psychology. My mother was a teacher. I had been a camp counselor. I had a degree in occupational therapy. These all contributed to it being easy for me to understand what Zac was experiencing. Once I appreciated how much I had known before all this started, it was hard for me to appreciate all that Bill had to learn.

I was lucky that my husband did want to learn about NLD and he counted on me to translate and summarize information for him. At times, I wanted him to know as much as I did, but I recognized that was unrealistic. I would say to him, "I want you to *want* to read all the stuff I'm reading and understand the way I understand." When I accepted that it made more sense for me to be the parent to take this educational process on, I began to appreciate Bill's fears and concerns as well as his contributions. Bill made sure I knew how much he appreciated all I was doing for our son, and having him acknowledge and appreciate my efforts became something I could be grateful for, too. I am a lucky woman to have such a rock for a husband.

Tell Your Child

Some parents do not want to tell their children they have NLD. They don't want the child to think anything is wrong with her, yet they take her to therapy every day of the week. I strongly urge you to tell your child. You are *not* helping your child or sparing her any pain by withholding the truth. In my experience, the kids who do the best are those whose parents say to them, "You know what? You've got some things to work on. It just so happens that we know some people who can help you."

Telling your child about his NLD is an opportunity to empower him. Talk to him about his learning style and explain to him what supports you will put in place for him. If your child knows what he needs to work on, he's empowered. I see this every day in my clinic. A child who knows his diagnosis and his learning style will come for a session. I'll say to him, "Bounce five times on the trampoline and turn around and catch this ball and throw it back to me."

"Oh," he'll say, "is this working on my vestibular system?"

"Yes, it is."

"So at home if I were to jump a lot, that would help me to do my homework?"

"Why, yes, it would."

This gives a child an active, empowered role in his growth and learning. I love it when a kid comes in and says, "I'm not as angry now. If I start to feel angry, I go jump on my pogo stick or take time on my Rollerblades, and then I can calm down and do my homework."

I also believe you will feel better if you tell your child the truth. Secrets eat away at us. Parents who withhold the information from their kids are fearful and stressed. One such parent asked me for a referral to a psychotherapist for herself because her son was making her "crazy and exhausted." This woman was trying to live a myth—that her son did not have NLD—but every time he did something to shatter her myth (which was hourly) she felt crazy. It takes too much energy to fabricate a myth. It takes too much energy to live in denial. You can take that energy and put it to good use elsewhere if you can be honest with your child and yourself.

After telling their child, some parents say to me in surprise, "But she didn't even cry!" For children with NLD, anxiety does not come from the same place that yours or mine does. It doesn't come from "I don't fit in." It comes from "Nothing I do works," or "I make that mistake every time, and I don't know how to fix it." It comes from not ever knowing what to do.

Explain the Diagnosis

Children with NLD have an enormous capacity to understand reason and logic, but not emotions. They will gobble up any fact we give them. That's their learning style. Take advantage of it. However you tell your child, your explanation should be clear, logical, and factual. Here's what I told Zac: "Guess what we just found out? We just found out that some things are harder for you than others. And we found out why. We found out that the left side of your brain is really strong. It's so strong that it's caused the right side of your brain to be lazy and stop doing its job. But the fact is, brains grow, and there are people who help the brain grow. We're going to start working on making the lazy parts of your brain stronger, and then all the things that are difficult for you, like tying your shoelaces and handwriting, will get easier. Not all at once but little by little." Every time I take him to speech therapy, I can remind him that he is exercising his brain to make it stronger.

I have found over and over with these children that if I talk about their brains, to them it has the same sort of weight as if I talk about their fingers. It's just information, not a judgment. If a finger is broken, we put a splint on it and it will heal. It may always be crooked, but it will work. Talking in this mode about their brains locates the problem in their brains and not in *them*.

I think it's important to make explanations appropriate to the child's age. For a first or second grader, simply saying "Part of your brain is strong, but part has gotten weak, or gone on vacation, and needs some exercise to get strong again" can be enough.

For a kid in fourth grade or older, I discuss brain anatomy more specifically. You may want to take your child to the library and look at illustrated books on brains. It can be useful to talk about your own strengths and weaknesses as well as your child's. For example, I say, "My brain isn't so strong on that side. I'm not that good in math. But look, this other part of my brain is really strong. I'm really good with words and with people."

Your child might answer, "Hey, Mom, I'm like that, too, only I'm good in math but not good with people."

Then you can say, "In our family, we all have a weakness, something that's hard for us to do, and we work on it. You know how I didn't know how to change a tire? Remember how we had to wait two hours for a tow truck? Remember how when we got home, I had Dad show me how to change a tire? That's what we do in our family. It makes our life easier. Just like Dad worked hard last summer learning that new computer program for his work, and just like when Aunt Martha hurt her back, she went to a physical therapist to get it stronger. Did you know Uncle Joe went to a speech therapist? Well, we all have areas we need to work on. If we work on that part of your brain about making associations—remember, we saw that in the picture, it's on the right side—if we work on strengthening that, then you'll be able to do that on your own, and you won't need us to help you."

I take the same approach with kids in my clinic. I'll say, "Did you notice how your dad holds a pencil? He holds it just like you do, and he's okay, right? So it's really no big deal. But if you hold a pencil that way, your hand is going to start to hurt, just like your dad's hand hurts a lot. And you don't have to have that, so I'll show you the tricks I know to make it easier." This is not minimizing the child's difficulties, but helping her have a sense of belonging in her community and seeing herself as okay.

When I'm explaining the diagnosis to a sixteen- or seventeen-year-old, I focus on what he is good at. If a child has not been diagnosed until that age, it's probably been a long time since he heard that he is good at anything. By this age these kids are terrified that they're going to be broken forever, because they've felt broken for a long time. They are also terrified they won't be able to function in the world. People rarely address this issue with them directly.

I suggest focusing on older kids' strengths and interests and how those strengths have real applications in adult life. Talk about vocational opportunities, go to the library and pore over the reference section on careers that require precision of language, logical reasoning, and advanced language facility. For example, "You are really great at identifying patterns. Do you know the kind of jobs that people with your talent have? Let's go to the library and find out."

No matter what age your child is, if you offer him a logical explanation of his NLD and show him you can now put the appropriate supports in place for him, he will be empowered by this knowledge. As your child learns about himself, he will be able to get along better in a world that frequently bewilders him and the fact that you explained it to him will let him know that he's not alone; he has you, and there are others who share his world view.

The Gift of NLD

My own experience as the parent of a child with NLD has taught me many things. One of the most important lessons I've learned is: We do not have to do things on our own. Let's face it, most of us would prefer to stay in our own world, have it all our own way, and need nothing. But the reality is the more we take on in life, the greater the stone to roll away, the more we need to seek and accept the help of others.

There is a reason some of us study stars and some love cultivating soil and some love the smell of babies and some the smell and feel of bread, pliant and resilient beneath strong, prodding hands. We each have gifts and not one of us is here complete. All myths and fables and fairy tales tell us this same moral—we need each other. We need each other.

Unfortunately, my personal preference would be to do everything on my own because if I do it all myself, then I know it will get done just right. I have learned that I can't do it all. Life is too big for that, and I think the reason is to force us to connect with others. Connecting is not always easy for me. It takes a ton of energy for me to engage with others. When I do connect, I gain immensely.

My personal belief is, when you just don't have that energy to reach out, you have to have a prayer in place that someone will come and help you. That's what I do. I know there are times when I just can't reach out. I pray and pray for a caring one to show up at my door. Sometimes it's the UPS man. He's having a great day and he says something wonderful to me that gives me a little bit of energy to call the psychologist about my kid. Sometimes it's Oprah or Dr. Phil on the *Oprah* show saying something inspiring on TV. Sometimes it's a book with a sentence or two that speaks to me. I was once moved to tears watching the cartoon *Pinky and the Brain* when Pinky *finally* did something without ruining the Brain's plans, and the Brain said, "Well, Pinky, I can see that the occupational therapy is working." Somewhere in my life I find a little bit of inspiration, something that renews my spirit, and I use that inspiration to take a tiny step forward.

For the parents who are open and receptive, children with NLD transform their lives in significant ways. When I first understood what Zac's NLD meant for him, I thought of the gap between his understanding and the world as a chasm I had to help him cross. I thought I had to go back and forth between the gaps enough times so that he could walk across the web. More and more I'm realizing I'm not the one who's going across and bringing him over. It's the other way around. For the parents who are open to it, I see them do that, too. While we're busy making it safe for our child to come across the gap into our "better" world, we wind up realizing maybe the child's world is better. At times, it's a world of honesty, of caring, of sweet innocence, of straight shooting. It's a world of simplicity, it's a world of beauty. It's a world where injustice isn't tolerated. It's really a much better world in many ways over there. I'm moved by their world. I'm moved by my child, and I'm moved by who I get to be because he's here. I didn't know I was on track for that. I didn't know to ask for that or pray for such a transforming life experience, and I am grateful I was given the life with my child that I have. I'm amazed by who my husband and I both got to be, and are still getting to be, because of this gift in our lives: our uniquely gifted child.

The Innocent Mower

For all the hard work of parenting children with NLD, there's also a lot of laughter.

One of Zac's chores is to mow the lawn. He uses a push mower for muscle development and safety. Part of the chore is picking up the fallen lemons in the yard. This week, Bill and I were watching him from the kitchen window. Each time Zac came to a lemon, he picked it up, held it for a minute while he listened to see if he heard anyone. Then he innocently—bloop!—threw them over the fence and into the neighbor's yard and went on his merry way. Bill and I were howling! This is such an NLD moment. It would never occur to Zac that he might hit someone or that there might be a social rule about not pitching rotten fruit over a fence into someone else's yard.

When Zac came inside, Bill said, "Zac, can I tell you one more little social thing?"

"Sure."

"It's rude to throw lemons into the neighbor's yard."

"Why?"

"Well, you could hit someone with the rotten fruit, and they probably don't want our rotten fruit on their grass."

"Oh, okay, I didn't think about that."

That's when Bill and I started to crack up again. Zac said, "Why is that funny?"

"Well, because we can imagine the lemons flying into a yard and folks wondering where the heck they are coming from. And then watching you do it, it was so clear you hadn't considered any of those things, you were just solving a problem the NLD way, and we thought it was so great to have NLD and just be able to pitch lemons over a fence with such a carefree heart—and it was just so funny."

Zac started to laugh, too, and said "Well, they won't know who threw them, now will they?" We all started laughing at that, and Zac started to dance through the house singing, "NLD rules, oh yeah."

Six

Implement Your Plan

WHEN Bill and I learned I was pregnant, we realized there were only a couple of things we could be sure about: We didn't know anything about the person who would join our family, and our lives would change. It's true that when we're expecting a child, we have hopes and dreams for who that person will become. We may picture ourselves playing soccer with the child or reading books with her. We may imagine the child growing up to be a successful scientist or artist. But once the child is born, we realize pretty quickly that our child is a unique being with his or her own attributes. When we take care of our infants or toddlers, we learn we have to work with them to help them unfold their personalities instead of imposing our personalities on them.

The same is true when you discover your child has NLD. If you want your child to grow up to be a happy adult, you need to let go of your preconceived ideas of who you wanted your child to be and, instead, accept the gift of who he really is. You have a child who is very logical, very vulnerable, and somewhat innocent. Your child has a particular set of interests and a particular set of strengths. Like everyone, he also has challenges to work on and overcome on the way to becoming a happy adult. If you think about his learning disorder in these terms, then it will become a manageable issue instead of an overwhelming problem.

Break Everything into Manageable Pieces

Remember, nobody can do everything at once. For a long time I thought that if I were a good enough parent, I would be able to do everything. If I could just get strong enough, or smart enough, or good enough, or drink more coffee, or drink less coffee, or weigh less, or weigh more, then I'd be able to do everything. Eventually I realized nobody can do many things well. So before making a grand plan for helping your child, break down the things you need to do into manageable tasks. Then pick just one or two to work on at a time. It will be far less stressful for you and your child. Remember, we're all working on something at all times and compassion helps us feel better about our journey.

Identify Your Resources

When you begin to plan how your family will adapt to your child's learning differences, you need to identify all your resources: money, time, support, and information.

Money

Most of us have limited financial resources. If only one parent is working, and it's possible for the nonworking parent to take a job, that will increase your family's income, but it will cut down on the amount of time you have with your family. It may be possible for your family to raise a little money by selling some valuables, holding a yard sale, or by approaching your extended family or your employer. Some employers have special programs for parents with a child who has special needs— ask your human resource department, which may be able to barter for some professional services.

Money is a real factor in planning treatment for the child with NLD. A therapist can design a great treatment plan for your child, but if it doesn't fit your family, it's useless. Some parents start by asking, "What does my child need?" and then try to find a way to pay for it. Although your child may need a lot of therapy, she does not need many therapies at once. Too often I see parents signing their kids up for lots of therapies without figuring out how they will really pay for them and without stopping to consider which ones are the most important. This creates stress in the family and probably resentment as well. A better place to start is to identify how much money you can realistically spend on the child with NLD.

Time

As with money, we all have a finite amount of time. We spend and save and waste time and money, as if they are one. While you and your family will need to establish your own priorities, I'd like to share with you a few things that have worked for me and my family, bearing in mind that what works for one child may not work for another:

1. We decided to do only two therapies or extracurricular activities at any given time. If Zac was enrolled in OT and soccer, that was it.

2. We initiated slug nights. On slug nights, we set out a picnic blanket in front of a movie or TV or play board games and eat take-out food, or leftovers warmed up, and hang out as a family. Friends are welcome on slug night, but the rule is we get to act like slugs—we're lazy, all chores are postponed, and we get to relax. We think of it as cheap family therapy.

3. We lightened the load of housekeeping. Several times a week we set the timer, and whatever we can pick up or clean up before the timer goes off (ten minutes is the maximum setting) is enough. Then we sit down and read or play a game.

4. I took on the project of being less spontaneous and more consistent, while my husband worked on being more flexible. Between the two of us, we can usually provide a strong, reliable foundation for our child, who needs a unified parental front.

5. We used television, books, and the comic pages as an opportunity to teach social skills and deepen therapeutic lessons. *The Simpsons* is a great study in the "don'ts" of good behavior. We dubbed Bart the Poster Boy of Poor Social Behavior. Using humor and observation of behavior helped my son think about the rules of social interaction, and talk about them. Then, when a real-life situation occurred, we had a reference to point to.

6. We make weekly trips to the library, using books as we might conferences and therapeutic sessions.

7. We let our neighbors and friends help and often rotate child care, dinner, and holiday hosting rather than always doing it on our own.

When parents come to me and say, "What more should I be doing for my child with NLD?" my answer is almost always, "Do less." Children with NLD are typically under enormous amounts of stress. Doing less—simplifying your lives—is a basic guideline to keep in mind when thinking of your priorities. Overall, we found that to be a good way to help our son learn the many things he needed to know, but without pressure.

Parents and families have to set priorities so that the child has time to be a child. That seems so obvious, but we can forget it when we get on a mission to "fix" something.

In the most smoothly run households, it's easy to let time with your spouse get eaten up by other demands. You need to set your priories so that doesn't happen. You have to make some choices in the short term that build a long-term foundation of strength, mutual respect, support, and love. Obviously, this is easier said than done, and it's important for you and your family to think through your priorities to make this possible.

Support

As you and your family begin to identify your resources, make sure you consider the people in your lives who can offer you support. Identify those family members who will understand your child's NLD and whose insight you value. Just because someone is family doesn't mean they'll be able to listen well and give you good advice, but if you're fortunate enough to have family who can do that for you, make use of them and count your blessings. Which of your friends are good listeners? Which friends are as much like family as family? Who among them will agree to listen to you complain for only so long and then promise they'll say, "Okay, so what are you going to do about it?" Can any of these people baby-sit your child once in a while to give you a break?

One of my friends, Cathyann (CA), can talk with our son on a level that we feel he is lonely for, as if they're both from some distant galaxy with a foreign tongue. They're both intelligent, and when Zac is really confused by some earth-based cultural oddity that we can't explain, Zac calls CA. She lives in New England and comes to visit often. Zac counts on her to make his life more understandable, more reliable, and more certain. For example, once CA was visiting when Zac was trying to learn division, and he was in total meltdown. She sat with him and drew elaborate *Star Wars* battle plans and taught him to understand that the number of bombs per plane had to be determined with division. For two hours they sat at our kitchen table, planned battles, reviewed the survivors, and divided the number of bombs used by the number of rebels and storm troopers remaining. Zac came away understanding and loving division. She made it concrete, real, and relevant to his world.

Another form of support could be as close as next door. Not all of your neighbors will be kind or trustworthy, but some may be. I know some parents are reluctant to talk about a child's learning disorder with neighbors, but if your child has NLD, people already know that she is different. Instead of pretending she is not, it may be more productive if you approached your neighbors and talked with them directly about your child's uniqueness. I told a couple of neighbors, "My child is very intelligent, but he has a very hard time understanding tone of voice. So sometimes he uses a voice that doesn't mean what he thinks it means or words that he doesn't understand are offensive. I just wanted to let you know that about him because it's something he's working on, and you may be able to help." If you ask for their cooperation, most people are flattered and pleased to be a part of helping kids grow and learn and see that he needs their understanding, not punishment or discipline.

We were unsuccessfully trying to break Zac from the habit of always saying things "sucked." We weren't getting through to him when we explained that some people consider it offensive. One night we went to visit our neighbors for dinner. During the conversation, Zac said something "sucked." The mother, Jennifer, whom Zac adores and respects immensely, said, "Please don't use that word here. I find that very offensive." That was it. He stopped using it right then and hasn't overused it since.

I truly believe children with NLD are a gift to our society. As we figure out what they need, we put in place things that will benefit all of us. One of the gifts these children bring is showing us that we do need a community to raise a child. Frankly, I think one mother and one father is not enough for any kid. We have been blessed by many people in our community. The mother of one of Zac's friends has become a second mom to him. She talks to him about his thoughts and impressions and leaves him feeling clearer. Fathers in the community coach our son or teach him woodworking or take him flying. Big brothers of friends taught him to surf the Web, beat video games, and build robots. Most kids would flourish if they felt they were part of a community that valued them, but they can probably get by without that. Children with NLD *must* have a sense of community and feel people are out there to help them.

When Zachary was selling candy for a school fund-raiser, he went to four neighbors' houses. They knew to help him through the process of counting change and writing out an order. When Zachary came back with an extra 50 cents, at first I thought he'd made a mistake and was going to send him back to return the money. But Zac said, "No, Mr. Brown gave me an extra fifty cents for doing a good job." An experience like that means there are people in the community who want him to succeed, who are in support of his successes, and who are willing to tell him when he has done a good job. That 50 cents was worth 200 times it's worth to my son's self-esteem.

Other ways to seek support in your community include parenting classes offered at the YMCA or local schools. These are usually inexpensive or free. Calling your local special-education office can help you locate such resources. Not only are they a great way to learn to be a better parent, but they'll also help you network with others in the community who are committed to being better parents. These classes may also direct you toward resources or give you ideas you wouldn't have thought of on your own. Community recreation centers and churches have a lot of programs that are free or inexpensive.

Finally, whatever faith you have, it's important to find time to participate in that faith. Whether you find support in prayer, church, or meditating, honor the power you can find in the practice of your faith.

Information

The library is a great resource. Children with NLD love books, so take your child to story time, and use those fifteen minutes to sit down and take a nap or read your own book. Bookstores are also good resources and many encourage you to assess books before you decide to buy any of them and are set up to invite browsing.

Put a Plan in Action

It is important to determine what bothers you most. For some families it will be meltdowns. For some, it will be that the child with NLD can't sit still through an hour church service on Sunday. For others it will be that the child has no friends.

Let's say you have 50 dollars a week to spend, and you can give your child with NLD an hour of concentrated individual attention per day. You've decided that for your family, the issue that bothers you most is that your child has no friends. So how do you apply the time and money to this problem? Twice a week you could have a kid over to your house for a play date, with you there mediating as necessary to help your child understand the nonverbal rules in effect, using what you learned from a book, workshop, or therapist. If your child is not doing well in the social skills group because he can't sit down and attend, you can stop the social skills group and spend that money on an occupational therapist who can help him organize his body so he can sit in a chair without needing to take flight. Once that skill is in place, your child can rejoin the social skills group. That way, he'll benefit more efficiently. You're wasting time and money if your child attends a group for social development, but spends much of the group in the hall because of poor behavior.

When you choose your priorities and break each problem down piece by piece, life becomes manageable. Doing that is really important for these kids. They need linear, logical, sequential interventions and lifestyles, and to whatever extent we can build those into their lives, they tend to do pretty well.

Making Choices

When you set your priorities, you need to keep in mind the principle of "first things first." Even though we live in a society that tells us we should be able to do it all at once, we can't. Even if we could, our children with NLD will remind us that that's not helpful to them. Just as in a treatment plan, we have to decide what's the most important thing, on a daily basis we have to look at what's the most important thing.

Examine your priorities and question your assumptions. Do you and your family have to comb your hair every time you leave the house? Do you have to have the latest style haircut? Can you get a haircut every six weeks and not every five? Do you have to have a sandwich at lunch, can you just have a glass of milk with some protein or fruit mixed in it? This is all part of simplifying and asking yourself, who do you need to do this for and is it something I feel I must do? Sometimes we need to reweigh the balance between how we look to the world and our own authentic priorities. My personal belief is that kids should always leave the house clean and neat, and sometimes I'll settle for clean teeth and a messy shirt.

As you and your family make a plan for helping your child with NLD, remember you don't have to do everything at once. Break each problem into manageable pieces and tackle them one at a time. The more you can do this, the better for all of you.

Math in the Morning

One recent morning as I was in the bedroom getting ready for work, I heard, "Parental unit alert! Any parental unit, report to kitchen for homework assistance!" That's our Zac. He was at the kitchen table, working on word problems for his math homework. He'd been able to independently read, interpret, and solve all but one of them. When I went in to help, he pointed out this problem: "Make an organized list of the possible pairs. Count the number of pairs. Oscar, Max, Norma, Pasha, and Hank want to ride. There are four horses: Spanky, Rita, Buttercup, and Ebony. In how many different ways can the horses be assigned if Max and Oscar ride on Spanky?"

After I read it, Zac said, "I think they've left out some essential information."

"Like what?"

"Like how many riders per horse? Pairs and riders aren't the same."

I reread the problem, and sure enough, I could see it had left out that important detail. The problem identified the one exception, but there was an unstated, implied assumption that there is one rider per horse. Knowing Zac, and knowing something about NLD, I could also see that this was a leap of inference that most people would have easily made, and I had the words and skills to make it clear to him.

"I think it's fine if you start your answer with, 'Assuming no more than two riders per horse and no fewer than one, then . . . ' and continue with the problem. That's what all scientists and mathematicians have to do when they get into higher math. They have to state their assumptions."

"Oh, that makes sense," Zac said, and off he went.

What's so great about these moments in our lives is that I have been keenly aware of his growth, his learning, and his progress. I have worked hard to pay attention to where Zac's been and where he is now so I can celebrate moments like this morning rather than be annoyed. (I did have to skip a shower to make up for the time it took to solve this mathematical quandary.) The true breakthrough is that Zac did not scream and fall to the floor, or tear his page up, or say "this sucks" or use any of those other behaviors that he used to use out of sheer frustration at not understanding. We've come a long way.

I told my husband about the math problem, my husband from whom this learning style was bequeathed. Bill problem solved the language for Zac and said, "Well, I would have told him, 'it appears that the essential information is missing in this problem, and there is an implicit understanding of the number of children per horse, but given that the specific assumption is not revealed, I would assume that there is one child per horse, possibly two. Of course, we *could* put all 3 remaining kids on Rita. That would leave Buttercup and Ebony riderless. I know! How about if Buttercup rides Ebony? Well—they don't specifically say that one horse can't ride another, now do they?'" It has helped that Zac has a dad who thinks like he does and can problem solve the language, and a mom who doesn't ever get tangled up in such details of precision when a clock says there's two minutes to complete an assignment and who can translate when there is a problem. A mom who can calculate when .01 percent of his overall grade in math is absorbing more than 30 minutes of time and who guesses a great deal in her life, but doesn't sweat the slivers of grades. Between the two of us parental units, we seem able to cover most of the ground missing (and in place) with our Zac.

Seven

Parenting the Child with NLD

IF you ask successful adults with NLD what made the difference in their lives, each one of them will say, "My parents never, ever gave up on me." Therapy will make a difference in your child's life, as will a school that fits your child's learning style. But it is your role in your child's life that makes it possible for your child to grow to be a happy, successful adult. Your thoughtful parenting is irreplaceable.

Parenting children includes discipline, not punishment. Discipline is what we need to achieve a goal; punishment is a payback for what was done. Parenting entails protecting and nurturing, teaching your values, teaching skills for membership in society, and teaching children how to live independently in the world. You know your values and your hopes for your child, and it helps you develop a touchstone for assessing your parenting.

Balance Growth and Well-Being

Upon first receiving the diagnosis, many parents of children with NLD (including the one in my mirror) want to rush out and do everything we can to "fix" our child's learning disorder. We think, "This is my child, for God's sake," and sign up our kids for every possible intervention. What Zachary taught me, and what I have discovered as a therapist, is that they need downtime—time to just think and process. When they're tired, they don't learn as well. Most important, they will not have the time to be children. If your child is always in some kind of organized program, then she'll never have time to invite a friend over to play. Inviting a friend over can be as or more important than learning to bring her hands together or how to form legible letters.

Of course we love our children. Loving them and caring for them, however, are not necessarily the same thing. You can love someone and not have a clue how to care for him. You can care for someone that you do not love. (Nurses do that all the time, and they do it well.) Loving my great little kid is an absolute for me. But I had to learn how to care for him. My loving him didn't necessarily mean I knew what was best for him.

When we think about what would be caring for our children, distinguishing between the "good" parent and the responsible parent can be useful, as I learned in a Parent Effectiveness Training class. In our "more is better" society, it's very easy to fall into the trap of believing that we're good parents only when we sign up our kids for every single enrichment program we can afford. That's what "good" parents do, we're told. But responsible parents don't buy into the "more is better" myth. Responsible parents are responsive to their child's energy levels and honor his need for rest and downtime. So instead of booking their child for therapy and sports every day, responsible parents choose a few activities, keeping the child's rhythm and pace for life in mind.

Understanding the distinction between the good parent and the responsible parent helped me be more centered and confident about my choices. My husband and I will often say to ourselves, "Is that choice being a responsible parent or a good parent?" Then when other parents say to me, "He's not in karate?" I feel comfortable saying, "Well, no, right now he's in soccer, and that meets twice a week, so that's all we're doing now."

As parents, we try to balance growth and well-being, we try to be caring, and we try to be responsible. It's not always easy.

Build Roots and Wings

When I got my BA in psychology, I learned about ego development, but it seemed like meaningless theory to me. It wasn't until I started working as an OT that I understood what ego development was and how important it is for all children, and especially children with NLD, who are at high risk for anxiety, depression, and even suicide. Once I thought about it in the context of what we were working on with my son, I understood that when people talk about ego development, they're talking about developing deep, firm roots.

Nowadays it's fashionable to talk about the importance of self-esteem, but I think self-esteem is a watered-down version of the key issue of ego development. My definition of ego development is a sense of truly knowing who you are: "This is who I am. This is who I am not." This knowledge is clear and unbreakable in any situation, which means you can let the criticism of others roll off you. We teach Zachary: "I am more important than any object. I am more important than any of my actions. I'm not defined by any of those because I'm me, and these are things I do. I'm always me, whatever I'm doing, and I am loved, and I have strengths, and I know who I am."

Ego development is having an inner center, a home to return to. When your ego is strong, those roots are clear and reliable and unchanging no matter what happens in your life. When your roots grow strong and deep, you have a solid foundation to grow from. It's the best insurance against anxiety and depression. That's why part of raising our kids to be happy, healthy, functioning adults is helping them grow those deep roots.

What grows the roots of a strong ego?

Unconditional love and knowing that no matter what you do, your family loves you. If you break a dish, your mom doesn't hate you forever. If you crashed your dad's brand-new car, he'll forgive you.

Strong roots confirm that you have some strengths as well as some weaknesses, and knowing you're doing your best. A sense of place, a sense of stability in your life, and a sense of community grows with deep roots.

I think a lot of adults with NLD have a hard time because they haven't developed a community. They don't have a home center to return to, so they are always looking for something to fill that void of "Who am I?" and "Where do I belong?" They sometimes seek community in unsafe places, like cults. You can't grow deep roots if you don't have a community, however small or large it may be. Our son knows his community. He knows the neighbors and friends who love and care for him, he knows his family loves and cares for him, he knows his grandparents love him even though they live in different states. He knows these people love him, and he knows they will never give up on him.

Children need to feel safe in order to grow, risk, and explore. When they have deep roots, then they can grow big wings. They feel optimistic. They don't have to be fearful about making mistakes or looking stupid. They can take risks, try new things, challenge themselves, and grow tall.

Expose the Monkey Brain

An important part of parenting is helping children to learn healthy mental habits. Each of us has a little voice in our heads that makes negative, belittling comments such as "That was a stupid thing to say," "Who do you think you are? They don't want to be your friends," "You idiot," and so on. In my family, we call that the "monkey brain." Naming that little voice and calling it something that indicates cleverness and mischievousness helps us separate that voice from our real selves. It takes the criticism out of talking about our negative sides and replaces it with humor.

I've often talked with Zac about his monkey brain. We talk about how loud that part of the brain can be and how it wants to grow big and powerful, to take over our actions if we'll let it. I explained that he had to question each negative thought. He has to see if it helps him feel good about himself and accomplish what he wants out of life. If not, it's the monkey brain up to it's dirty tricks again.

For example, on Saturday mornings, Zac likes to be the first one up, roll up in a blanket in front of the TV, and watch cartoons. When I get up, I'll say "good morning" to him. Often he will jump, panicking, and say, "What did I do?" This startled reaction is part of the fight-or-flight stress reaction. Because he's on sensory overload so much of the time, my saying "good morning" can feel like an assault.

I'll answer, "Your monkey brain is telling you I'm yelling at you, but you need to tell it, 'This is my mom, and she loves me and I have permission to watch cartoons and this is my house and I know the rules and

I've done nothing wrong.' " He'll repeat that, then he'll smile and we'll hug. We've done that ritual about forty times and now he doesn't flinch. More importantly, he has increased his tolerance to failures, is more resilient and when he falls prey to negative self talk, we can say "Nice try, Monkey Brain but I caught you! Now, go away."

One day he told me his monkey brain wanted him to hurt himself. I was glad he told me, glad he had the words to tell me, and glad that he knew that the voice was not a loving voice, and that his job was to not listen to it and also to tell me about it.

Choose Discipline Rather Than Punishment

As a parent and an occupational therapist, I have found that some parenting styles work well for children with NLD. Others, I have found, are either ineffective for these kids or make their problems worse.

If you go to the parenting section of any bookstore or library, you will find dozens of books by "experts" to tell you how to discipline your child. The majority of these base their methods, at least in part, on the field of psychology known as *behaviorism*. Behaviorism is based on the discovery that behavior can be learned as the result of negative and positive responses. When a rat in a maze gets an electric shock for taking a wrong turn, it quickly learns the correct path through the maze. This discovery was significant because it departed from psychoanalytic theory. It wasn't concerned with an unconscious cause of a behavior or the psychodynamics of a relationship; it just studied cause and effect, reward and punishment.

B. F. Skinner, the father of behaviorism, did not intend his work to become a technique to be scripted and followed, but a dynamic intervention that could help people change their behavior with as little emotional pain as possible.

Behavior modification is primarily a *nonverbal* form of discipline. If you smile at a child with NLD for putting her dish in the sink, she is unlikely to perceive your smile, and even more unlikely to connect it to the act of clearing her plate. If the reward is not perceived, then it's not a reward and will have no effect. If your dad puts you in "time-out" or spanks you and you have no idea why, you'll be angry and indignant, or afraid and anxious, but you're not likely to be contrite about the mistake you made, nor will you be capable of "knowing better" next time. A child who cannot perceive his own behavior cannot know how he looks and needs verbal assistance to link that raised eyebrow with his annoying mouth music.

Spankings, in particular, can escalate the NLD child's difficulties. He is likely to perceive spankings as random and arbitrary, even sadistic, because he does not connect the swat to his behavior and has little hope for understanding and anticipating the consequences of that behavior in the future. Spanking is an old form of punishment and gets handed down from generation to generation, but all the research is clear: it doesn't change behavior and it instills resentment. Spanking is a bad habit, not a thoughtful, loving form of discipline and is, in my opinion, a form of child abuse. Children with NLD have a keen sense of fairness. If you tell your child, "Never hit someone, that's the rule," and then you turn around and hit her, she will be confused and feel this injustice very deeply. I have never heard a parent say that spanking helped a child with NLD. Any extreme punishment is not going to help.

When parents punish misbehavior in ways the child cannot interpret, and the child doesn't change the behavior, parents often assume the child is being defiant, and the child is punished further. This sequence can make children with NLD anxious and depressed. Children treated this way are at the highest risk for suicide or dysfunction because, from their point of view, they are subjected to random, harsh punishment they can't control or prevent. Such a punitive approach to childrearing will turn a difference in learning into a full-blown disability. I know of kids whose parents scream at them, tell them how stupid they are, and spank them when they fall out of a chair or when they hold their ears and rock when the blender is turned on. Tragically, some children with NLD are treated so abusively they have little hope of growing up to be healthy adults.

Children with NLD are verbal creatures. They are very logical, linear, sequential thinkers. If you explain your rules to your child in a linear, logical sequential mode, chances are your child will be happy to obey them. Children with NLD are in fact very compliant once they know what's expected of them. Their noncompliance is usually because they don't know what's expected or because they are confused by mixed messages or they are neurologically incapable of doing what has been requested.

Learning a specific task like putting on a pair of pants is the one situation where behavior modification can work for children with NLD. As long as it's a behavior they can control (that is, not due to a neurological deficit), behavior modification can be a very effective form of treatment. We used behavior modification for Zac to help him learn his morning routine. He got a star when he was independent with tooth brushing and another when he combed his hair. This is a positive reinforcement of the positive behavior. But if we only gave him a star when he "got ready independently," then he would fail over and over because he didn't have sufficient organizational and sequencing skills to hold a picture in his head of what he needed to do each morning. Now, he's totally independent and it's terrific. He's actually more efficient in the morning than Bill and I.

We also use behavior modification for turning off the TV or video games. If we ask him to, and he is pleasant about it, he gets more time the next time. But if he is rude and angry, we say, "It seems that when you play too long on a glowing box, it takes away your ability to be pleasant. So I guess you're telling me that we need to help you by limiting your time more."

Use Logical Language

If you explain your rules to your child, presenting them in a linear, logical, sequential style, he is very likely to comply. For example, when Zac was very little, long before I knew he had NLD, I used to prepare him to go to the store with me because I knew stores are challenging for kids. The rule was he could have one treat each visit to the store. I taught Zachary, "If you want a treat at the store, and you cry for it, you cannot have it. That's the rule." I would rehearse this with him each time we went to the store. "If you want something, even if I really want to give it to you, if you cry for it, what will happen? That's right. I can't give it to you because that would teach you that the way to get something is to cry. That would be a bad thing to teach you. I don't want to do that to you." In the grocery store, he'd really want something and his little lip would start to tremble, but he learned to hold it together and ask for his treat without crying. Sometimes he'd see other children crying for a treat and get it and he'd say, "Mom, look, that parent is teaching that kid to cry. Isn't that really sad?" Because he knew the rule and had practiced it over and over, he was very accepting about the rules.

One of the many blessings of a child with NLD is that once he learns your rules, you can count on him to follow them. The downside to this is that he will expect everyone else, including adults, to follow the same rules. If they don't, he'll be quick to correct them. If your child knows that when the movie begins in the theater, it's time to stop talking, but the adults sitting in front of him are still chatting, your child is going to be the one to tell them to stop. To handle this with Zac, we talk about how some grown-ups aren't really grown up on the inside, so they have a hard time hearing what they did wrong. We also tell him sometimes it's not a good time to correct an adult, because if you tell someone they did something wrong, and there are a lot of people around, they might get embarrassed. We help him understand by pointing out that sometimes we will wait to correct him until after his friends go home or do so in private, practicing public praise and private criticism.

When you are teaching your rules to your child, it's important to say what to do, not just what *not* to do. If you say, "Don't throw the Frisbee in the house," you're actually implying a lot of nonverbal information that your child may not infer. You've told your child not to throw a Frisbee indoors, but he may still think it's okay to throw a basketball in the living room. "Please throw things only when you're outside," is a much clearer communication. As children with NLD must learn to take the perspective of others, we have to take their perspective, too, to understand what our words mean to them.

Never assume your child knows something just because he "should" or because "everyone knows that." There are no "shoulds" for children with NLD. Just the other day I said to Zachary, who was watching TV in the living room, "Don't eat popcorn in that chair. I just vacuumed."

"Okay," he said.

A moment later I went back, and he was sitting on the floor watching TV and eating popcorn. "Zachary, I just told you not to eat popcorn in here."

"No, you didn't. You said not to eat it in the chair."

"You're right. I said don't eat it in the chair. I'm sorry. What I meant was, don't eat it in the living room."

"Well, why didn't you say that?"

"I don't know. I goofed. I'm sorry. Would you please take the popcorn into the kitchen?"

"Okay."

Apologize

It's easy for us to assume that our sloppy way of talking says what we mean it to say. We're used to having people fill in the missing words for us. But children with NLD won't do that. I believe it's so important to apologize to our children when we make a mistake.

Some parents and therapists I work with disagree with me on this. They say, "He's manipulating you," or "You're just a softy." Well, perhaps, but I have evidence that supports my belief. When I apologize for my sloppy speech, kids change their behavior for me. They grow calm, and become ready to do good work.

I am proud of my son, who went from being severely affected by his symptoms related to NLD to being a strong, competent, adorable, straight-A, athletic, typical ten-year-old. I have a kid who is happy, content, successful, and a "typical kid," according to his teachers. He's successful where others said he would surely fail. He's successful in areas other parents say it would be impossible for their child to succeed. I think apologizing to him is one of the keys to his success.

Still, as a parent, I know it can be hard to apologize to our children. If we think of ourselves as authority figures, apologizing to children might seem backward. I think it makes a big difference if we say, "You're right. I'm sorry. I didn't say that." Particularly because these children have a keen sense of fairness, it can be very confusing to them when we make mistakes but don't apologize. An apology helps keep your child from becoming confused and anxious about your rules. Apologies help make your home a safe and accepting one.

Have Appropriate Expectations

Because of their astounding vocabularies and factual knowledge, children with NLD can speak like little adults. When your seven-year-old child can recite the Gettysburg Address, it's easy to assume she can get dressed. But remember, there are no "shoulds" with these kids. If your child has difficulty sequencing and problems with fine motor control, getting dressed will be a major challenge for her. If you don't recognize this, you'll be frustrated and angry at her "failure."

It's only a failure if you define it that way. When your child fails to meet your expectations, you may be upset. If you have an *inappropriate* expectation, you'll need to realize, then, the problem is not the child's, and therefore it's not fair to blame her. You know if your expectations are appropriate by paying attention to what your child can do. If you expect your child to get dressed independently in ten minutes, and she never has, that's an inappropriate expectation.

Parents often receive misleading information, which leads to an assumption that their child "should" be able to do something independently long before their child is really able. Instead of taking advice written by someone who doesn't know your child, consider what you know to be true of your child. Start where she is, set up ministeps for moving forward, and take things slowly. Then you will develop appropriate expectations. If it takes your child 20 minutes to get dressed in the mornings, try to reduce the time to 18 minutes and celebrate the progress. Children can learn anything when it's presented to them in a way compatible to their learning style.

Say It Over and Over

As a parent of a child with NLD, you will probably need to say the same thing over and over again in different contexts to compensate for these kids' inability to generalize from one situation to the next. Rules and lessons need constant reenforcing.

For example, when Zac is doing his homework, it's okay to put his elbows on the table. But at dinner I'll say, "Don't put your elbows on the table." That's a different context. Instead of getting angry when your child breaks the rule, it can be helpful to ask, what part is different this time? What didn't my child understand? There is almost always some kind of reason. So you need to keep telling them over and over until you and your child have dealt with all the situations the rules apply to. Children never get the wrong answer or act wrongly, they are responding to a different question or request than the one we intended. It is better to find out what question their behavior is an answer for before jumping to conclusions. In the same example above, Zac's persistant behavior (elbows on the table) was an answer to his question "How do I hold my head up when I'm so tired and I have to eat and this is a novel, socially demanding situation?"

Some children hate being told the same thing over and over, but children with NLD don't seem to mind as long as they are being told in a matter-of-fact way. I think they don't experience it as repetition. I think it's new for them each time, especially if you say it a little differently. Zac has never said to me, "Stop telling me over and over." I know he'd let me know if it were bothering him.

Explain

Recently I was on the phone talking about NLD with a colleague while my son was getting ready to go to school. He came into the kitchen wearing a dirty shirt, and I interrupted my call to say, "Hey buddy, you've got cotton candy on that shirt. You can't wear it to school."

"Why not?" he wanted to know.

"Because it makes you look kind of dorky and that's not what you want to look like at school, right?"

"Nooo."

"And you could fix that really quickly by just changing your shirt. Go see Dad for help."

"Okay." Off he went to change his shirt.

My colleague said, "Rondalyn, that was a great example of what you were just talking about."

"It was?" I had to stop and think what I'd just done.

"You stopped to explain why he should change his shirt, and you did it calmly, explaining the reasons and suggesting a solution."

If I had said, "Zac, what were you thinking when you put on that shirt? You wore that yesterday, it has cotton candy on it, and you look stupid." Then he would have had a meltdown and his whole day would have been horrible. But instead of a meltdown, he gave me ten kisses on his way out the door.

Preview and Rehearse

Children with NLD have difficulty with novel situations. Previewing upcoming events with them can make a big difference in how they handle a new situation and how anxious about it they will be. Before an event like a visit from someone or a birthday party, we rehearse with Zac what the social expectations in that situation will be.

Zachary's grandparents were coming for Thanksgiving. Zac adores them, but we don't see them that often, so I knew he'd need to preview his greeting. I said to him, "When Gram and Grandad come, how are you going to greet them?" Our rule is you can give a handshake using good eye contact, or a hug, or just say hi. The choice of greeting is Zac's, no matter who the person is or what that person expects of him.

Zac said, "A hi, a handshake, and a hug."

"Oh, I think it might be a little awkward to give them a handshake and then a hug."

"Oh, how about a hi and a hug."

"I think that would be better." When they arrived, Zac was ready to give them a hug. Otherwise, because it's so exciting to see Gram and Granddad, he'd start one action, stop, start another, and it would have looked goofy. Of course, all of us do goofy things, as when you reach to shake someone's hand and they give you a hug and a kiss on the cheek. Most adults can recover and handle this fairly smoothly, but for children with NLD, thinking it through ahead of time is helpful.

Part of previewing requires keeping in mind the next thing coming up and getting ready for it. Most people do this automatically, creating a mental picture of how a situation will play out. But kids with NLD don't have the ability to make mental pictures about future events, they need to use words to get them prepared. If you ask your child to talk through a scenario with you, you're helping him learn to preview a process through language: "You're going to Johnny's birthday party this afternoon. Let's talk it out. What will happen when you ring the bell? Think it through out loud for me."

When children with NLD ask persistent questions over and over and over it can be maddening. They ask repeated questions because they don't have the organizational skills to ask the real question they have, so they repeat an approximate question. When this happens, I think they're really saying, "Help me rehearse, help me think something through out loud." I have learned to say, "I have answered that question several times now so I'm thinking you actually have a different question for me. Can you think of a different way to ask me that so that you can get the information you're looking for?" Then the child changes the question and the repeated questions stop.

If something doesn't turn out the way they expected, children with NLD can become very stressed and anxious, resulting in a meltdown. If you can anticipate what might go wrong with a plan—the things that might not turn out the way you hope they will—you can help your child prepare for the unexpected turn of events. By talking about the things that could go wrong, you prepare your child and then the unexpected is not overwhelming. If you prepare for those possibilities, whether they happen or not, you've got a plan in place. Some glitches will arise that you've never considered, and you will have more resources to deal with them.

Interpret "Controlling" Behavior

If you ask your child to do a task—putting on her shoes, for example—and you meet with a lot of resistance and verbal fencing, it may well be because the task is beyond the child's ability, and she would rather look disobedient than stupid.

I worked with a little boy who didn't want to button his coat. He would ask me in the sweetest voice, "If you could just help me with my buttons, you're just so good at it." Some people would call that manipulative. But I think a more helpful interpretation is that the child was trying to save his dignity because he knew he couldn't button his coat. Children will resist in order to avoid the humiliation of failing. Another child I worked with wasn't so sweet. When it was time for his handwriting lesson, he would lie on the floor, throw a pencil, and start a verbal battle with me. As we continued working together, and I made it safe enough for him to fail and to succeed, this behavior stopped, and we developed a good relationship. More important (to his parents), his handwriting improved, and he felt more confident and competent in his written work at school.

When we see this kind of thing in younger children, it's fairly easy to see the cause and effect. In a six-year-old, it's easy to see that he only acts like this when we ask him to do pencil work. It's pretty clear that the motivation behind this behavior is to avoid a difficult task. They can often experience failure as a failure of self and not as difficulty with one task. In older children, avoidance behavior is easily misinterpreted as controlling behavior. Older kids will sigh a lot, use lots of verbal bantering and negotiation, and act like usurpers.

These kids have the raw intelligence to create some very savvy avoidance strategies. But it's important to remember that these children are not calculating how to push your buttons. They really don't have that calculating ability. It's just that they know what "works." That's why calling the behavior "controlling" is inappropriate. It's really an expression of frustration at being asked to do things they can't do. It's the only strategy these children have.

When I see kids engaged in this behavior with their parents, I always envision a bull and a matador in battle. It can get very ugly. In my experience, a more effective approach is to say, "Wow, that looks like it must be pretty frustrating to you. You've banged your pencil and you've kicked the table, and you're really very frustrated. So let's take a break, have a drink of water, and come back to it." Zac really didn't have many controlling behaviors. Partly this is because we started intervention early, but more because we didn't set ourselves up for battles with him. We didn't force him to do things, and we were always asking ourselves "Why would he be acting this way?"

If you work from the assumption that your child won't obey you, then you start from a premise of an antagonistic relationship, and the things that occur to you to deal with the situation will probably be punitive: confining her to her room, spanking, or withholding food. If you let go of the idea that the child is resisting your authority, let go of the idea that the kid *won't* and instead assume that the kid *can't*, then you're working from a different frame of reference. Then you can start providing your child with ways to do what you want her to do. This might be an environmental intervention, like Velcro-closing sneakers, or a therapeutic one like strengthening her fine motor skills, but ultimately it changes the child's perspective of herself and develops her understanding that she can succeed with the right support and in the right environments.

Although I know that certain parenting styles will make a child's difficulties worse, of course I acknowledge that my own style is neither perfect nor the only effective one. If we perceive NLD as a series of problems to help them solve rather than see them doing something "wrong," we have started the journey of being better parents. Parents, like children, are searching for mastery, and sometimes we are not using the most successful strategies available.

Support Siblings

Every family has to balance the competing needs of all its members. In families with one child, that means balancing the needs of the parents with the needs of the child. When there is more than one child, the competing needs of siblings have to be addressed. Parents of a child with NLD are often concerned that their other children are not getting enough parental attention or a fair share of the family's resources because a lot of money gets spent on the child with NLD. Furthermore, siblings often spend several afternoons a week in the car while Mom drives the child with NLD to therapy. Then the sibling waits in a waiting room, and when the brother or sister comes out of the therapist's office, often he or she will have made a craft or earned a small prize for filling up a sticker chart, while the sibling gets nothing. It's natural that the sibling would be sad about this.

The social deficits of children with NLD also affect relationships with siblings and family friends. A sibling's friend comes over and the NLD child's behavior causes him to say, "What a geek." Even among good friends, an occasional intolerance or a misinterpretation of behavior can make get-togethers pretty challenging. We have family friends who do not understand Zac. It's stressful for us to visit with them, although he loves them. It's almost painful to watch him with them because he has so little skill in interacting with them. We try to anticipate and practice the social challenges of such situations, but we always come across new ones. This is a loving and generous family, but it is a social stressor for Zac and thus for us all to spend time with them. We've solved *that* problem by letting Zac take a friend when we go on vacation to visit this family, then, Zac's not the "odd boy out."

Often the homes of children with NLD are volatile homes. Things seem to be going just fine, and then, boom, there's a meltdown and chaos. It can seem to siblings that the parents are more lenient with the child with NLD. It's natural that the sibling would feel stress and anxiety, and it's natural that the parents would feel conflicted.

Although I've seen this very natural response in both parents and children, I've also noticed that the siblings of children with NLD often have a good understanding of their brother or sister's unique needs. They seem to make allowances for their sibling and to be generally accepting.

If you're concerned about handling your children's competing needs or avoiding creating the role of "problem child" for the child with NLD, what I suggest is going back to your family discussion of what each of you is working on. Then you can explain the child's need for therapy in terms of your areas of knowledge.

"Right now, Johnny needs a little help with his posture. I don't know that much about posture. I know about riding bikes, so I can help you learn to ride your bike, but I need someone to help Johnny because I don't know how. Someday if you want to learn the piano, we'd have to get someone outside the family to help you because I don't know how to play piano. Right now, Johnny is working on something we need some outside help with."

If you show each of your children that you are working with him or her on something, then you don't create the perception that the child with NLD is the "problem child" and everyone else is either okay or unimportant. I think it's important to establish the value that everyone in the family is committed to each member of the family's growth.

One family I work with has five kids. When the mom is not feeling well, the teenage brother brings the boy to his therapy. He'll say, "Looks like I'll be the one helping you this week." Often when I show the boy something new, the big brother will say, "Hey, that would help me, too, can you show me?" The brother makes sure he knows what the boy's homework is and how to help with it. And the little boy will say, "I can show this to my sister," or "Can I have one of these for my brother?" Families like this one do well because they are aware that everyone has something to work on and they are supportive of one another while they do the work.

Handle Criticism ASAP

Many parents of children with NLD report that even before their child was diagnosed, they had an intuitive sense that he needed more protection and care than their other children. These parents frequently interceded for or shielded their children when they thought they needed to. Most of these parents report receiving criticism for being overprotective, overinvolved, clinging, or having unclear boundaries.

Once we learn our child's diagnosis, we have the assurance of knowing that our instinct to protect our children and guide them through social situations is right. But that doesn't change the way others perceive us. If you are the parent of a child with NLD, you've probably received plenty of criticism for your parenting.

I would say that 90 percent of parents of children with NLD have been accused of making it all up. We get called "crazy," "hysterical," "overly involved," and "overly protective." The irony is, the parents who are doing their best are the ones that get this criticism the most. It's really devastating to parents to have to fend off so much criticism. They should be given awards for how hard they are trying. Instead, they're more likely to hear:

"If you'd just give her a good swat."

"What he needs is more discipline."

"What she needs is less control and authority in your family."

"He has too much power in the decision-making process."

"If you'd just spank him."

"Let me spank him."

Parents of children with NLD take a lot of grief and get called lots of things by teachers, administrators, family, and friends. People want to know what's going on in our marriages and offer all sorts of inappropriate psychological examinations of our motives. Some of us even get criticism from our spouses. Strangers feel comfortable voicing their criticism. Holding your own in the face of so much flak can be hard.

When you are bombarded by criticism of your parenting style, it is easy to lose sight of your own values and priorities. It's easy to doubt yourself. When this has happened to us, we've gone to the people who share our values, people who know us and care about us and whose advice we respect. We've had long talks about our parenting with the friends we trust. We've learned to listen to the advice of the people we honor and to ignore the criticism we get everywhere else.

The Pleasures of Parenting Children with NLD

Parenting a child with NLD is a challenge, but the rewards and pleasures are many.

Children with NLD are good editors of our language. Even though it's annoying to be corrected, it has helped me be a better speaker. Since I had Zac, I've realized I'm a sloppy talker. He's taught me to be precise.

Another great pleasure: Zac believes what I tell him. If I say to him, "If you eat five servings of vegetables a day, you'll be a healthier boy," he believes me and he does that. We don't get the "Oh yeah? Says who?" attitude many kids have. It's really nice to have a kid who is not challenging me on some of these essential things. (There's a responsibility attached to that that I hold sacred.) I think that when he's a teenager this will pay off even more. We'll be able to talk about our beliefs and values, and he'll listen and believe us.

Children with NLD can be charming because they don't censor what they say. The other day I said to a kid in my clinic, "Oh, you threw the ball over my head again and I have to run and get it. Try to throw it right to me, I'm getting to be an old lady here." He looked around the room and said, "Where? Where's an old lady? I don't see an old lady." I get that kind of stuff all the time out of these kids. These kids make me laugh every single day and etch the laugh lines more deeply into the corners of my eyes.

These children are persistent. The younger kids especially will try forever to please you. They'll be so wrong and so off, and they'll keep try-ing so hard for you long after most of us would have given up. Zac is working on learning to control his tone of voice. Now he'll say, "Oh, I'm sorry, was that a rude tone of voice?" It usually was not—he usually doesn't catch his tone when it is a rude one—but he's very sweet when he asks. Every time he does that I want to fall to my knees and hug him for his courage. He has so much courage on a minute by minute basis as he tries to guess, "How did I do for you right there?" He cares so much even when he's clueless.

Children with NLD follow the rules. If they understand that some-thing is a rule, they will follow it to the letter. The rule is you always wear your seat belt, and my son always does, even if he's in a friend's car. We've given him support to learn the rules, and we've practiced them, but now I know that even when I'm not there, I can count on him to fol-low our rules.

When he was as young as ten months, I could explain things to Zac. I think we intuitively knew he understood us. He would roll his eyes if we spoke baby talk. As he got older, we could chat with him. He didn't go through the terrible twos because he had the language skills to ask for what he wanted. When he was four, we read stories from my anatomy book together and discussed the kidney well into the night. We never had to talk down to Zac. Our friends are amazed that he listens and interacts with them like a teenager. These days, if I need to know some-thing about history, he can tell me. He's always right. It's like living with a lovable old college professor.

Zac and Bill have long conversations about gravity and relativity and history. They delve deeply into time travel and warp drive and physics. I think this started by Zac trying to figure out his world—asking ques-tions over and over about everything. For example, when he will ask questions like, "Why do some people beat up others because they're gay?" or "Why is my penis big when I wake up in the mornings?" or "Why do I have to brush my teeth?" or "Why is it five servings of fruits and vegetables and not three?" All his questions are clean and clear and not based on wanting to embarrass or offend, just attempts at gathering information. Zac is fascinated by the details of life, and he has the verbal skills to hang in there and persevere with a detailed inquiry.

One Saturday Zac and Bill spent the entire morning discussing the Korean War, looking at an atlas and finding the important rivers and boundaries. We love to see him so curious about so many things, and whatever we can do to support those curiosities, we do. If we don't know the answers, we can speculate and look it up. I am amazed to behold his insatiable curiosity. When clinicians list the traits of a gifted child, they describe this characteristic as "persistent and curious, able to tune out the world and concentrate deeply." Interestingly, in the world of disability, they more often refer to this as "perseverative, fixated, obsessed or having an intense interest." What we've noticed is the observers decide if the conversation is obsessive or deep and satisfying, and it depends on the degree to which the observer shares Zac's interests. We are happier with some of our son's passions than with others. We prefer World War history over video games. We have to realize our perceptions are based in our values, so we have found it is important to show him, with our time, what we value and what to value.

Another great pleasure is that when we (Bill or I) are too tired to read a bedtime story, then Zac will read one to us. I think most adults love opening up a piece of the world for a kid, and these kids are fertile ground for that. You can open up their world with the tiniest thing. And the greatest pleasure is seeing who your child really is.

Big Feelings

Recently Zac, Bill, and I went on a walk with Bill's parents. It was Christmastime in California, a blistering 60 degrees. We were walking around Shoreline Park, right on the bay, observing various West Coast birds and enjoying the beauty of the day.

Zac was Rollerblading. He passed by us so closely that he almost knocked down my mother-in-law, scaring her. I told Zac he needed to apologize to her, but time passed on the walk, and he didn't say anything. I caught up to him and asked him why he hadn't apologized. Zac said, "I don't know how. What should I say?"

I was so glad I hadn't gotten mad at him or assumed he was being a little brat. He had some big feelings about scaring his grandmother, whom he loves. Those feelings were so big, he didn't know how to apologize big enough to match the feelings. I role-played with him and then he was able to relax and apologize. His grandmother, of course, gracefully accepted his awkward apology. It was another one of those moments when Zac appears so aloof, but in fact he's lost in another gap of social rules and confusion.

Eight

Teaching Moments and Other Parenting Strategies

As you choose your priorities and make a plan to help your child, keep in mind who your child is likely to be when she grows up. Focusing on the immediate problems is easier, but alternatively, an holistic approach to treatment would explore the problem in the context of who the child is going to be when she is twenty-five and what her social role will be when she is an adult. Asking this question helps us choose priorities. If handwriting is so difficult, should we allow the child to be the kindergartner who's proficient on a computer, or do we force her to do everything with a pencil and produce a child who's very anxious around expressing herself?

When I am treating a child who has problems organizing himself, problems expressing himself on paper, and has poor motor coordination, the first thing I ask is, where is this kid going? What is he interested in? For example, Britt, a child in my practice, is interested in opera. She wants to sing the greatest arias. Britt's handwriting is a huge problem, and she has very little postural control. Although I need to address her handwriting, my first approach is to work with her on developing postural control so that her breath is sufficient to hold a long note. She needs to be able to maintain her posture when she walks on stage. The exercises I give her are not intended directly to support her handwriting, but to support postural control and allow her to target and respond to something moving quickly in her environment. One needs that skill in order to be successful where one wants to go. She needs to be able to express herself when she writes an essay or when she fills out a form, but she doesn't need award-winning penmanship.

If we consider the challenges our children will face as teenagers and adults, we can work with them now so they'll be ready. For example, if your child is 11, in five years she'll be learning how to drive. Without intervention, she'd be a very dangerous driver if she doesn't pay attention to anything in her environment. (Therapists have a lot of anecdotal evidence that many kids with NLD die driving cars because they didn't see something coming.) So part of the therapist's and parent's job in treating an 11-year-old is to think about the 16-year-old who's going to get behind the wheel of a car. Driving is made up of small components, and those components need to be addressed before a person will be successful at driving. A therapist can work with the child on responding quickly to visual information in the environment with the goal of attending to two and eventually three or four moving objects and orienting her body to that movement.

If you think about where your child is now and where she will be in two or three years, you can anticipate what skills she will need to learn in order to be successful at the challenges she'll face later. I knew that going to amusement parks with his friends would be important to Zac by age ten. So when he was eight, we started working on the skills he'd need to help him be safe there. I started by letting him go up to the counter and purchase a bagel with me standing right beside him. Eventually I could stay in my car and watch him through the window while he went into the store. Before he went inside, I'd ask him, "How much do you think it's going to cost? How much change should you get back?" When he got back in the car, I'd break down the transaction for him. I'd say, "Did you notice three people got in front of you?"

"Yeah, they didn't wait on me."

"Right, so next time you need to walk right up to the counter and say 'excuse me.' And did you notice you forgot to get your change?" Or if he'd remembered, we'd count his change and make sure he'd gotten enough. We also worked on safety issues: what you do if you get lost, what you do if someone threatens you. After we'd worked on all these skills, he was able to go to the amusement park with two friends, but he had to check in with me every two hours. Next year it might be every three hours, and by the time he's 15 he can go all day. We had one problem when I told the boys to meet me either at the roller coaster or the spider ride and, of course, we kept missing each other countless times until I was in a panic. Now we say, "Meet me at this one spot," and then we have a "plan B" in place. If something doesn't work with our first plan, we move to the second plan. We also played a game for about three months called, "and then what would you do?" to help develop some of those reasonable choices we might expect Zac to make. Guess what I learned? Zac always makes good, logical choices, just different from those I'd make. Now that I have learned his way of thinking, we don't lose each other.

Sexuality

One big challenge all our children will eventually tackle is their sexuality. Before they become teens and adults with intense sexual feelings, we need to address the needs of children who are impulsive, have poor insight, are unable to anticipate consequences, and have some sensory issues like not wanting to be touched or always wanting to be touched. These are issues we need to break down into manageable pieces for our kids before they even know what sexuality is. We can talk to our sons about the role of girls in their lives, how a girl can be a friend. We can start early pointing out the nonverbal rules that govern how you talk to a girl and how those rules differ from how you talk to a boy. When they're ten, they think sexual issues are all gross and silly. But what you're really doing in these early grades is helping your son attend to the fact that girls are in his class and that the social rules about girls are different. The same applies to our daughters.

Talking about intimate topics can be very uncomfortable for parents. However, many adults with NLD report being sexually violated and those are the survivors we can speak with. I wonder how many teen pregnancies have occurred as a result of a girl or boy with NLD not understanding the consequences of intercourse or insufficient bilateral coordination and motor planning to don a condom. One form of sensory seeking behavior typical of children with NLD is seeking deep pressure and proprioception (the pushing and pulling of the bodies joints and muscles), both of which are gained during sexual relations.

Like other activities of daily living, children with NLD need to learn the rules of intimate touching and inappropriate touching to be safe in their lives. Learning the rules of touching will be part of any good social skills group. Parents can build on those lessons and help their child apply them to intimate touching, sexuality, and safety. For children who are five to ten years old, we talk about the nonverbal rules of space (proximity) and touch. The rule is, we have an entire six inches of space surrounding us, like an eggshell, that is our intimate space. Children need to consciously identify who has the right to be in that intimate space—Mom and Dad, a teacher, a grandparent, close friends—and what to do if anyone other than those folk enter the intimate zone without permission. Children with NLD need to learn to tell a teacher or a parent when this rule has been violated. This simple lesson helps to establish boundaries. Children and adults with NLD are vulnerable, trusting, and a safety risk. They often have that look that predators seek. We must speak to them, teach them the rules, and teach them that if they come to us with questions about the rules, we will listen and help them.

Teach Activities of Daily Living (ADLs) Early

In past generations, passing on the skills needed to run a household was a standard part of childrearing, but nowadays our society doesn't place much value on household chores. If we need to heat our homes, we push a button, to cook, we take something from the freezer to the microwave, if we want a new shirt, we push a button, point and click, and the shirt is delivered to our door. Even groceries can be delivered to our door this way. We tend to assume that upon reaching adulthood our children will automatically know how to do laundry and dishes, cook, and take out the trash. This may be true for some children, but children with NLD will not learn these skills unless they are taught. Everything that you do for your child each day, your child will someday have to do for herself. Children with NLD will not pick these up. It's important that children with NLD learn basic cooking skills to prepare nourishing meals, learn how to do laundry, learn how to grocery shop, how to wash dishes. A new set of social opportunities opens for folks who keep a tidy home, who can cook a meal to share with others or bring to a potluck, and who have sufficient health and vitality to get out of the house to join in activities in the community. These basic skills have ripples in the social world that make a big difference in social success.

Shielding your child from these chores is not a caring act. If you excuse your child from chores because "he's so tired and he's already got so many things going on, so I'll just do it for him," you might be helping his wellness in the short term, but not his growth in the long term. While it may, at first, be easier to do the chore yourself, ultimately you want your child to be a helpful contributor to your family. Pick one or two chores you have time to let go of.

Teach Organizational Skills

Keeping organized is a challenge children with NLD need to cope with now and as adults. When I work with children on this skill, I teach them an organizational system that can last through college and throughout life. I use a system that is easy to use and simple enough that, once a child learns it, she can use it forever. I use a simple day planner and have him log all his daily assignments and scheduling. Long-term assignments are broken into their sequential parts and logged in as well.

Helping your child organize her home space can make a big difference in both reducing his stress and teaching him life skills. It makes a big difference in the day-to-day levels of stress if your child has learned to organize homework, clothes, toys, etc. While I struggle to maintain organization of all my various papers and projects, I put forth the daily effort to clear clutter, label drawers, and empty leftovers from the fridge. Each member of the family sees how helping Zac stay organized makes our lives calmer and more successful. When Zac was younger, we borrowed an idea from Kathy Allen's book *Star-Shaped Pegs in Round Holes*. Our way of keeping organized was to pretend his belongings were in jail. If his shoes were in the living room, I'd say, "Oh, no, the shoes have escaped from jail. Let's take them back to jail." Jail for the shoes was in the closet on the left, and jail for the backpack was in the closet on the hook. Jail for the books is inside the backpack.

We also organize his workspace. Zac's pencils and pens belong in a box on his desk. He's allowed to bring them out to the kitchen table, where he prefers to do his homework, and they always go back on his desk so he can find them next time.

Zachary has a bulletin board hung at his height in the kitchen, where he knows to look for important papers. We also hung a white board there for him. When he gets home from school, he writes his afternoon schedule on the white board. "Okay I'm going to do homework from four to four-thirty, and then I'm going to take a break and watch my show from four-thirty to five, and then I'm going to skateboard, and then I'm going to do the rest of my homework." He writes it all down on the white board every day. It's a little unusual for a ten-year-old, but it works. He'll be doing the same when he's fifty. For a child with organizational deficits, providing him with a place to write this and places for all his belongings helps enormously.

Think Aloud

We often think to ourselves about what we're doing or need to do. Speaking our thoughts aloud is helpful to our children. We model our organizational process for them and show them that we don't just start a task in a random place; we have a plan we follow. "I'm opening the dryer and checking to see if the clothes are dry. They are. Now I empty them all into the laundry basket. Now I find all the socks and put them in a pile. Now I fold Dad's T-shirts, then mine, then yours."

Or, "Let's see, I have to go do my errands. Let me check, do I have my list? My wallet? Do I have the clothes for the dry cleaner? The returns to the store? Do I have Zac? Okay, let's go." I watch Zac go through his list in the mornings: "Do I have my binder? My lunch? A jacket? My book for after school? Okay, I'm ready."

Exploit Moments

As a parent, you will need to become your child's primary teacher. Therapists can help you, but your child spends far more time with you than with her therapist. And you know your child best. You know what she needs to work on. To make the most of your special role, you can take advantage of what I call "teaching moments," using the opportunities that daily life provides to develop your child's skills.

Sometimes when I begin to work with a family, the parents will say to me, "I don't know how to become a model or a teacher for my child. I don't know enough." They're intimidated and overwhelmed and don't know where to begin. As with every other problem, you have to break it down into manageable pieces. What I suggest is that you pick one thing you'd like to help your kid with. Otherwise you'll be teaching your kid to death, and she'll hardly be able to stand being around you.

You might ask a therapist or another parent or a friend for ideas. You can get books from the library or bookstore that address the issue that you want to work on. You will probably find that opportunities to address an issue will appear in your life. Even Pokémon starts to look like a teaching opportunity. You don't necessarily have to orchestrate a lesson plan to teach your child, because once you're paying attention, opportunities arise and you can use whatever shows up.

For example, at one point we were working with Zac on the importance of looking clean and well-groomed. Appearance is a part of nonverbal communication. If you have trouble with nonverbal communication, your appearance is one of the areas in which you can have a deficit. Zachary couldn't have cared less about his appearance. I'd say, "Comb your hair," and he would go into a meltdown and scream, "Why do I have to comb my hair?"

I'd explain to him that we didn't expect him to win any awards for his looks, but that people's responses to him would be based on how he looked. Like it or not, that's how our world works. A lot of adults with NLD do not look clean and well groomed, and are consequently set apart. They can be almost slovenly, with greasy hair, dirty faces, gunky teeth, wrinkled clothes, mismatched socks, and shoes with holes. Regardless of my own aesthetics of dress, I don't want my son to be treated the way our society treats people who look that way. So when I wasn't getting through to Zac with simple explanations, I looked for teaching moments.

We were in our car waiting at a red light when a man walked across the street. He looked as if he would be dirty and smelly with disheveled hair. I looked at Zac and said, "Why don't we give that guy a ride?"

"No way!"

"How come? Let's just take him home with us and hang out with him and see who he is."

"No!" Zachary was just adamant.

"Why?"

"Well, look at him! He's dirty and gross."

"But you said that stuff doesn't matter. Maybe he's a physics professor, maybe he's a teacher, maybe he's a champion bike rider or a video game champion."

"I don't think so, Mom."

"Well, why? Why don't you think so?" Of course it came down to the way this man looked. "So Zac, you're making a judgment and forming an opinion about this man just based on the way he looks?" There was a long moment of silence, and that was our little epiphany.

When we're looking for good teaching moments, we look to the child's interests for opportunities. For a while Zachary was obsessed with Superman, and though he was only six, I used this as an opportunity to talk with him about issues that would eventually affect his sexuality. We would watch his *Superman* video over and over, and whenever Lois Lane was mean to Superman, I would say, "Was she nice to him? No. Would you like a girlfriend like that? No. Would you want to marry someone like that? No. Is she a good friend? No." Everything that mean Lois did to poor Superman, I would talk to about in terms of Zac's eventual sexuality.

Teaching moments can be small victories for your child. Right now we're working with Zac on being able to talk about the main point. We recently saw a PG Arnold Schwarzenegger movie. Zac was psyched to see it because he loves Arnold, but we don't let him see R movies. At dinner that night I said, "Zac, what do you think was the main point of the movie?"

He looked at me in a very ordinary way, as if I'd just asked him if he wanted the salt, and said, "Do you want the marketing version, the speech therapy version, or the Zac Whitney detail version?" That was a great moment, because it showed he knew the difference.

I said, "Give me the speech therapy version," because I wanted the succinct answer, not the mass of details he usually likes to give, nor the advertisement I knew he could parrot. The speech therapy version was the one I picked!

We recently watched a videotape of *Cocoon*. Zac asked me at the end, "Mom, they never covered why the guy stayed behind on the boat. Or is that easy for you to infer and I just didn't get it?" This showed us how much Zac has learned. Before intervention, he would have just been confused. Now he can articulate his confusion and ask a question about it, knowing that's okay, instead of feeling like, "Oh, here's another thing I didn't get."

Admit Your Idiosyncrasies or Personal Quirks

We used to have a society that allowed for people to be a little eccentric and idiosyncratic, but that is disappearing. Now people who differ from the so-called norm tend to be thought of as mentally ill or disabled. We all have our quirks. I can't do simple math if I'm asked to calculate on the spot, and I forget names when I'm stressed, even names of my family members. I make a point of admitting my idiosyncrasies to my son, just as I acknowledge other people's. We'll talk about his grandma Maggie, who isn't very organized. "But isn't she so caring? She never forgets your birthday present. Sometimes it's late, or even early, or she sends you these quirky little gifts like seeds to grow giant loofa sponges. She is kind of odd and we really love her." Instead of focusing on faults or weaknesses, we talk about people's idiosyncrasies.

This allowance for variation from the societal "norm" also extends to appearance. Once Zac said to me, "You really have a kind of big butt."

"I do," I said, "and I don't think I can help it much."

"How come?"

"Well, let's think about it. What's Grandma Maggie's butt look like?"

"It's kind of big and soft."

"Okay, what's Andrew's butt look like?"

"It's big and soft." We went through the Varney clan and he realized all my relatives have big, soft butts.

"Now, what do the Whitneys look like?"

"Tall and thin."

"And who eats the most ice cream?"

"Uh, Whitneys."

"And when we go out to dinner, which family eats the most?"

"Well, Grandma Maggie usually just eats a salad. But Grandma Whitney eats a regular meal plus dessert and we always have potato chips. I've never seen Grandma Maggie eat dessert or potato chips." Then Zac added, "Wait a minute, that's not fair!"

"You know what, it's not fair." I explained that my butt is something I have to work really hard on and this is as hard as I can work and this is the butt I have. He understood. Then I said, "When you say I have a big butt, it hurts my feelings because I'm doing my best."

"Okay, I won't say that."

Rather than respond to his comment with anger, (and I certainly had a moment of wanting to do that), I used logic and sequential thinking to point out I was doing the best I can, and that's good enough. Zac was giving me information. He did not intend to insult me. It is helpful to Zac and to others to talk through struggles with sensitive issues, to take their perspective and explain my own in a nonjudgmental manner.

Foster Their Intellectual Lives

As parents of children with NLD, it can be easy to focus on their deficits. However, we need to remember to give our kids time for their strengths. You might wonder, if your child's verbal skills or his knowledge of history are already so good, why work on them? Because they give your child a chance to be who he is.

Our kids love words. Words are their strength and their comfort. It's an amazing day when my son sits down with my friend Cathy, and they talk about words. I feel as if I'm in a college classroom. When he wanted to learn swear words in other languages, he called Cathyann (a linguist by training). They discussed the power of language and came up with some words with adequate force but no offensive connotation. Zac will ask her, "What are the dirty words in French? How do we get dirty words? Why are they dirty?" and off they'll go. Then she'll say, "But swearing in any language is still offensive." Zachary is so fed by these conversations. Our kids really need this nourishment in their lives.

For some children with NLD, finding this stimulation in their lives can be difficult. Even if they have friends they enjoy playing with, those friends might not be their intellectual peers. As he grows older, other kids will catch up to him, and as an adult, he'll probably have an easier time finding common ground with peers. But if we didn't make this experience available to him now, he might not know to seek it out as an adult.

Finding intellectual peers for your child may not be easy, and it is very important. Otherwise life can be empty for them. They can get frustrated being with kids who aren't their intellectual peers, just the way a mother will say, "I love my kids, but I'm going nuts without adult conversation." The same is true for kids who are gifted, as a lot of kids with NLD are.

You can look for intellectual peers at museums that offer classes. In our area, we have Lyceum, where parents teach gifted children, and other programs through the gifted association. You may also find mentors among your neighbors or friends with whom your child can form friendships with folks who share his interests. We found a guy who works at the local store that sells Dungeons & Dragons sets, magic cards and comic books. He's offered to host a Dungeons & Dragons group for Zac and a few friends.

Make Learning Fun

Children with NLD don't just pick up information or skills, they have to consciously learn almost everything. The best way for them to learn is for it to be as fun and engaging as possible, but sometimes they need a day off. Zac gets four hooky days a year, days he can stay home from school and just do nothing. We let him decide when he needs them.

It's also very helpful for children with NLD to add multisensory input to any lesson—movement, song, colors, etc. If your child is learning multiplication, you can write the problems on colored paper using different colors of ink. You can have your child sing the multiplication tables while bouncing on a ball. Your child has a better chance of receiving information through one of these sensory channels than if she relied only on a visual mode of learning. Or for spelling a hard word like *February*, you might write out FebRUary, then when you recite it, yell the RU as loud as you can.

You can help to build math skills by using relation concepts such as bigger, smaller, light, heavy, tall, and short, all of which build mathematical thinking skills. Group toys (categories) by putting all the square toys into the toy chest, (puzzle boxes, blocks) and round things like marbles balls and such in a basket. These are sets and subsets. Matching games teach math concepts such as equal, odd and even, and more, less, greater, etc. Teach counting and numbers with real world items that a child can touch and hold to develop strong connections between the tactile and visual systems.

One night we were walking home from the Tech Museum here in California, and Zac was running around getting rid of some of his energy. At the curb he kept hopping up and down like a runner. Meanwhile, 60 mph traffic was whizzing by twelve inches from him. Zac didn't have a problem with this, and Bill and I were trying to get him to stop and stand still. Finally, Bill put his hands on Zac's shoulders, got his eye-to-eye attention, and explained that if Zac fell or even lost his balance and bent forward, his head would be in 60 mph traffic. Zac got it and stopped. But when Bill said, "I want you to stand five feet from the curb," we got into a debate about what five feet would be. Zac imagined it such a huge distance that he would not be able to run a sprint on the sidewalk and follow the rule. I stood about five feet from the curb and said, "This is about five feet."

"No, it's about two or three." So there we were in California winter weather (okay, so it's only 50 degrees, but we were cold), and I had Zac (who only wears shorts and T-shirts) lie down on the sidewalk at 9:30 P.M. with his feet by my feet and his head at the curb. Thank God, I was right and my "about five foot boy" fit snugly into the space, not an inch to spare. Zac surrendered the point. This experience helped him get ready for geometry and to understand space and distance, not to mention safety, and yes we did look like certified wackos!

Opportunities to teach math can arise daily. Estimate a half a cup of nuts when the package says a half a cup is a serving. This helps to build concept formation, spatial relations, and visual memory, which is very hard for many children with NLD.

Counting out silverware for the family dinner, sorting socks and matching them, dividing cookies and pizza slices evenly, estimating how many pizzas to buy for a party with 12 kids, all involve math skills. One game we've enjoyed is to place a bunch of numbers in a jar. Zac can pick a number at clean-up time, and he has to pick up that many items.

We also use lot of board games with dice and spinners. Dice are a great way to teach parts to whole thinking. Spinners are practice for counting, and all these increase math concepts. With dice, the players have to look at the numbers (say six separate dots), and eventually they see the whole concept "six" (whole) when they see that pattern of dots, not having to count them (parts) all the time. We used to make big dice out of a half-gallon milk cartons and throw two of them against the wall. Then we'd race the clock to shout out the sum of the two dice. Now, a six on a die is a six, and no one has to count the dots anymore.

Use Television as a Tool for Learning

I know many people question the value of television. I understand their concern, but my son has learned a lot about the world watching TV. Television, in limited doses, can also be very soothing to children who are overstimulated and need downtime. While I am definitely not advocating letting your kid sit and watch TV all day, I do believe TV can be a useful tool.

Choosing TV shows can help kids learn about prioritizing. You can help your child plan his day: "What do I want to do today? How much time does that leave me for TV? How big of a priority is it?" My husband and I have explained to Zac that watching a TV show is not a priority for our family. Friends are a priority, and being with family, and those things take precedence over his show at five-thirty. So if there is a show that he wants to watch at five-thirty, then that's the *one* show he may watch, and he can tape it and watch it at a time that's not for friends or family. That compromise has worked for us.

The History Channel is geared for adults, and my son devours it. We usually sit and watch it with him so we can talk about anything that's a little confusing. Some shows on TV I use as lessons in social skills. To me *The Simpsons* is a thirty-minute story about what not to do socially. Whenever we watch it, I always sit down with Zac and talk him through it. What's great about that show is that even though Homer and Marge do a terrible job at being parents, it's obvious they really love their kids. That gives us a chance to talk about people who love someone, but don't really know how to do a good job caring for them, or people who don't know how to be a good friend, or people who don't spend their time well. The show makes those ideas pretty clear. Sometimes we'll be watching a show and something inappropriate will arise, and I'll say, "This show doesn't fit with our values, and I think we need to turn it off," and we do. Now Zachary will say, "This show doesn't fit with our values, does it, Mom?" as he's learned to recognize more and more and turns a show off himself when it doesn't meet our values.

Sometimes finding intellectually appropriate movies and TV shows that are also appropriate to my son's emotional age can be difficult. Zac loves forensics, for example, and took a class on forensics for kids at the Tech Museum here in San Jose. That got him hooked on some of the forensic science shows on television. Sometimes they're a bit graphic, but he completely focuses on the science of the show, and we think that's an appropriate trade-off for him at this time.

Encourage Appropriate Reading

When Zac was in fourth grade, his class read *Charlotte's Web*. He was so annoyed. "I read that in kindergarten. Why do I have to read it again?" Finding appropriate reading for children with NLD is a challenge for parents. Our kids love to read, and they usually read far above grade level. Intellectually, they are capable of reading adult material, but they are still children. How do you balance their intellectual needs with their maturity? The best guidance I've found is through the Gifted Society, which has lots of materials you can use. They recommend choosing books for your child not necessarily because they're age appropriate, but because they're developmentally or intellectually appropriate and one of their interests. Think about what your child is ready to learn about or ready to hear. For example, we try to find books for Zac that are intellectually challenging and that don't have sexual issues in them, because we know he's not ready for them yet. Science fiction is great because it tends to be linear and logical and isn't that concerned with relationships. Sometimes we read books before we give them to Zac. I also ask other parents, the librarian, or Zac's teachers for suggestions. You can help your child by paying attention to what she's interested in and finding applicable reading.

Of course, we take some heat from time to time for this. When Zac was seven, he was reading *The Hobbit*, and at eight, the *Star Wars* series and books about WWII. Then at eight and a half, he decided to reread *Stuart Little*. His grandparents said, "Oh, we're glad to see he's reading more appropriate books for his age." However, giving him those books would be like giving a college freshman Dr. Seuss books, so it's tricky. We have to use the resources available to us to help guide us in the selection process.

Ask Your Child

One simple parenting tool is asking your child what he wants. If you ask your child to choose between Disneyland and staying home, she might surprise you by choosing to stay home. If you say, "You can go play with your friends, or you can watch TV, or I can read to you," your child might just prefer to be read to. Children with NLD are unusual in that they sometimes want things you wouldn't expect, and those things are usually ones you would be happy to give them. Sometimes, when we're being "good" parents, we feel as if we have to provide entertainment all the time or as if we have to buy our kids all this stuff or go to exciting places. Sometimes kids really prefer keeping things simple. Once, for his birthday, Zac asked for 25 feet of rope. I would have been embarrassed to give a kid rope for a present, but now I consider it every time there's a birthday. We had so much fun with it. We ran over it with the car and Zac had to pull it out from under the tires (a good proprioception exercise), we tied people up with it, we strung it through the tree limbs and made swings with it. Try asking your child what he or she wants. You might be surprised.

Hide-and-Geek

Zac was at my clinic one day while I was working on a report. We had to leave by two to get him to a therapy appointment. A little before two I started looking for him. I looked everywhere for him and I could not find him. These are my offices so it's not like I don't know where to look, but I could not find him. I was ready to throw up. I was thinking either somebody came in and stole him away or else he went out onto the street and got killed. It was one of those nightmare moments. Plus, there were clients everywhere, so I couldn't run around calling "Zachary! Zachary!" I'm supposed to be the therapist in charge, and I can't even find my own child.

Really upset, I asked one of the other therapists, "Have you seen Zachary?"

"No, but do you think he's hiding like he did the other day?"

"I don't know. I've looked everywhere for him." Just then I saw Zac scoot around a table and hide in a new place. As I walked over to him, my first thought was "I'm going to kill him." Then I really quickly realized he was just playing a game, and he had no clue what I had been going through. Just then I had a moment of being aware of my choices. I could have yelled at him, and Zac would have been destroyed. I knew what he would look like if I did that. Then I'd have to throw him in the car and drive through traffic and get him to his therapy appointment and he'd be upset and not be able to benefit from the appointment. I said, "Okay, Zac, come over here and let me kill you." Zac comes over and I was pretending to choke him. I was being really goofy because I've learned that if I do that, that changes my mood. Zac laughed and I laughed, and yet I got to pretend I'm killing him, which I needed to do! We got in the car and I said, "I know you're playing a game, but we need to find a way for you to play this game without giving me a heart attack. "Zac, when I was a kid in West Virginia, we used to call out 'ollie ollie in come free' when the game of hide-and-seek was over. So Zac, if I call out 'ollie,' you know to come in." That was all it took. Now I know if I say "ollie," he comes out of hiding. If I had yelled at Zac or punished him, we would not have gotten to that point. Zac would have been a puddle. I don't always choose the right fork. I am thankful for the times I do.

Nine

Reduce Stress

Our society is not set up well for children with neurological differences. Children with NLD are on sensory overload most of the time. We can't protect them from everything in the world, but we can do a lot to reduce stress and provide opportunities to rest and relax.

Schedule in Extra Time

When you learn your child has NLD, you need to understand that you don't just have a child who learns differently, you have a child who processes much of the world with a slower rhythm and therefore needs extra time on almost everything. The more you can schedule that extra time into your daily life, the less stress your child will experience. I can get ready and out the door in ten minutes. Zac needs at least 20. I need to plan for that. By allowing your child extra time, you can reduce the feelings of stress that make her so tired and make it hard for her to focus on a task. Gradually, she will need extra time less frequently.

Count how many times a day you say to your child, "Hurry up! We're going to be late!" If you allow extra time for the daily breakdowns of life with the child with NLD—the spills and the falls—then you have time to deal with them. Instead of considering those events to be things that derail your schedule, you can look at them as part of your schedule. If you were to write them into your calendar, allowing thirty minutes a day for incidental problems, then both you and your child would be less stressed when they inevitably occur.

Anticipate and Avoid Trouble Spots

Maintaining an awareness of your child's deficits can help you immensely in being aware of potential trouble spots. You can reduce stress in your child's life by anticipating and avoiding the situations that cause extra stress or meltdowns. If you know your child has low muscle tone and poor endurance, you can use that information to prevent downward spirals. You know not to sign up that child for activities every day after school because you know she will be too tired to benefit from them. If your child can only tolerate a small amount of novel social interactions, you can expect a meltdown at a family reunion instead of being surprised and mad about it, and you can plan to have breaks or activities that will increase your child's tolerance.

If we recognize potential problems and plan appropriately, we can put some limits into place instead of getting mad at our children for something we could have predicted. If you need to do your Christmas shopping at Toys"R"Us for half an hour, your child can play a video game the second fifteen minutes, or you can find some other way of decreasing the overstimulation of that experience. You can always pack a juice box so that your child can take a minute to drink something. That sucking behavior is very organizing and helpful to the body. Or give him a big squeeze every fifteen minutes.

Monitor your child. If he's starting to kick things, know that there is a meltdown approaching and *leave*, even if your shopping isn't done. Once the meltdown begins, you won't be able to shop anyway, so make the decision to go. Eventually these interventions will build your child's trust in you and he'll begin to tolerate these situations better. Your child will start building up a reservoir of strategies, and you start building up a tool kit of interventions. Gradually these strategies will allow you and your child to manage more stressful activities without meltdowns.

Schedule in Rest Times

On weekends, my husband and I used to say, "Let's go to the play-ground, let's go to the beach, let's go to the amusement park!" and Zachary would say, "Can I just stay home?" Finally I understood that we were doing too much and what he needed was rest. A lot of children with NLD are frequently tired and overstressed and look for ways to decrease their stress by sitting on the couch. We can honor that need by scheduling in times to do nothing.

Decrease (or Increase) Sensory Stimulation

You may think of your home as calm and quiet, but it may not feel that way to your child. How many times a day do you use a blender? How often do you run the vacuum cleaner? Most parents don't think to check in with the children and say, "I'm getting ready to run the vacuum." We need to prepare children with NLD for sensory stimulation and give them the option of going into another room. If they are prepared, their sensory systems can manage, but the unexpected intrusion is difficult to organize and control. Small, apparently innocuous noises, like tearing off a sheet of aluminum foil, can be painful for a child who is auditorially hypersensitive.

For some kids, music at a manageable level can help mask smaller noises, like a ticking clock, dripping water, or rustling blinds. For others, music can be overwhelming, so you need to check with your child before you make any assumptions. For some it depends on the music. I find the soundtrack to *Mortal Combat* so intense as to be stressful, but some kids need that high intensity input to bring them up to the normal level of arousal.

Members of your family may well have competing needs for different levels of sensory stimulation. In this case, you may have to take turns. If you as a parent need a lot of stimulation, and your child needs very little, then you can set up a safe place in your house for your child, some-place without noise or light or whatever it is your child finds irritating. Remember that children with NLD can be either hypersensitive or hyposensitive to any sensory input. Almost all children with NLD have problems with modulation, meaning that if they receive too much or too little stimulation, adjusting their bodies to just the right level is hard. When they can't adjust, expect a meltdown, disorganized behavior, and excessive chatter. One night Zac had a report to write, an activity that always makes him anxious. Dad had just gone out of town for two weeks (which makes us both anxious), and it was the end of the school year (which makes us both anxious). He and I were working together at the kitchen table—Zac on his report and I on paperwork. When I'm anxious, I pull back and retreat into quiet, calm spaces, and minimize all sensory input. I clear all counters, clean away clutter, take out the trash, and sit quietly. It was 5 P.M. Zac was chattering away, asking questions like, "Why don't children have more rights? Why do we have to go to school? Why do I have to do homework, aren't I covered under the Constitution to be a free citizen with rights? Can't I have free speech and tell that teacher what I think about her stupid assignments?" I suggested, "How about something to occupy your mouth? I'm having trouble concentrating with all your talking." Zac said sure, helped himself to some gum off his shelf (full of mouth items for just such moments), and sat back down quietly for about an hour while we finished our work. We moved on to dinner and the talking resumed—yack-yack-yack-yack-yack . . . I was trying to cook, get the trash out to the curb, wash the dishes, organize my day, organize Zac's school day, pack lunches, and all the while dancing around my yacking son. Eventually, at 9 P.M., I met my threshold for sensory input and said, "Shh, my ears are full. It's time for you to brush your teeth and go to bed."

"Bedtime is at 9:30."

"Shh, look at me, look at my face. I can't hear you, I can't process anything else today. You need to be thoughtful to me—my ears are full and can't listen to you anymore—go to bed and read, let your body rest and my ears unwind and tomorrow you can tell me all your ideas. I want to hear them all, I just can't listen anymore tonight. I need some quiet time to finish my chores and get us ready for tomorrow." Zac quietly slung his arm around my waist, patted my back, kissed me, and snuggled into his bed, quiet, with a book.

Put People Before Objects

Beyond making practical changes in your home by scheduling time for upsets and reducing noise, a change in attitude can go a long way toward reducing stress in your child's life. When you live with a child with NLD, you live with someone who frequently spills or breaks things because he doesn't think through his movements. I could get angry at Zac every time he spills. I would prefer he did not spill. But what is much more important to me than a pristine carpet is that Zac knows he is more important than any object in our house. Before I made that explicitly clear to him, he would be in meltdown every time he broke something. He'd be certain we'd be so angry we might even abandon him. He knew he couldn't promise not to break something again; he knew he would break something again because he couldn't help it. If we got furious over a broken lamp, that was a very scary experience for him.

Before Zachary was diagnosed, we knew we valued our son over anything else, but he didn't know it. It's heartbreaking to think of, but Zac lived in a constant state of fear that he would lose our love. When he was seven, we sat holding hands on New Year's Eve making wishes for the coming year. I said, "My wish for the year, Zac, is that you would know we love you." We expect children to know they are loved whether we verbalize it or not, but children with NLD may not know it till we tell them over and over that they are more important than anything that can break.

We learned to say, when we hear a crash, "First of all, are you alright?" and then "What's more important, a lamp or you? I can replace a lamp, but I can't replace you and your emotions. I'm sorry the lamp was broken. But we can get a new lamp. We can't get a new Zac." We acknowledge that he broke the lamp, but we don't blame him for a consequence he could not prevent.

On the other hand, we have a rule that if he breaks another kid's toy, or something important to us, then he has to replace that item using his allowance. We have taught him that that's what good friends do for each other. Sometimes we may step in and help him financially to replace a toy. Responsible people respond and offer to repair or replace things they've broken. He's not to blame for the toy breaking, he didn't intend to break it, but he has to *respond*, to be *responsible* and offer to replace the toy.

Vocalize Your Rules

Once they know the rules, children with NLD will follow them. In many families kids assimilate that there are a lot of unspoken rules as they grow. But children with NLD need to be told the rules. Knowing the rules gives her a sense of safety and of boundaries: She knows what to expect and how to comply. It makes for a more peaceful household. If your child does break a rule, ask yourself if you have really explained it clearly. Chances are you haven't.

Anticipate and Prepare for Challenges of Travel

For children with NLD, travel is stressful. It involves many transitions and many novel situations, which are challenging for these kids. Before we got Zac's diagnosis, any time we would travel, anywhere we went, Zac would get a sinus infection. Now we know to help Zac prepare his body for the stress of travel ahead of time. Just as you might prepare yourself for a stressful trip by increasing your exercise or your vitamin C, or by making sure you get enough rest, you can do the same for your child. We have also found it makes a difference if we help Zac get his body ready for stress with appropriate sensory techniques. Helping him preview and anticipate the new people and situations we'll encounter is also important. We've found that these strategies can make the difference between a great trip and a miserable trip.

Reduce Stress

Stress is the mechanism in our bodies that tells us to pay attention. It helps us get exciting and achieve our goals. Too much stress creates a state of hypervigilence, physiological and psychological illnesses, and can eventually become a disease in and of itself. By our actions, as parents and teachers, we can help children live in a world that is safe and secure or one that is volatile, chaotic, and uncertain. A secure world allows for learning, growth, and self-awareness. Prolonged production of corticosteriods, the chemicals of stress, work in the body like acids, breaking down organ tissues, blocking transmission of vital functions (such as deep respiration and digestion), and inhibit organized thought.

The first step to reduce a child's stress at school and create a calm environment there is to make sure you have a school that's a good fit and that your child's teacher is willing to work with you to support your child. Assuming those things are in place, the next step is to work with the child's teacher to find ways to reduce stress in the classroom. If it's at all possible, reduce sensory stimuli. Make sure the child's seat is not beside a source of constant noise or something that blows air on him, like a heater or an air conditioner. Insist that he keep his desk tidy so he can be better organized. Some kids will wear headphones in the classroom to shut out distracting noises. Some will chew on something or suck on a sports water bottle to help them pull their organizational system together.

It's also tremendously helpful if the child's teacher knows to anticipate your child's idiosyncrasies. Zachary used to freak out whenever there was a fire drill. After the kids came back inside, he always acted out and got sent to the office. So we made sure to include in his IEP that he would be supported to reenter the classroom after a fire drill.

We have found that accommodating the idiosyncrasies of children with NLD actually helps teachers become better teachers. They start to recognize the idiosyncrasies of other children and can make accommodations for all the children who need them.

Zac and the Bully

At recess, Zac was playing on the school playground when he thought a bully cheated again. Zac, being the king of fairness, just couldn't take it anymore. So Zac threw the ball at the boy's foot. In response, the boy grabbed Zac from behind, covering his nose and mouth with his elbow so that Zac couldn't yell or breathe, so Zac bit the boy. The boy let go, and Zac started walking away because that's our rule: Get away from the bully. But the boy followed him, grabbed Zac's head, and started yanking his head around. Zac got away again. The boy grabbed the basketball, threw it really hard, and it hit Zac in the head. Zac walked away again, so the boy went to the teacher and said, "Zac Whitney started a fight by throwing a ball at me and biting me and look at my arm," which was by then good and purple.

The intervention specialist, who I had never met and didn't have a clue as to who she was, greeted me when I arrived to pick Zac up at the end of the day by saying, "I really think it's quite important that Zachary learns to take the other child's perspective." Though this woman might have been great with some kids, she clearly didn't understand Zac. She read the incident report to me, "Zac threw a ball (missed), bit another child (self-defense). In the future Zac will 1, walk away; 2, tell a teacher; and 3, avoid the situation." She presented this information and suggestions for resolving the problem as if it were new, easy, and possible, not realizing these were, in fact, his annual IEP goals.

I turned to Zac, who was standing there waiting to find out what would happen and said, "Wow, Zac, it sounds like you did a good job defending yourself. I'm really proud of you."

The intervention specialist didn't like that and repeated, "Well, it's really important for him to learn to take the perspective of another person."

I told her: "We have been working for ten years to teach Zac to defend himself when he's faced with a bully, and it sounds like he did a good job. I certainly will talk with him about this incident and strategies other than biting and"—turning to Zac—"I'm really proud of you, Zac. Good job." The intervention specialist's face was pinched and red.

By the time we got home, Zachary was nearly hysterical—crying and laughing at the same time. He kept saying, "So what am I supposed to do? If someone holds a gun to me, I'm supposed to say, 'Thank you for shooting me'?"

At that point, Bill, in his infinite wisdom, stepped in. "Well, Zac, the best way I can explain it to you is to teach you the three rules of robotics. Isaac Asimov wrote books in which humanoid robots are invented. People are very frightened, so all the robots were programmed with laws. The first law is, you will never harm a human. The second law is, you should never allow harm to come to another human, unless it breaks the first law. The third law is, you are to never harm yourself unless it would break the first two laws. But then there's a zero-th law, which is you are to protect humanity. Because sometimes you might have to harm a human or yourself in order to protect humanity. For robots, the zero-th law trumps everything." Then, Bill went on, "The laws for humans aren't quite in that order. The first law for humans is, let no harm come to yourself."

"Oh, I see," Zac said, "So humans have a trillion rules and shifting priorities. So that makes it really tough, right, Dad?"

I sent an e-mail telling Zac's teacher we were keeping him home the next day for a mental health day.

Zac's teacher called shortly after and said, "I'm sorry to hear that Zac's so upset. It sounds like it was a good decision to let Zac stay home, but please give him three messages from me. Number one, tell him I am absolutely not mad at him. Two, I think he did his absolute best in a no-win situation, and three, tell him I'm looking forward to seeing him on Thursday." When I told that to Zac, he transformed. The red splotches left his face, his breathing relaxed, and his shoulders came back to where they belonged.

Ten

Safety

CHILDREN with NLD are at high risk for both serious physical injury and emotional damage. As their parents, it's our job to get them safely to adulthood with the skills they'll need to protect themselves. To balance their safety with their need to grow and explore, to run and play, and to be part of a community, we need to provide therapy to increase their physical competence; we need to teach them social and safety skills so they can recognize and avoid dangerous people and situations, and we need to be vigilant in protecting them from people and situations that can cause our kids severe emotional distress.

In her pioneering work, *The Sourcebook for Nonverbal Learning Disorders,* Sue Thompson relates heartbreaking stories of children with NLD who were not protected. An eight-year-old boy jumped off a water tower because his "friends" convinced him their Superman cape would let him fly. After her parents were told by a psychologist to stop being "overprotective," a ten-year-old girl was raped by her "friend," the manager of a taco shop where teens hung out. Countless other children with NLD have suffered similar abuse whose emotional wounds have lead to deep depression and even suicide. Many adults with NLD report past histories of date rape, incest, molestation, and abuse. It's our responsibility to make sure this doesn't happen to our children.

If the boy who jumped off the water tower had discussed with his parents or a therapist to figure out "What are the rules of being a friend?," he may not have jumped off that water tower. He could have known a friend doesn't ask you to hurt yourself. If the parents of the girl who was raped had not allowed their daughter to be alone with an unsafe adult in a social situation she couldn't interpret, she might have been safe. Or if her parents had taught her to tell them at the first sign of an uncomfortable touch and if she had said, "That man touched me and it didn't feel good, but I didn't know what to say," she might not have been raped.

As parents of children with NLD, we are often accused of being overprotective. However, we know how high the risks are for our kids. We know they are at high risk for debilitating head injuries, and for anxiety, depression, suicide, institutionalization, or marginal lives if they are not given the proper support and coping strategies. Teachers, neighbors, and friends may not realize how vulnerable our children are, so it is our job to educate others, to disregard ignorant criticism, and to insist above all else, on safety for our children.

Assure Physical Safety

Occupational therapists have an extensive body of knowledge and experience in teaching safety judgment to adults who have any kind of impairment, from a stroke to a hip replacement. Unfortunately, our knowledge has not yet been adequately transferred to our treatment of children with neurological differences. Even as a professional in the field, I haven't found anyone talking about safety on an IEP team or Student Study Team.

Children with NLD don't anticipate consequences. They have impaired perception in their bodies and joints as well as poor spatial awareness. If you aren't thinking about what will happen next, if you don't get accurate information from your senses and don't know where your body is in space, you're going to fall. Parents of children with NLD tell countless stories of biking accidents and falls off monkey bars. Children with NLD have been hit by cars because they either didn't think to look or they were unaware of the spatial relationship between them and the car.

Zac almost always has a cut or a bruise somewhere on him. In years past, he would be sitting quietly in a chair, not fooling around or doing anything dangerous, and the next minute he'll be on the floor and he'll be bleeding. This is typical for children with NLD. For their parents, it's terrifying. My mother has seriously suggested we make Zac wear his bike helmet all the time. I've resisted going that far, but she has a point. Parents of children with NLD know that head injuries can happen at any time. These days, Zac's sensorimotor system is functioning like a typical kid's and he doesn't fall out of his chairs, but he still runs into poles or trips more frequently than other kids.

These kids have so many accidents that it's not unusual for their parents to be accused of child abuse. We are in a no-win situation, we'll be labeled "overprotective," or we'll be accused of hurting our kids or of incompetence. I can't tell you the number of times I have wanted to call my mother and have her come and get my child because I clearly was incapable of keeping him safe. I'd be sitting right beside him, and then he'd be on the floor with a bleeding chin, and I'd be sobbing, "I can't keep him safe, and I've got to leave for work and he's bleeding again." This really is typical of our lives. And it leaves us feeling helpless, incompetent, and frightened.

When our children get hurt, it's not because they're impulsive. They are not like children with hyperactivity who are always into something because they're so curious and attend to so much in the environment. Instead, children with NLD don't understand the gestalt of a situation, they don't attend to enough of the environment to anticipate safe maneuvering. They don't think through steps two, three, and four. When they act, they don't necessarily anticipate a consequence: "If I put my fingers up there while my mother is opening the hatch, will my fingers get pinched?" So we need to anticipate for them. Now when Zac's in the car, I never, ever, close the door or power windows without saying, "All heads clear? All fingers safe?" I never move my car without checking where he is, just as if I had a toddler living with me.

You help your child be safe by increasing your child's awareness of her body. As much as you reasonably can, you need to change her environment to make it safe. Childproofing your home has to continue well beyond the toddler years so that when your child does fall, she avoids permanent injury. Our children *must* wear helmets when biking or

Rollerblading. This is a nonnegotiable rule because they are at a high risk for head injuries. They must also have prescribed boundaries of play and firm rules for electrical and heat safety. You also need to teach your child safety precautions by vocalizing your own safety checks: "Did I turn off the stove? Did I move the potholder far enough from the burner? Did I close the screen to the fireplace?" All the things you say in your head, you need to speak aloud so your child can learn to go through that list for herself. Most people develop these mental checklists on their own, but children with NLD don't unless they have been helped to learn good safety habits.

Up until about a year and a half ago I considered Zachary to be a person who required "standby assist," which means you are within an arm's length distance of a person (meaning you can catch the patient if he falls). When Zac was on the playground or whenever he was climbing something, I considered him standby assist. If he was in the mulch on the playground, standby assist meant I could hear what was going on. But if he was off the ground on the monkey bars, for example, standby assist really meant I needed to be within arm's reach. My husband's version of standby assist was five to ten feet away, because he could get to Zac so much faster than I could. We got criticism for standing so closely to him ("back off, he's eight"), but we knew we needed to be there because he *would* fall.

Our kids spend a good part of their day in school, where there are many safety risks. In the classroom, our children frequently fall out of their chairs, which wouldn't be so bad, but there's usually a desk or an elbow in the way. Your school can have an occupational therapist work with your child to increase her physical safety in the classroom. (Lack of safety judgment is a documented disability for which the school must provide treatment, and an OT is the only professional trained to do so.) The OT can teach your child ways of sitting in chairs that don't risk tipping the chair over, using cushions or wedges, sitting on balls, sitting on their feet, or taking frequent breaks. Sometimes an OT will put tennis balls on the feet of chairs so they slide better, don't make as much noise, and are a little harder to tip over. OTs can also consult with teachers about room layout to minimize or eliminate safety risks.

Playgrounds are potential danger zones for our kids. When Zac was eight, he fell four or five times off the top of the monkey bars, which were about 12 feet off the ground. Each time some angel eased him to the ground, but his falls got progressively worse. For a long time we had on Zac's IEP that he was not to be more than eight feet off the ground at any time without standby assist supervision. At first, the teachers thought this was ridiculous because they had no idea what kind of risks we were really talking about, but at the same time they knew they were responsible for something that was going to be hard to maintain. There was only one ten-by-ten area of the playground, where the monkey bars were, where anyone could get more than eight feet off the ground, so the principal insisted that a teacher be stationed there. He also posted signs in all of the rooms that said "Safety judgment important on the playground."

Every child has a federally mandated legal right to be safe at school, both in the classroom and on the playground. Safety is never optional. The schools know this, but sometimes they will not understand what is required to keep children with NLD safe. You may need to be vigilant in making sure your child is safe at school. If your child frequently gets hurt on the playground, you can check to make sure it meets the legal safety requirements. Anyone who has a professional involvement in playgrounds, such as your city's parks and recreation department, can explain the safety requirements to you. For example, if the monkey bars are eight feet off the ground, there must be eight inches depth of ground cover, such as tan bark. Professional consultants can help you, or you can find the information on the Internet for free. At recess, is there appropriate adult supervision? If there are 600 kids on the playground and two adults supervising, which does happen, that's not adequate supervision. You can lobby through the PTA for more supervision. A lot of schools hire parents to provide additional supervision at recess.

Part of keeping your child safe at school is educating teachers to recognize when your child is injured. Children with NLD frequently have hyporeceptive nerves, so they don't register pain, or they register it inconsistently and inaccurately. When my son is seriously injured, he's likely to say "Ouch" or nothing at all. Because teachers generally expect kids to scream or whine, they tend to underreact when children get hurt. I told Zac's teacher, a very conscientious woman, "You need to send him to the office if he even says 'ouch.' " She agreed, but Zac kept getting hurt without her seeming to notice. He'd come home and say he fell off the monkey bars and show me a huge bruise. One day he came home and said, "My back really hurts." There was a four-inch gouge in his back. His shirt was stuck to his skin with blood. He said, "I was sitting in my chair and I fell backward."

"Did you tell the teacher?"

"Yeah, but she just said 'Okay.' "

Zac's shirt was bloody. Most kids would be screaming over an injury like that. I took Zac in to his teacher, showed her his wound, and said, "This is what I mean." I thought she was going to cry or throw up. She said, "Okay, from now on I will send him to the office if he says 'ouch.' " And she did. That year we added a new IEP goal for Zac: for him to go to the office with an injury and to let the grown-ups decide whether or not he needed attention. The school secretary was informed and worked as our partner, commending Zac each time he came to see her and *never* suggesting he was overreacting.

Assure Emotional Safety

If the only risk to our children were frequent falls, cuts, and bruises, maybe a broken bone, or possibly a head injury, that would be frightening enough. But children with NLD are also at high risk for disabling emotional injuries. It's critical to understand that chronic anxiety, depression, and suicide are real possibilities in our children's lives. Given their vulnerability, we have a great responsibility to keep our children emotionally safe. We know the risks of anxiety and depression are too high for us to expect our kids to negotiate the world on their own.

A Great Resource

Dr. Martin Seligman has done a tremendous service for parents by researching and organizing information on preventing depression. His research has demonstrated quite convincingly that optimism wards off depression, and optimism can be learned. Optimism, according to Seligman, lies in the way one thinks about causes. Each of us has habits of thinking about causes, what he refers to as our "explanatory style." In his remarkable book *The Optimistic Child*, he outlines a clear, comprehensive program, called "psychological immunization," that parents can use with their kids.

Seligman makes an important distinction between self-esteem and optimism. Reading Seligman's work helped me understand that Zac, who would rip up his paper after making a mistake in handwriting, didn't need more self-esteem; he needed to know that mistakes never get better when we quit. He needed to learn that calling himself stupid was mean and made his heart hurt. He needed to know we could talk to ourselves in a way that makes us want to get up and try or give up and quit. Optimism, the ability to look at the events in life and have them serve you, be instructive, and be an invitation for more effort, resources, or resolve, made sense to me as a tool for success and, in fact, our family found it very helpful.

Protect Our Kids

While we can take steps to prevent depression by helping our kids build a community and make friends, we also need to protect our children from emotional abuse, no matter what its source. We need to empower them by teaching them how to protect themselves. Until they know how, we need to be ready to step in again and again. If, for example, a teacher yells at your child every day, he will not develop the antidote to depression in her classroom. Instead, that teacher will *make* your child anxious and depressed. So get your child away.

If your child is being bullied, you need to intervene. I know of a child with NLD in a Boy Scout troop that rotated leaders. The boy's turn was next and two other Scouts were plotting to set him up to fail and be humiliated. The Scoutmaster's response was, "That's just boys being boys." Fortunately the parents refused to accept that stupid remark and they refused to condone a situation in which the boy would be devastated and quit Boy Scouts. The parents insisted that when their child was leader, the Scoutmaster would be present and insist on respect and good friendship when any of the scouts were in the leadership role. When the Scoutmaster didn't perform this role, the parents stepped in, did a talk about respect to the Scouts, and sat down with the Scoutmaster to explain NLD. Other things I might have done would include asking a Scoutmaster from another troop to come and observe, or I might have turned the tables by having the Scouts role-play a mock meeting where the boys who were setting up a child got to be the leaders of an uncooperative group, then do another role-play with reversed roles, and then discuss the experience as a group.

Our children are innocent and vulnerable. They are very trusting. They believe what they are told. Adults who say mean or inappropriate things to them can cause considerable damage. If a parent or a teacher tells a child with NLD that she is lazy or stupid, the child will internalize that belief and "know" she is lazy or stupid. Over time, this poor self-image can contribute to depression. Our children are vulnerable to anxiety because they don't find reassurance in their environment through nonverbal cues. If a teacher has yelled at a child, and then smiles an apology, the child may not think, "Oh, my teacher is smiling now. She isn't mad at me anymore." Instead she may well continue to believe that her teacher is angry with her all that day, all that night and maybe even forever. The world is emotionally very unsafe for these children. The casual obnoxious comments so common in our culture can really eat away at these kids. They won't know that the grin that goes along with an insult is meant to convey that the insult is a joke. They don't recognize hyperbole. When a teacher says, "If you don't finish your report, you'll never get out of fourth grade," most kids shrug it off as an exaggerated threat. But a child with NLD will believe this and panic, even if he's a straight-A student.

Children who are difficult to calm and who don't get reassurance from their environment because they can't benefit from nonverbal cues are going to be prone to depression and anxiety. Children who are unable to protect themselves grow helpless and hopeless, leading to depression or anxiety or both.

Anxiety is more than just a feeling. It is a response that can have physiological consequences if allowed to persist. Scientific evidence consistently demonstrates that prolonged anxiety causes deterioration of our vital organs and eats away at our brain cells. Too much anxiety prevents us from learning, and it compounds a disability so that children can't function.

Anxiety triggers the sympathetic nervous system, the fight, fright (freeze)-or-flight stress response. When you're hiking and you see a bear, you experience intense anxiety. When you see the bear, you don't have to think, "I'd better get my muscles ready for running." Your response is an instantaneous reflex, not a cognitive process. Your sympathetic nervous system forces blood into your legs so you can run. Your physiological responses—fast breathing, sweaty palms, flushed face, blood moving to the external body—help you run away from the bear. It's a physiological fact that when you are in fight, fright-or-flight mode, your cognitive processes will not be working optimally. A child with NLD sees "bears" everywhere. If the teacher is yelling at him, a bully is sitting next to him, or he knows he's going to get picked on at recess, he is in a constant state of anxiety and the more we can reduce a child's anxiety, the more we can increase her learning potential. Our kids' clumsiness also gets worse when they're anxious, so they are also at a higher risk of injury.

Emotional safety and anxiety are opposites. Anxiety is very frightening. If it continues long enough, it can become depression. Clinical depression is a constant, ongoing state of feeling unable to overcome the obstacles in your life. Depression is marked by feelings of helplessness and hopelessness. If a child remains in an anxious state long enough, depression becomes a real threat. We owe it to our children to prevent this by avoiding prolonged anxiety.

Some specialists advocate medication when our kids are anxious or depressed. Taking an herb or a pill that will negate the body's physiological, chemical response to anxiety is certainly possible, but the physiological response is generated by our thoughts and feelings, so if we can change our thoughts and feelings, we can change the body's response. We can change our anxious thoughts in two ways: through relaxation/ stress management techniques or through eliminating the source of the anxiety (getting rid of the bear). We can teach our children to recognize the symptoms of stress and tell us about them so that we can help them name their feelings.

There are children who need medication to help them manage their anxiety and depression. It gives them a longer wick. Research has demonstrated pretty clearly that medication alone is only part of the solution and should be used in combination with other services, not used as a substitute for therapy and is never the place to start. A child must also learn the skills to self-monitor, self-control, and self-regulate. When a four- or five-year-old is treated with medication, but no other intervention—no therapy—then he's not learning skills for the long term. A more appropriate treatment would be to remove the source of the anxiety, teach the child coping skills, and, if his anxiety or depression remains, then consider medication.

Bullies

Children with NLD are the ideal targets for bullies. Because they are desperate for friends, they are easy pickings. Our kids can look different, so they're more likely to be singled out and picked on, they have that innocent look of a good victim. Because they don't pick up on nonverbal cues, they are easily teased, insulted, and lied to. Because they are trusting and they don't anticipate consequences, they can be convinced by bullies that it's okay to do risky or foolish things. Unless they've been taught to, children with NLD usually don't think to tell grown-ups about the bully's behavior.

Any parent of a child with NLD has had to deal with bullies. It's our obligation to intervene to protect our children from them. We need to teach our children how to recognize a bully, how to stay away from bullies, how to stand up to them when necessary, and how to tell a grown-up when bullies pick on them.

Our rule for Zachary is "walk away from bullies." When someone attacks him physically or verbally, he knows he's supposed to leave. He is not supposed to retaliate, and he's not supposed to stay and take it. But a child can only apply these rules if he knows how to recognize a bully, when to walk away, and when and how to defend himself, and not all children with NLD can do that.

In preschool, Zac was attracted to bullies. Perhaps because he couldn't read their nonverbal signals, he didn't know when those kids were taking advantage of him. Kids with weak social skills may not recognize a bully. So part of protecting your child is making sure she knows the definition of a friend and the definition of a bully.

For the longest time, I wanted Zac to get angry when someone bullied him. When kids were convincing him to use his money to buy them Popsicles, I tried everything I could think of to make him get mad at them, but nothing worked. He was so accepting. He thought those kids were just teaching him the rules. "Okay, I have to buy them Popsicles because they said I did." He didn't know they were not being his friends. The difficulty is that children with NLD are so compliant, such rule followers, that standing up for themselves can be hard to teach. While I didn't realize it at the time, his difficulties with bullies were in part due to problems in social perceptions. We saw a tremendous improvement in his ability to deal with bullies after language therapy.

In interacting with others, there are spoken rules and invisible rules. The spoken rule is, "You are never to hurt another child." Most kids hear that and think, "But if another kid hurts me, I can break that rule." That is the invisible rule. Children with NLD miss the invisible rule and follow only the spoken rule. Honorable as this may be, the result is that they seldom hurt others and are almost always the ones who get hurt and they feel helpless. The message here is "shut up and take it." The most effective way to prevent a bully from targeting you repeatedly is to make the first occasion so unrewarding for the bully that he never tries again. Depending on the situation, this can mean either ignoring or retaliating. While I am certainly *not* advocating responding to violence with violence, as parents, we have to step in and say to our kids, "We expect you to defend yourself. We don't want you to use violence, but you do need to learn to get away from the bully and to tell a grown-up."

It took a few years for Zac to learn to tell me when he'd been bullied. In the early years I tried grilling him, but it didn't help. Eventually I learned that if I make it clear enough that I am very interested to know if someone is picking on him, and if the way I handle it is to protect him, but not embarrass him, then he will come to me.

We need to say to our children, "I'm interested in hearing what you have to say. I want to know what happens to you. I'm one of the grown-ups who can help you and who will love you no matter what. Let's remember who are the other grown-ups who will help you and love you no matter what." When our kids know that they are loved no matter what, when they know that we will step in and protect them without embarrassing them, then they have an antidote to anxiety and depression.

Our rule is, "Get away from the bully, tell the teacher, and tell Mom or Dad." We rehearse over and over, "What three people at school can you tell when someone hits or pushes you?" and Zac will answer, "The principal, Mr. Kappa, Mrs. Orkiss." We can't say, "Tell me when there is a bully." We have to say, "Tell me when someone insults you, or tell me when someone hits you or pushes you."

If your child is being bullied, and you know your child isn't going to tell or doesn't know how, what can you do? You can ask the school to write into the IEP that your child will learn to tell when she's been bullied, because then the IEP team will work together on this goal. By federal legal mandate, schools have two fundamental rules that supercede every other rule: Your child has the right to be safe at school, and your child has the right to a secure learning environment. It doesn't matter whether the bully is hitting your child or saying mean things to her, emotional safety is the school's responsibility as much as physical safety.

I know of a child who was tormented by a boy in his school for *two years*. The parents eventually caught on and tried to get the school to take some action. After applying a lot of pressure, they convinced the principal to shadow the bully. After *two hours*, the bully was permanently expelled from the school. As parents, we need to teach our kids to tell when they're being bullied, and we need to step in and make sure the bullying stops. When Zachary was buying Popsicles for the other boys in his after-school program, eventually I had to approach the teacher and have her intervene with the bullies. Every once in a while it's the kid with NLD who's the bully, but it's pretty rare. If your child is a bully, the school is mandated to help you with him, too.

Be Undauntable Around Abusive Teachers

So far in Zachary's education, he's had four terrific teachers, one who was completely clueless, and one terrible one. That's pretty good odds! If you're lucky, you'll never have to deal with one of those awful teachers, but what if your child is placed in a classroom with someone who is abusive or hateful?

Most children with a difficult teacher will be unhappy, but they can still more or less function. While I don't believe any child should have to tolerate that kind of behavior, children with NLD will take this treatment personally. Zac didn't believe our reassurances and was confused and scared. When Zac was in this woman's classroom, he began to talk about suicide again, and she said that wasn't her concern.

Your child is guaranteed, by federal law, that his or her classroom will be an emotionally safe environment. When Zac had a horrible teacher, we got the school's attention by insisting, "This woman is not providing a safe environment for our child. My child is emotionally unsafe in her classroom." Meanwhile, Zac was planning things like pulling the fire alarm to get out of his classroom. I used that as leverage. I said, "My child is making these grand schemes to get away from her. You need to protect him."

We had to be extremely persistent. I had to look the school principal in the eye and tell him, "I understand that you need to protect your teacher, and you know what? You have an obligation to keep my child safe. I understand that you don't have a space in the other classroom, but you *will* keep my child safe." He offered a bunch more excuses, and I said, "I understand that, but you *will* keep my child safe." I must have said that 30 times, and I would have said it 30 more times if I'd had to before he finally agreed to implement any alternative plan. I swear he was afraid of that witchy teacher.

If you find yourself unable to be this persistent, hire an advocate to do it for you. You can find them through parent and community groups, churches, or schools. You can call the state board of education, ask to speak to someone in special education, and ask for help with advocacy.

Do whatever it takes. I've learned over the years that when I scream and yell, people ignore me. But when I say calmly and slowly, "I am so furious," when it's clear that I'm upset, and I repeat the same thing over and over in a very firm, measured voice, people listen. Dads seem to get a little more attention partly, I think, because a male's position in the school is still perceived to be higher on the status ladder and partly because when a woman gets upset, we consider her emotional, but when a man gets upset we feel we need to listen and take him more seriously.

Then, choose your battles well, and say, "I'm not budging. I don't care about your budget, personnel, or the number of desks in the class-room. I know that my child has a legal right to be safe. I will hold you accountable for that."

You do *not* have to accept that any unsafe situation is the best the school can do. Too many parents think, "We just have to put up with it for this year," but that's one-twelfth of your child's education. Are you willing to pay one-twelfth of your child's education and teach your child they are powerless to get away from an abuser? Parents need to know they have the power to do something. Then we wouldn't have any more abusive teachers.

If the school can't provide a safe classroom, for whatever reason, you *can* take your child out of school. As long as you tell the authorities you're doing it to keep your child safe, you can do whatever is necessary. As parents, that is our primary responsibility. It might make everyone angry and frustrated, but it will get them to take action because, by law, your child has to be in school.

When Zac's school insisted they could not change his classroom assignment because of laws about the number of desks and other bureaucratic reasons, I said, "Okay, no problem, I'll just keep him home till you figure that out."

"No, you can't do that!"

"Well, the only consequence that I know of is in thirty days the truant officer will show up at my door, but I can keep him home until you find an appropriate, safe environment for him." I applied for home schooling, knowing that the paperwork would take a while, which gave me some leeway. I knew I didn't want to home school my son because he needs social interaction, but in case a truant officer did show up, I could say I'd applied. That forced them to act because they know they will get a call from the state governmental agencies if they have a kid out of school, and they can't explain why.

I told them on a Tuesday that I would take Zac out of school on Friday. That gave him a chance to say good-bye to his friends. We made an agreement with the school that he would be allowed to leave his classroom whenever he needed to get away from the teacher. He was to go to the secretary, who would call me. I promised him that no matter where I was, I would come and get him.

When I took Zac out, they did not have another placement for him. The school district insisted I had to have him in school, but by law I knew my first right was to keep him safe, and until I found an appropriate placement, home was the safest place for him. Fortunately, I found another school I really liked, with a very caring teacher. If I hadn't, I would have home schooled Zachary rather than subject him to his horrible classroom environment. Parents, whether they know it or not, are in charge.

I was once consulted by parents of a child whose teacher was insisting that the child be put on Ritalin or taken out of the school. Only the school psychologist or an MD can make a medical diagnosis, not a teacher. What you can say is, "This teacher-child interaction is not a good fit. We need to find another placement for my child. I'm not willing to start with medication, but I am open to exploring other strategies." If the school resists and claims medication or expulsion are the only options, you have the right to demand more open-minded options. I'd like to see someone call educators on prescribing medicine without a license. There is talk of passing legislation in several states to prevent this from happening, but to date these measures are not available to parents.

Recognize Evil

We all know people who enjoy demeaning others. We need to know, and our children need to know, that evil, mean, or dangerous people do not just wear black robes and masks. They look like ordinary people. We say they have no conscience and researchers have found these people have an incapacity to feel anxious when they cause harm to others. Timothy McVeigh is a good example of this. He looked like the guy next door, but he caused great harm to the people in the Oklahoma City bombing, and he never showed any remorse for his actions. Evil doesn't have to look dark and ugly. People who enjoy hurting others are often drawn to working with children or the elderly because they have ample opportunities to find vulnerable targets. Bad life experiences, mental illness, and sadistic tendencies can cause people to prey on our children.

Most of us recognize evil or dangerous people because we feel sick to our stomachs and our life energy begins to drain away. Kids with NLD will not have an intuitive sense for who is dangerous, and the children believe words like "I won't hurt you, just get into the car and you can have your bike back," not the insinuation from the situation. You can't teach that sense to someone who doesn't have it. What you can try to do is teach children that when they consistently feel bad around someone, when they feel put down all the time, when they're completely unable to succeed around a person, it's our job as parents to protect them. Children need to know when they come to us as their parents or teachers that we will listen to them and help them.

When our children are not able to succeed in an environment, we step in and help them. We have to teach them rules to follow, since they won't pick this up intuitively. Now Zac knows, "If a teacher yells at me I can leave. If she makes me cry, I can leave. The rule is the adults are not supposed to make me feel this way. These people are not following the rules of being respectful around me, so I can leave and go to one of the safe adults around me, like my teacher or the principal or my neighbor." He knows there are people around whom he is unable to trust, and that his father and I or the safe people we have identified for him will get him away from those people.

Educate Thoughtless Adults

I have had to teach myself to not let mean comments go by. I have become notorious for saying to people, "Do not speak to my child that way." They may consider me obnoxious, but this is something I consciously model for Zac *all the time*. He needs to see me advocating for him so that he'll learn how do it for himself. For example, I took Zac and his friends to the swim club the other day. The boys were throwing tennis balls into one of those floating basketball hoops because a little girl was hogging all of the plastic balls. I thought her father could have told her, "You need to share the balls because they are community toys." But he didn't. Instead he yelled at Zac and his friends, "You don't throw tennis balls at that. What are you, stupid or something?" I said to the dad, "This is a community toy—do you think your daughter could share?" I addressed the boys and said, "That man has spoken to you in an inappropriate way. I'm really sorry that some grown-ups feel like they have the right to be mean, so let's go play over here where it's safe." One of the boys replied, "Grown-ups are mean to kids all the time." I still cry every time I think about that.

Adults also often make comments that are confusing to our kids. Parents on the playground used to say to Zac, "Oh, you're so cute and pretty, you look like a little girl." I never let comments like that go because I knew they would be confusing to Zachary. "Wow, Zac, isn't that sad, he doesn't know the difference between a boy and a girl." I would say something to negate every weird comment he got, because they fester in our kids. They don't have a context for those comments, and they don't have a good vocabulary for feelings, so they can't identify or sort out the feelings those comments provoke. Zac didn't have the ability to say "Well, that's stupid" then, but he does now.

Or in grocery stores, people would say, "Wow, he's really hyperactive, isn't he? Does he have ADD?" I'd say, "You know, I just got him out of school. It was a really hard day, and we have to come to the grocery store, and it's really loud in here, and there's a big long line he has stood in now for fifteen minutes. I think he's doing a really good job, and I think the fact that he's pushing the cart back and forth now a little bit is really okay." I always verbalize it all so Zac can hear it, too.

Or if I'm really feeling like a snotty redhead, I'll say to Zac, "Here is a person pretending to be a psychologist when she is not because she clearly doesn't know what attention deficit is. You clearly don't have that."

He'll say, "I don't think I have that, do I, Mom?"

"No, honey, you don't have that, but they do have delusions of grandeur, which has been known to respond to medication."

Or I'll say something to the person like, "It's really hard for a boy to stand in a big long line like this. We need bigger yards so he has a place to run and play, but hey, we're in California, where we get a postage stamp." I try my best to use humor to defuse a situation when I can, and sometimes I have to be blunt and sassy. Some adults seem especially intolerant of boys. On several occasions, parents of girls will expect quiet play from boys. Testertosterone is the strongest drug on our earth and boys play with more vigor and tumble. We expect the impossible if we ask them to hold their exuberance in check and play quietly for extended periods.

It was a real victory for us when Zachary first showed he could advocate for himself. One day his math teacher said, "You didn't finish your worksheet, so you need to stay in at recess." Then she went to the teacher's lounge. I have drilled into Zac that he needs recess. It's on his IEP that he's not to be held in from recess, but this teacher somehow didn't know that. So Zac wrote at the bottom of his paper, "Read my IEP," and went out and played. I was so thrilled for him. Of course, I also knew that the teacher was likely to regard Zac as an insolent, defiant kid. I made sure to talk to the teacher the next day to make sure she understood that this act of self-advocacy was an important milestone for Zachary.

Teach Basic Safety

Many children with NLD need to be taught social skills, but social skills are not just about being nice—taking turns and sharing social skills are about responding to the rhythm of conversations, knowing what is expected in various social events, and having a range of appropriate responses available. The skills we teach have to be balanced. Children with NLD need to know what to do when someone is mean to them. They need to be taught how to say, "Stop what you're doing or I'll tell." We need to teach our kids a full repertoire of protective language. These children typically don't think much about other people's motives, so they'll assume other people are like them, nice and good. You can use movies where someone gets tricked as teaching tools to help them understand how to protect themselves. We also talk about how real bad guys don't dress like they do in the movies. Real bad guys can look just like anybody. In fact, in reality, they pretend to be nice.

We need to teach our kids how to be safe if they're separated from us. As with so many things, we cannot assume our kids will just pick up appropriate safety judgments. They need to be taught it as a rule to follow. Saying what not to do is not enough. We need to teach, "This is what you can and should do," and practice it with your child. I taught Zac, "If you get lost in a store, going to a woman is always safer. Go to the person behind the register." Because a register clerk can get him to the right person. I taught him "If you get lost in a store, it's okay to break the rule about interrupting a grown-up," because otherwise he'd just stand there. "Then what do you say? 'My name is Zac Whitney and I've lost my mother.' " We practice these things regularly, and I've been paged in stores a couple of times, so I know it works for Zac.

We also practice what he should do if he hurts himself playing. Which neighbor's door can he knock on? What should he say? We rehearse what to do if the house is on fire or if he's locked out. For example, when we had the talk about what to do in a fire, we said, "How would you get out of your room if the hall was on fire?"

Zac said, "I'd use a chair and break my window."

We said, "How about just opening the window?"

"Oh yeah," he said. Then we talked about how to knock on a neighbor's door for an emergency, what to say, and so on. Of course you can't predict every situation, but if you practice and rehearse enough of these, you'll be building a bridge in your child's mind so that he'll know how to get help when he needs to.

Once I dropped Zac off at a therapy appointment. Usually I walk him to the office, but since we're always increasing his independence one step at a time, this day he was to go up the steps and into the therapist's office while I parked the car. I dropped him at the curb, parked the car, and within five minutes I was in the therapist's waiting room. Ten minutes later the therapist came out and said "Where's Zac?"

I didn't respond, but got up and ran out of the room, looking for him everywhere. It was a distance of twenty-five feet from the curb to her office. How could he not have gotten there unless someone had taken him or he'd fallen and killed himself? I looked for him first on the ground, expecting to see his mangled body. It turned out there were two sets of stairs and he had taken the wrong one. Thank God I had said, "If for any reason you can't find the office, let's meet under the sign for the pizza parlor." That's where he was. He had followed the rules. He had gone up the wrong set of stairs, gotten turned around, found the pizza parlor, and sat under the sign, while I was looking on all the stairs expecting to see him sprawled at the bottom. Finally I remembered what I'd told him and found him waiting for me. He looked at me very calmly and said, "You told me to go right here, I did what you told me." I was furious and he was upset, but he actually did the right thing, I was the one who forgot what I had told him. For children with NLD, it's always a good idea to have a contingency plan and to practice with them what they can do if something unforeseen happens.

I believe it's essential for all children to know that their body is theirs. If anyone—Mom, Dad, grandparents, a friend, a teacher, anyone— touches them in any way that they don't like or give permission for, then that's wrong. We don't have to explain that it might be illegal or it might be sexual. It's enough to say, "It's wrong because it's *your* body. So when

Grandma comes to visit, you have a choice: You can say hello with good eye contact, you can shake her hand, or you can give her a hug. It's your choice. She's not supposed to give you a hug unless you say that's okay, because your body is yours. Even though she may think she has the right to hug you, we want you to know she doesn't." In our family, Grandma is a good example to use because she's not threatening, then we also explained that this rule applies to everyone.

When we learned about Zac's NLD, we put him into a class for self-protection taught by a teacher and a karate expert. The class was offered by Kidpower, a national organization that teaches safety and self-defense to kids. Some safety classes have the effect of making kids so scared of kidnapping or other dangers that they feel helpless, but Kidpower's goal is to empower kids by giving them tools without leaving them scared and fearful. One of the things Zac learned was how to not be so vulnerable to people who are good at telling stories. For example, the teachers will ask the kids, "When Aunt Susie touches your hair, and you don't like it, and you say 'stop,' and she doesn't, then what do you do?" Little kids will usually say, "I don't know." They teach the kids to say, "Stop or I'll tell." But if Aunt Susie says, "I'll stop if you promise not to tell," they teach the kids to promise not to tell. Then the teachers ask them, "What do you do when you see your mom? You tell. That's right. You promise Aunt Susie that you won't tell and then you go tell." Because they use many innocuous examples, and some harder ones, it helps these kids be prepared for more serious dangers. Our kids have to have those programs. We can't close our eyes to their vulnerability or to the dangers of the world. Children with NLD can learn anything, including safety judgment, if it's taught according to their learning style. It's our job to keep them safe while we help them learn.

The Rules of Farting

You just haven't lived as the parent of child with NLD until you've explained in a linear, logical manner the rules of farting. We have explored all the medical words for farting, including flatulence, expulsion of intestinal gases, and turbulence from the anal canal. We have examined how many farts a day are typical. (You'll be interested to know it's about twenty.)

We have read about the types of farts, the ones that make noise, the ones that don't, and examined all the peculiar attributes of those distinctions. We have gone into the depth that only families of children with precocious, insatiable, verbal curiosity can go.

When expelling gas from any part of the body, the rule is, we say "excuse me." But at home, when gas comes out we ignore it and accept it as part of our high-fiber lifestyle. This has always worked out. Zac recently read Mark Twain and Twain says the most underrated pleasure in life is a good bowel movement (my medical phrase). Now, another rule is that anything that gives pleasure is followed by an "ahhh." Who knew Zac would connect those rules.

One night we were at the museum's IMAX movie theater. The docent was giving his talk about the new Egyptian film we were about to see. Zac not only added musical accompaniment to that man's talk, but also followed it up with an audible, "Aaahhh." I realized in that moment that I hadn't told Zac about the rules of farting in public.

Most of us all know that if you fart in public, we are not supposed to say anything. If it makes a noise or not, you're to act innocent and oblivious. You should never announce your pleasure at having released an uncomfortable bubble. If you do, you should never, *never* do so in a quiet, built-for-maximum-reverberation-sound theater. If you do, you should *never, never, never* do so in the center, front seat.

Other rules we discussed on the way home included never saying, "Yuck, what stinks?" Never acknowledging that we know another person has made a contribution to the environment, and never acknowledging when we hear someone fart in public. If you're with a friend or at school, you need to excuse yourself, go to another room, make your music, and return to the room quietly. Those are important rules that govern our world and make it a better place, according to many.

One could argue that Mark Twain would love my son and agree that he has it right—why go to all this trouble to pretend to ignore what's most basic and most obvious? But as the mom of a preteen with NLD, I'm on a preemptive search for even more rules of farting. Yesterday we were in a restaurant, and Zac looked at me and said sincerely, "Mom, if I fart here, what am I supposed to say?" As it turns out, the humor of farting is, in our culture, one of the foundations of laughter from about preteen and beyond. Some of the biggest laughs come from movies with fart scenes, like *Blazing Saddles* and the latest Nutty Professor movie, *The Klumps*. . . . I think the joy of scatological humor lives on in guys and the laughs they get out of farts is a real, male bonding thing. At some point this year, we may have to teach Zac the rules of laughing about farting. Just a thought. . . .

Eleven

Social Skills

B<small>Y</small> definition, a deficit in social skills is part of the NLD syndrome. If a child has all of the markers of NLD, but has good social skills, she might have another learning disorder, but not NLD.

What are social skills? When a teacher says of a child that she "gets along well with others," she's referring to the child's social skills. The skills that enable a child to get along with others, accurately reading others' facial expressions and gestures, producing facial expressions that match one's feelings, understanding the rules of proximity and touch, recognizing the meanings of tones of voice, and producing appropriate tones of voice. All these nonverbal modes of communication are an essential part of good social skills. Most children learn them without direct instruction; they "pick them up" from their parents or peers. But as with so many things, children with NLD will not just pick them up. They may be completely unaware that these nonverbal forms of communication even exist.

Clinical psychologist Steve Nowicki has made an important contribution to our understanding of nonverbal communication by breaking the invisible language down into distinct areas. Children with NLD have deficits in one or more of these areas of nonverbal communication:

- **Paralanguage:** All those aspects of sound that communicate emotion and are used either independently or with words fall into this group. Whistling and humming are paralanguage, as are tone, intensity, and loudness of voice.

- **Facial Expressions:** Facial movements and poses communicate emotion. Effective eye contact and the appropriate use of facial expressions, like smiling, are two of the most frequently noted characteristics of socially adept children.

- **Postures and Gestures:** Hand and arm movements that communicate meaning are called gestures; positions of the entire body that convey meaning are called postures. Both postures and gestures can convey messages that conflict with spoken words, confusing communication efforts.

- **Interpersonal Distance (Space) and Touch:** We all carry a portable territory and boundaries around with us. If a child stands too close to others while having a conversation, that child is violating the rules of personal space. Similarly, a child who touches others inappropriately, either in terms of the location or the intensity of that contact, is breaking one of the unwritten laws of touch and stands an excellent chance of being rejected without knowing why.

- **Rhythm and Time:** Speech patterns, attitudes, and speed of movement or speech all fall into the category of rhythm. A child from New York City has a different "rhythm" from that of a child from Baton Rouge, Louisiana. Their speech patterns and attitudes are indicative of the differences in their environments. Problems can arise when they are "out of sync" with one another. This area also includes habits of time management, such as arriving promptly or being late for appointments.

- **Objectics:** Personal hygiene and style of dress indicate that individuals are part of a group, and keep them from being singled out as strange or different. People frequently judge others by the clothes they wear, the way those clothes are worn, and their personal hygiene. (Nowicki, 1992)

Deficits in these areas of nonverbal communication can be either receptive, meaning they don't know how to interpret the nonverbal information coming from others, or expressive, meaning they don't understand how others will interpret their own nonverbal communications. For some children with NLD the deficit is very obvious; for other kids it's very subtle. (Nowicki and Duke provide a very helpful checklist to identify your child's deficits in their book *Helping the Child Who Doesn't Fit In*.)

Zachary's major deficit is tone of voice, which is subtle but it pervasive, meaning it would show up in many different situations. It was both receptive—he could not interpret the meaning of other people's tone of voice—and expressive—he could not hear how his own tone of voice sounded to others. If someone said, "Would you like some juice?" he'd say, "NO!" in a loud, rude tone. Of course that made people, including Bill and me, angry with him. He'd say "Duh" a lot in a very sarcastic, or angry, loud tone. But he didn't mean to be sarcastic or angry, and he didn't know that's how he sounded to others. His problems with tone of voice made him sound arrogant, pretentious, and obnoxious, even though he really is not any of those things. When Zac began to realize that people were perceiving him that way, he was sad and frustrated and angry. His change in behavior can confirm what the person thought and around them he becomes angry; it's a self-fulfillment prophesy. That sadness propelled him into the depression he went into at age six, because he just couldn't figure out why people, even his grandparents, aunts, uncles, and cousins, thought he was rude, mean, or arrogant when he was none of those things.

Almost everyone assumed his "offensive" tone of voice was intentional. It was really painful for him, and for us, to learn about that. I knew Zac was a beautiful, together, charming child, but I saw him being negatively judged by people who didn't know that he had a deficit.

Because Zachary's deficit was also receptive, he did not hear intonations of voice the way we assume everybody hears them. Think about how much we communicate when we shift our tone. Just a simple phrase like "Please stop that" can be said to indicate anger, impatience, distress, humor, flirtation, or a dozen other attitudes, each intended to elicit a different response. Most people pick up on these subtle distinctions, but the information conveyed through tone of voice is unavailable to children with NLD who have that deficit. These kids miss a significant portion of a communication, and therefore, people's behavior and responses appear to be arbitrary and random. Zac had to guess at people's meaning all day, every day. His effort to comprehend the incomprehensible was quite exhausting for him. He needs to be conscious about his communications, an exhausting effort, and if he slips, he often ends up offending someone.

Even though Zac has made phenomenal progress with his social skills, tone of voice continues to be an area of deficit for him. When he's stressed, or in a new situation, or around people who aren't quite tolerant, his skills decline. Sometimes that's very upsetting to him. Recently at his dental checkup, the dentist said to him, in a matter-of-fact voice, "You need to do a better job brushing because you have four cavities." Zac perceived that as "the dentist is making fun of me" and, because of, that he didn't want to go back and see the dentist ever again. I called the dentist before our next visit and explained what had happened. I said, "this visit, you have to point out at least three things Zac is doing right for every one he's not."

Even though we have made an effort to ensure that Zac's doctors are kind and gentle, sometimes our efforts are not enough. When we went back to have the cavities filled, I took the receptionist aside and told her, "I need you to remind the dentist he has to say something positive to my son today, something that makes Zac feel like he did a good job, because he doesn't want to come anymore." I have to run interference with people to explain that they have to go over the top to make a point clear to Zac. It's hard for people to imagine that they have said something that would be upsetting to a child who seems so together. It's another one of those gaps: the child in the dentist's chair talks like a little adult, yet he didn't understand what the dentist meant to say.

I work with a little boy named Ravi who has a major deficit in interpersonal distance and touch. Most people's idea of intimate personal space is about six inches. That's how close you would want to be to someone you felt very safe with. It's the appropriate distance between parents and young children, between teachers and students, or between lovers. For most people in American culture, social personal space is about an arm's length radius around us. Ravi's idea of social personal space is literally two inches. He is always right in someone's face.

If someone gets within two inches of your face, it puts you into a fight-or-flight response, which is the way people respond to Ravi: They perceive him as aggressive even if he is just attempting a normal conversation. When Ravi actually is angry or frustrated because someone hasn't gone by the rules of a game, he's perceived as being extremely aggressive. He has also some difficulty with tone of voice, and this combination makes him appear to be a very aggressive, mean child, when in fact, he is one of the sweetest, most delightful children I have ever known.

This is obviously a major social deficit. Ravi can't play successfully in unstructured playground time because he is considered aggressive and a safety risk to himself and others. He rarely actually hurts people, but he makes kids so apprehensive that they react to him negatively. Sometimes he'll touch someone or push someone, and because he's a very strong kid and because he doesn't get good sensory feedback through his joints and muscles, his idea of a small push can send a kid onto the ground. As a result, Ravi is in trouble all day, every day. If he goes into the bathroom with a group of kids, the school is practically on red alert because if he accidentally gets in someone's face or pushes, there's a high risk someone could get a head injury falling against a sink or a stall.

For Ravi, this is a confusing, frustrating situation. Intellectually, he understands the distinctions of intimate space, personal space, and social space. When asked, he can reel off the definition. If you say, "Ravi, who is allowed in your intimate space?" he can tell you that his mom and his teacher are allowed in, but strangers are not. But even though he grasps the concept, he can't integrate it into his body because he doesn't have that visual perceptual ability. The deficit in visual-spatial integration—a primary deficit of NLD—means Ravi doesn't see the distance others see.

Tomo, another boy I work with, has learned a lot of social skills in a rote manner, but he doesn't understand the nonverbal back-and-forth of language and social exchanges. For example, if he wants to play with someone, he'll leave ten messages on the answering machine because he hasn't heard back from them today. Consequently, his peers perceive him as needy and annoying, and he has no friends.

This is a fairly common problem for children with NLD. They want so badly to have a friend, but they don't understand that their perseverative, persistent behavior is extremely off-putting. They fail to grasp that time is also a kind of personal space, that you have to put forth a request to someone and then give her time to respond. This is even more subtle than the concept of physical space, but because "everyone" knows about it, people assume that children with NLD know about it, too, though many of them do not. They can be taught it through rote lessons, but it will take a while for them to pick it up.

With Tomo, for example, we might say, "After you call someone you must wait forty-eight hours before you call him again." Or maybe, in his case, we might need to say, "You must wait and allow him to call you back. The rule is, after you call and leave *one* message, you must wait."

When I was trying to arrange for him to get together with another little boy, I kept saying to him, "Tomo, this boy's out of town."

But Tomo was frustrated. He'd say, "He didn't call me back, and I'm really mad at him for that."

"That's because he's out of town."

"Well, I left four messages."

"But he's *still* out of town."

Tomo also has a deficit in eye contact and facial expressions. Seeing and interpreting facial expressions and gestures is related to the visual system. But if you haven't made good eye contact for ten years—if you're literally not looking at facial expressions—then you've lived ten years without attending to them. That's ten years of not collecting a vocabulary of expressions and attaching meaning to them. All you see is a face.

Many studies have shown that infants are highly attuned to their mothers' facial expressions. When a mother avoids eye contact with her baby, the infant becomes depressed. What has yet to be studied is what happens when an infant doesn't *perceive* her mom's expression. It's been widely assumed that all babies naturally tune in to their mothers' faces. Children with NLD, however, can't do many things we assume children do naturally. I think that it is not an accident that children with NLD are so prone to depression. If you're a three- or five-year-old, and you can't perceive your mom's smile, it seems reasonable to assume you would always be anxious and confused. Or at best, you'd have missed essential, foundational social knowledge. You're also unlikely to be motivated to explore your environment or to engage with people, two deficits of many children with NLD because infants look to Mom to know what to explore and what to ignore.

Although Zachary did not have a significant deficit in gestures and facial expression, this might have been because Bill and I intuitively knew to exaggerate our emotions when we needed to communicate something important to him. For example, when Zac was just a baby learning to crawl, he would crawl straight off the bed. We'd gather him in our arms as if he were something very precious that had broken, and we'd make lots of alarmed, concerned noises. Zac learned pretty quickly to stop at the edge of the bed. We didn't realize that we were doing therapy from an early age, but that's probably what it was.

Often we would look at people and say, "Look, Zac, she looks sad to me, do you see that she looks sad?"

"No."

"Well, why do you think I think she looks sad?" and we'd discuss eye position or lip orientation.

Or I'd say, "Look at my face. I'm feeling sad right now, and you just came over and hit me. Why do you think I'm feeling sad right now?" I intuitively talked that way as a mother. Without realizing it, I was giving Zac information about his world that he might not have gotten otherwise on how to take another's perspective and his effect on others.

Or I'd say, "Zac, look how beautiful the sky is! That beautiful sky makes me feel so happy." I think that helped him link an external event with an internal sensation, which is something we work on in social skills training.

It all goes back to those foundational deficits. I believe Rourke was mistaken when he says the primary deficit of NLD is a social deficit. The social deficit is really a secondary problem resulting from the primary neurological deficit. That's why even though the problem we're addressing is social skills, each family has to work on the underlying neurological deficit. With Ravi, the family has to work on increasing his body awareness and visual discrimination so that he can integrate proximity into his sensory system. He also has to develop his proprioceptive system so that he can be in control of his body and know how much force he's exerting when he touches his peers. Tomo has to increase his visual-spatial system so that he can look and attend to gestures and facial expressions.

Develop a Socially Appropriate Appearance

Children with NLD sometimes look different and are regarded by their peers as "goofy" or "geeky." For many children with NLD, this is the result of an expressive deficit in "objectics," a term defined by Steve Nowicki. People with an expressive deficit in objectics literally do not know how they appear, and they will be equally unaware of how their appearance is interpreted by others. They can't see themselves as others see them; they can't judge their own appearance.

For better or worse, people are judged by their appearance. This is as true among children as it is among adults. If a child has a deficit in objectics, it's highly likely that she will be ostracized by her peers. When Zac began having trouble in kindergarten, my brilliant mother said to me, "You go to that teacher and you ask her, 'What do the other kids say about my child? Do they say he's stinky? Do they make fun of his clothes? Does he have a weird haircut that sets him apart? Does he make rude noises with his body? Tell me. Is there anything in his appearance or behavior that sets him apart? I want to know. Tell me.' If he's having trouble in school, you need to make the teacher tell you the truth about these things and be the mom who can hear it."

When my mother first said that to me, I remember thinking she was a little odd. In Zac's case none of those things were true. He was appropriately dressed and clean. After working with a lot of children with NLD, however, I've realized she had an important insight. Many children with NLD are set apart by an odd appearance that causes estrangement from their peers. I think it's important for parents to take inventory of their children. For better or worse, our society has very strong rules about grooming and hygiene. If you're trying to help your child grow up without social deficits, grooming and hygiene is one area where your child needs to conform. Maybe your child's style of dress fits with your family, but it might be causing her a lot of suffering at school.

For some children with NLD, grooming and cleanliness are very challenging because of their motor deficits. Those deficits need to be addressed in therapy and at home. But sometimes children with NLD look "goofy" because they don't know how to dress to fit in with their peer group, and their parents either don't know or don't consider it important. If, as an adult, you choose not to conform to the social norms for dress and hygiene, you can do so while understanding and accepting the consequences. However, I believe that in fairness to your child, you need to consider whether dressing her in a way that leads to rejection by her peers is a statement you want to use your child to make. If a child is unhappy, has no friends, and can't succeed at work or play, then I believe we owe it to that child to help her get to the point where she can make a choice about how to present herself.

Parents need to distinguish between their choice not to conform (because they won't) and their child's inability to conform (because she can't). For example, a little boy at Zac's school had very long hair. He was very pretty, and no one knew that he was a boy. The parents were making a statement about being cool and Californian, but the kid was really suffering.

Zac's always been a little messy. He'll say, "So I spilled something on me, what's it matter?"

I always answer him, "Clothes with food on them tell people you don't care about yourself, and in our family that's not okay. If you look like a slob, people will interact with you as a slob. We have a value that you demonstrate to the people in the world that we care about you and that you care about your own body, so you need to clean that up." We don't believe Zac has to wear the latest fashion, but we do believe that his appearance does communicate to people, and he is clean and well groomed. Children with NLD have to be taught this.

On the other hand, I do not believe in forcing a child to conform to a social norm when it makes them crazy. When we go to weddings, Zac's formal wear is khaki shorts, a Hawaiian shirt, and California sandals. People say he looks like Don Johnson of *Miami Vice*. His dress is appropriately formal for the situation, just different than the East Coast norm. I would rather have a happy, healthy child and enjoy the wedding than have a child who is in constant meltdown because I made him put something on his body that he cannot tolerate. Some of our family members believe we're giving him too much control, but we have made a conscious choice about this.

Learn Social Skills at Any Age

Adults with NLD who have never gotten treatment often are very isolated and lonely. They frequently have traits that quickly repel potential
friends. They don't know when to stop talking or how to listen. Then
they are shocked, frustrated, and sad because they don't understand
what happened for others to get angry with them.

One man I know, Paul, keeps asking the same questions over and over
because his language deficits don't allow him to ask the questions that he
really wants to ask. He doesn't have difficulties with objectics—he's a
very handsome man, well-groomed and dressed—but he doesn't have a
single person in his life who can tolerate him. A colleague of mine and I
both evaluated Paul and gave him the same recommendation, to call a
hospital and get into their program for adults, because we don't have
any equipment to treat an adult his size. Then I got a call from the hospital switchboard operator, who said, "We have this man calling us over
and over. Can you please tell me what he's looking for? Because we are
about to explode." Clearly, however he was speaking to them but that
was not getting him what he needed.

It's important to emphasize that this is what social skills deficits look
like in adults who have not gotten good intervention. Zac, Tomo, and
Ravi will not look like that as adults because they're getting good interventions. I often say children with NLD are going to be fine as adults,
many of them, if we don't crush their spirits, and if we give some support along the way.

Help Your Child Make Friends

Many children with NLD have never once had a friend prior to intervention. Many children are not especially tolerant or interested in
being with someone who is different. Children with NLD are sometimes excluded by the other kids because of their oddities—either in
behavior or appearance. Children with NLD often lack social cognition, the ability to think about what it would take to be successful
socially. Children with NLD make the same mistakes over and over
again, and they don't really understand the consequence of those

choices. However, I have never seen a child without friends who couldn't be helped with therapy.

We were really fortunate in that Zac was surrounded by lots of good kids who were willing to be his friends, and he always had one or two friends, and then a handful of acquaintances.

Play Dates

Children with NLD frequently have difficulty initiating play with others. They want to initiate, but they do goofy things like asking irrelevant questions (e.g., "Do you know what a google is?"), or mimicking something they've heard on TV that makes no sense out of context. Other kids perceive their attempts as so weird that they rebuff the overture. If your child doesn't know how to initiate play with another child, it will be up to you to set up some play dates for her. One way to do this is to get to know the parents of the other kids at your child's school. You can do this by becoming active in the PTA or just through hanging around, waiting to pick up your child, with parents outside the classroom door. Pick a parent you like and whose kid you like, and say, "Let's take the kids to the park."

If your child seems to be able get along with another kid for an hour, then you can say, "We'll meet you at the park from three to four and then we need to go run some errands." That way you have an out if the play date isn't working out, but you can stay longer if it is. Then your child gets exposed to these people. When you're with a parent who is understanding, you can say, "Oh, there's that tone of voice thing she's working on that I told you about. I'm sorry, but she's not quite there yet."

After you've had some casual dates at the park, you can set up more formal play dates. You can invite a child over for two hours in the afternoon and set up clear boundaries. You want to allow enough time for the kids to play successfully, but you need to give yourself an out in case you need one. Be specific: "Can Travis come over from three to five on Tuesday and play with Owen's new *Star Wars* Monopoly game?" That way when Travis comes over, Owen has practiced and is ready to play that one game. If Travis comes over and says, "Let's play video games," you can say, "We're just going to play with *Star Wars* today."

"Oh, but I really want to play videos."

"Well, I'm sorry, but that's not a choice today."

Kids were very clear that that was what they were coming over to play, and Zachary was clear on the rules of the game to be played. We would practice playing the game before the play date, and practice the social rules of turn-taking that went with it. That way the play date wasn't a novel situation for him. He knew what to expect. We would pick whatever the high-interest game at the time was, so that the kid would want to come. Sometimes they came for the game instead of for Zac, but pretty quickly they wanted to come because of Zac. It was nice. We don't have to do this anymore because now having a friend over is not a novel experience.

It's also a good idea to make sure your child previews and practices the rules of play. "Chi Young is coming from three to five, and when she leaves at five, what do we say? That's right, we say good-bye and thank you for coming to play. And do we cry when she has to leave? No, we don't. Why don't we do that? We don't do that because it makes our friend feel bad. What do we do if there's a fight over a toy? It goes away. Does it come back out? No, it doesn't come back out."

When the other child arrived, we always said, "We have three rules in our house. Let's tell you the rules so that you can play and not break our rules. If you fight over something; it goes away and it doesn't come back out. We take turns. We don't use mean words." We would say the rules very clearly, and we always had just three because we felt that was enough to remember. We'd rehearse the rules for both kids when the guest arrived. This worked very well. Our guests really appreciated knowing the rules. I think all kids really want to know the rules, and my kid really needed to know them, *and* he needed to know that the other kid knew the rules, too.

Preplan Birthday Parties

Parents often take for granted that their children will enjoy birthday parties and other social events. But there are countless stories of children with NLD walking into their very own birthday party, being scared to death, and hiding under their beds till the children leave. Parents don't realize that their child's sensory system is overwhelmed by the stimulation of those parties: the noise, the unfamiliar decorations, the unclear social expectations. If you're planning a party for your child or taking her to a party, try some of the sensory strategies (in the Appendix) to help get your child prepared for a fun, successful day.

Before we knew about Zac's NLD, we always stayed with him at birthday parties. When Zac started to seem overwhelmed, we would take him away and gave him some tight hugs, or we'd help translate for him, or help bring him into the group to play. Those things were just our habit. People could easily have said that we were overprotective, but our son needed us. We listened to his need and to our intuition.

After we'd found out about Zac's NLD, when he was six and seven, birthday parties tended to get bigger. They were often held at large, overwhelming places like The Jungle or Discovery Zone. To prepare Zac for the party, we'd find out where the party was to be, and the weekend before we'd go and practice finding the bathrooms, finding the person behind the counter in case Zac got lost, and figuring out how the games or rides worked. On the day of the party, Bill or I would go with him and stay. We'd sit off to the side with a book and say to Zac, "I will be right here if you need me." Most of the time Zac would never come to us, but knowing we were there was helpful. At one party, when Zac was eight, he got separated from the other kids. When he finally found Bill he was hysterical. Thank God Bill was there, because the other parents would have said, "What is wrong with this little baby?" But Bill knew to say, "Oh my gosh, it must have felt terrifying to feel lost. Why don't you just sit with me, let me get you a cold drink, and you tell me when you're ready and I'll walk you back over to the party." Bill's intervention was invisible, and no kid saw Zac in tears. Zac often did not look different because of the behind-the-scenes work we were doing. I think that was an important support to provide him.

Teach Play Skills

Another helpful behind-the-scenes support for your child is teaching her play skills. When other kids are playing on the playground, children with NLD are often the ones walking around and around the perimeter. They don't know how to join in a group, and they don't know how to play games. Find out from the teachers what the popular game is this year, learn it yourself, and teach it to your child. If you can't teach it, an OT can, or a PE teacher, a teenager, or a peer. It's also a great idea to include on the IEP. One of the annual goals can be that your child will be taught to play the playground games each year. When they know how to play, it's easier for them to join in. You might have to fight for why it's an important goal for the IEP, but for a child who has a primary deficit in social skills, you won't have to fight very hard. Probably the IEP team will respond, "Great idea! We should have thought of that."

Another gift of children with NLD is that they teach us about the value of play for all children. In a lot of his books, psychiatrist Stanley Greenspan addresses the need to get reacquainted with the value of play. He writes about how different learning styles show up in play and on the playground. In our society, occupational therapists and some psychologists have become the holders of the value of play. It's ironic that in our society you may have to hire a professional to teach your child to play, but as a parent of a child with a learning disability, it might be necessary. A child's inablity to participate in playground play is an academic need. The IDEA mandates that your child get remedial services for that. I don't think many people know this. Teachers may just assume, "It's playtime, so it doesn't count," but the law says it counts, and for children with NLD it counts a lot. It's perhaps more important than whether or not they work on handwriting. Children with NLD can type their way to success, but if they can't get along with the boss and coworkers, they will never succeed at work.

More and more, occupational therapists are being called in to work with kids on the playground because the children don't have the skills for unstructured playtime. We're also doing more consulting with physical education teachers to help them bring children with NLD and other learning disabilities into PE classes. PE teachers are not necessarily trained in some of those subtle learning disabilities, so if they're playing games that a child with NLD doesn't know how to play or if the child's clumsy with the ball, an OT can help.

All those years of working the behind-the-scenes intervention have really paid off. Now Zac has a ton of friends who really like to play with him. He makes friends easily on his own now. We don't have to orchestrate anymore. Now our job as parents is to make the time and effort to maintain friendships a priority in our lives.

Develop Their Interests
Another way to help your child make friends is to develop her interests. We say to Zac all the time, "People are interested in interesting

people. Let's develop some of your interests, and let's teach you to talk about what you're interested in and find out what a friend is interested in. It doesn't matter if what you're interested in is robotics and only three other people are interested in that. It still makes you interesting." So, for example, when Zac began his new school in the middle of the school year, I said to the teacher, "We need to make Zac interesting to his classmates because Zac is not going to initiate with them. We need those children to initiate with Zac." After Zachary had been at that school a few days, he brought in a huge bag of balloons and a balloon pump, and he made balloon animals for every kid in his class. At the end of the day, when I went to pick him up, he was still making them. Kids were coming from other classes, and they were all leaving with balloon animals. Immediately he'd become interesting to the children: "The new kid can make balloon animals!" That elevated him quickly. It didn't have to be balloon animals. It could have been anything he could demonstrate and share in an interesting way, and he chose the balloon animals himself.

Tony is very interesting to other kids because he is in drama and has had a couple of starring roles in community theater. Now his oddities are seen as creative and theatrical, not weird. His parents were brilliant in following his lead and helping him develop something interesting about him that's a natural outcome of his interests—it was not contrived. To help your child develop her interests, find out what she is passionate about and help her develop that into something she can share with others. If your child is just into reading books, then you have to help her learn to talk about her reading in a way that is relevant and playful, not a monologue of facts. Speech therapy can help with that.

Expect Setbacks

Sometimes when a child with NLD has made a friend, he will do something that is so goofy that the friend says, "You are way too weird for me," or "I'm really embarrassed by him all the time," and the kid goes away and won't play anymore. Of course the child with NLD is crushed. If children with NLD have waited a long time to have a friend, they may be overly dependent and overly needy.

These kids change schools a lot, and changing schools is often a social setback. New friends take time to develop. It's a good idea to ask the teacher to help your child initiate friendships with the other kids. When Zac went to a new school three-quarters through fourth grade, he spent recesses and lunch with his head down on the picnic table. Of course that made him look unusual. He was withdrawing, trying to make himself look invisible and not be noticed for not knowing what to do. I'd say, "Why don't you join in the playground games?" and he'd say, "Mom, I don't know how to do that." So we had an occupational therapist step in to alert the teachers and the principal to the importance of integrating Zachary into the social scene. An occupational therapist could have taught him some of the playground games, but play is better if it evolves internally. We were fortunate that his teacher stepped in and would say, "Come on, Zac, let's go play basketball!" or would run with him out on the playground and get him engaged, and then run off but keep an eye on him. If Zac disengaged, the teacher would run back again and get him engaged again. This was moderately successful. The following summer we took Zac to a camp where he learned how to play many of the playground games, and the next year he was able to join in because he knew how.

In some schools, principals or OTs will institute a board game group, like a chess club, and make those available at recess and lunch. Or you might ask them to open the computer lab once a week so that there is a quiet place where your child looks engaged as he's taking a break.

Evaluate Social Skills Groups

Not every child with NLD will need a social skills group, but for kids who really have a hard time playing with one other child, social skills groups can be a great way for them to learn and practice in a safe setting. Ideally, the child learns skills that he can then transfer into a natural setting, like a play date. There are four kinds of social skills groups, each lead by a professional from one of four fields: psychology (either a social worker, a psychologist, or a psychology intern in the school system); speech therapy; occupational therapy; and education (teachers). Each group will have a different focus and use a different framework of analysis. Each has its strengths and weaknesses.

Psychology-Run Groups

Psychotherapists who work with kids will have games or some way to keep the kids engaged. It will focus on the meaning of words and analyzing social exchanges: "Carl, what happened when you told your friend John at school today that you thought he sucked? Have the rest of you ever experienced that?" These groups try to explore the meaning of events and to reconceptualize them, bringing new understanding and meaning that the child can then take back into the situation. The good part about a psych-based group is it helps break down the invisible meanings and helps children feel a little better about themselves. Some of the drawbacks of these groups is that the skills learned in the group don't always transfer to situations outside the group. Children with NLD have a hard time generalizing. Your child might learn to apply the skills with the other group members pretty well, but the new skills might not transfer back to her school. Just because she knows how to do it with Susan doesn't mean she knows how to do it with Tessa. At psychology-based group is also going to operate mainly by talking and will be somewhat sedentary.

Speech Therapy Groups

Groups run by a speech therapist will concentrate on the use of language, both expressive and receptive. They work on speech pragmatics, the use of language in conversation, including idioms and expressions, and the invisible rules of turn-taking or responding to nonverbal cues and processing speed. They might work on the organization of language by taking a sentence that's been printed on paper and then cut up. The kids then have to figure out what order the words go in. They might look at photos of children and try to identify their facial expressions. They might come up with definitions for different idioms: What does it mean when someone says, "horse of a different color"?

Typically, speech-based social skills groups have kids sit around a table and talk. While often successful, this method tends to be sedentary, requiring children to sit for 45 to 60 minutes. Knowing that can be important. If your child can't sit and focus for that long, then that's not the place to start.

Occupational Therapy Run Groups

A social skills group run by an occupational therapist will teach social skills in the context of play. These groups teach play skills, turn-taking, development of the rules of the game, and frustration tolerance, while paying close attention to the sensory and motor skills needed to succeed at those activities. Occupational therapy–based groups use a lot of movement and sensory strategies. Whereas a speech therapist might start out a group with an ice-breaker such as, "Let's go around the table and everybody tell us your favorite color," in OT we use movement and sensory input to charge the body and get it "available for learning," as we call it. We might start the group playing with a huge wad of Play-Doh that's been scented with vanilla and mix some plastic ice cubes into the dough. The Play-Doh is very resistant, which is calming to the sensory system, and the ice cubes provide the sensory input of temperature. Then we can focus on some of the social concepts like turn-taking or figuring out how to form a line when everyone wants to be first.

The downside of an OT social skills group can occur when the activities themselves become the goal, taking the focus off of the child's progress, like using a Valentine's Day project because it's February 14, but not making sure it matches the therapeutic goal of the individuals in the group. It's also possible that the occupational therapist's training in the language deficits of NLD might be inadequate.

Teacher-Run Groups

Social skills groups run by teachers often use preprinted curricula. There are a lot of good curricula available drawing on psychology, speech, and occupational therapy. These groups take place in the child's natural setting (school) and tend to be with kids from the school, so they have the benefits of familiarity and accessibility. These groups are for all kids who are at risk at school, not necessarily just children with NLD.

These groups teach concepts: "John said, 'Give me back my ball, you jerk,' and what might he have said differently? Let's write that on the worksheet." They work on helping the child think about alternative ways of handling situations. The children might read a short story about somebody handling something well and somebody handling it not so well and discussing the two choices. This can very effective.

I have known many brilliant teachers. They often have a natural intuition and understanding of children that we would call therapeutic. They see the children in a natural setting (classrooms) and have a sense of what's normal and typical for kids of a given age. Teachers usually know what's appropriate to the age. Sometimes, because they use preprinted curricula, and because they don't have a clinical background, sometimes teachers are unable to go into the deeper causes of some of the behavior they're analyzing. They have a tendency to label issues "behavior problems" as opposed to identifying, for example, a breakdown of language, or a child's tactile defensiveness, or that a child felt very wounded by another.

Interdisciplinary Groups

The best social skills groups combine attributes of all four approaches or are run by teams from more than one field. You might find a really playful speech therapist who has worked with an occupational therapist or who just naturally knows the importance of movement, or you might find a group run by a psychologist who has good skills with language. Or the educator running a social skills group at your child's school might have worked with some of these other professionals or has had some training, or you might find an OT who has developed skills in social language. In these cases, even though the group is led by one discipline, they are pulling successfully from the other fields.

If a social skills group requires kids under 12 to sit still for 45 to 60 minutes, I believe that's an inappropriate group and an inappropriate demand. For younger children it's even more inappropriate. A group that lets the children move and be playful in learning these skills is far more effective. Children progress faster and feel more successful.

One way to tell if a group is effective is if your child looks forward to going; if he wants to go and doesn't want to leave when the time is up. Just because a social skills group might be "good for him" doesn't mean a child is benefiting from it. If your child doesn't want to go, you need to step in and find out why, because a social skills group for a child should be fun or it's not going to be as effective. Research has proven that people get better faster when they're motivated to participate in their own therapy. Some people believe kids should shut up and take their medicine, but I don't believe in that as a parent or as an OT. In my field, *any-*

thing can be made motivating and fun. The therapist just needs to figure out how to do that. If the concepts are fun and engaging, a child will be more likely to take them into other areas of her life. If your child spends most of the group time outside the group (in the hall or in a chair set aside for misbehavers), then that may not be an effective group for your child at that time. You may want to explore an OT group to work on body regulation, a speech therapy group to work on language issues, or a psychology group to work on emotional needs.

Getting the Most Out of a Social Skills Group

Children with NLD have difficulty transferring skills from one environment to another, so it's important for parents to make a conscious effort to make that happen. You can bridge that gap for your child by saying, "In your social skills group you learned this, and here is the same situation on the playground, so let's try it here." Let's say your child is working on asking a question. You can help your child practice that on a play date by saying, "We're working on questions, remember? So when Dylan comes over, let's see if you can ask him a couple of questions to find out something interesting about him." I'd keep it as simple as that and not harp on the issue.

A social skills group might be appropriate for some kids, but not the right choice for your child right now. There are some children for whom social skills groups require them to face their weaknesses, head on, for an hour each week. A child might dislike a speech therapy group, but really enjoy and succeed in an OT-based group because she gets to move and play and learn the same concepts in a way that's more fitting for her needs. For kids who are ready to sit down to concentrate for 30 to 45 minutes, a group with a speech therapist where they can really get in and work on language would be a good choice. Different kids have different needs at different times. My measure of a successful group is if the child leaves taller and more centered than when he arrived.

Final Note on Social Skills and NLD

For children with NLD who have relatively high-functioning social skills compared to those in most social skills groups, but low-functioning skills in the classroom, whose social skills deficits are subtle, a group may not be helpful. These kids need to work on social skills, but they need something other than what most groups offer. When you have a child with subtle social skills deficits, you can consult with therapists in one-on-one sessions and then go home and implement her suggestions. Another option might be to consult with the child's teacher or with an OT to learn the playground games and then teach them to your child on the weekend, or work with the PE teacher or resource teacher to help you. We have found that to be our most successful strategy.

Have an Inviting Home

For your child to develop social skills, she needs practice. She needs opportunities to play with other kids outside of school settings. She needs to have play dates in her home. One simple way you can make this easier is to make your home inviting for children. If you have white carpeting and a white couch, and you insist that all the toys and games have to be put away all the time, it's going to be hard for your kid to bring someone over to play. If that's the house you absolutely have to have, then you need to be willing to drive to a park, or be willing to take your kid and a friend on an outing once or twice a week.

Our house is considered a fun place to be because we often have playful activities for children set up ahead of time. We have lots of board games that are easily accessible. In our living room, for years we had two or three big therapy balls instead of chairs. They were a hit. There was also a huge blow-up toy kids could get inside of and jump in—I got it from Lilian Vernon for 30 dollars. *House Beautiful* will never take a picture of my living room, but I have a kid who is doing great, and I think that's more important. We often put down a picnic blanket on the living room carpet so kids can eat there. We're the house where kids always get to cook. It's something I enjoy doing, and a lot of kids don't have any opportunity to cook. Cooking is a rich social activity. They can make a pizza or cinnamon rolls, or if I'm making pancakes they get to come in and break the eggs for me.

We are lucky to know families who also make their homes child-friendly. One has a downstairs with overstuffed couches and huge pillows. Their home is full of kids of all ages, teens to five-year-olds. The teens do impromptu recitations, frequently break into song to express their ideas, and Thanksgiving dinners there are packed with family and friends. The kids often have grand games of Monopoly stretching over days of play with adults stepping over the players without a hint of annoyance. Another family has a huge heated rug in the living room where we sit close, warmed with the rug, hot tea, and the snuggling families. The children come and go, hanging out on a futon playing Playstation games or building robots that will scale a carpeted wall. Neighbors ring the doorbell and drop off all sorts of interesting food (bean cakes, freshly caught salmon, freshly pressed warm soy milk). The mom is always cooking and feeding us wonderful foods and teaching the boys about Korean history and language.

When we first started on this journey, we gave fun parties as a way of getting to know kids at Zachary's new school. At our "in the dark" party all the kids had to bring a flashlight, and we went to the park down the street at night. We played flashlight tag and did bat hangs on the monkey bars and hid plastic gold pieces in the sandbox. We had a piñata with glow-in-the-dark toys in it. It was an inexpensive party, but it was really fun. Once we had an "unbirthday" party. All the kids wrapped up toys they were done playing with, and they exchanged them at the party so every kid left with a "new" toy. Now that *Harry Potter* is the rage, we often have "A Train Ride to Hogwarts" parties. They're really sleepovers where we make a huge pile of blankets on the floor of Zac's room. We give the kids a picnic basket of treats, but we label them "pumpkin juice" (orange juice) or "butterbeer" (cream soda) or other things from the books. Then we put the *Harry Potter* tape on the tape player, dim the lights, and say, "See you when you get home from Hogwarts!"

Setting up a playful home isn't difficult. It just takes a little creativity, and if you don't have that, get a book from the library for ideas. There are many books with good ideas available.

Concretize Invisible Rules

One of the hardest things for children with NLD is figuring out the rules that "everyone" knows, but nobody ever talks about. You know the ones: Don't pick your nose and rub your findings on the car seat. That's not written down, and people don't discuss it, but it's a rule. At school, don't say "penis." No one talks about this unwritten rule, but Zac found that breaking it really got his teacher upset.

You can help your child by talking about why we have these invisible rules. You can label some of them for your child and even start keeping a list of them. What we began to do was to celebrate finding another invisible rule: "How interesting! So the rule is . . ." If you're always on the lookout for them, it can become a game of trying to discover another invisible rule. Try to enlist the child's teacher in this strategy. Have her help your child identify the invisible rules in the classroom and help your child write down each new rule he discovers. It was always cool when Zac's teacher would say to me, "Zac and I discovered another invisible rule today . . . ," and then he'd tell me what it was.

When you first read about NLD in the literature that's available, the facts can be depressing. The truth is, *children with NLD can learn any-thing*. We just need to get to work and help them. As they learn, they get better and better and stronger and stronger till they operate in a typical way. Zac calls it "becoming bilingual," meaning he has learned the social language. There are more and more kids like Zac, who at age ten is indistinguishable from other kids. Now all his charm is available—he has access to it—and the people who meet him can see just what a great kid he really is.

Learning a Script

When Zac learned to say "no offense," he used it a lot. It was a script he'd learned. But at the beginning he used to say, "No offense, but you suck at Playstation." He had to be taught that whatever comes after "no offense" has to be about yourself, not others. For example, it's okay to say, "No offense, but I don't like cabbage," but it's not okay to say, "No offense, but this cabbage you made stinks."

When he was first learning this, he said to me one day, "You said I could tell you anything, no matter how hard it is or how uncomfortable to say."

"That's right, Zac, you can tell me anything."

"Well, I don't want to offend you and I don't want to hurt your feelings, and I don't quite know how to tell you this but. . . ."

Long pause

"Yes, Zac, go ahead . . ."

"Well, guess who my favorite parent is now?"

Many people, grown-ups included, don't know this rule, and they offend others accidentally. But after they've made the error they can see what happened and fix it. Zac couldn't necessarily see that and had to be taught. Other times he would say, "I don't want to offend you, but my toe hurts." Learning scripts is not as easy as just repeating them. The child has to have someone to observe, translate, and correct while the child practices.

Twelve

Finding the Right School

M<small>Y</small> husband's job is working with computers that are not doing what they are supposed to do. He has to use numbers and logic to unravel problem after problem, and he's great at it. If I had his job, I'd feel so impotent. But Bill, who loves his job, would hate the work I do as an occupational therapist. When I am working with children who have learning disabilities, I feel inspired and enthused and invigorated. . . . I am transformed and humbled by each inch of progress they make. When I work to support a teacher who has a child she doesn't understand, I feel I am making a difference in the world. I know I'm doing meaningful work. When I tell Bill about my day, he feels overwhelmed, sad, and daunted by how far these kids have to go on their journeys, while I am focused on how far they've come and how many gifts they bring to all our lives. I love my work.

Most adults who work are usually engaged in activities that are aligned with their abilities. Even if our jobs are not ideal, we usually know what to expect, we feel generally competent, and when challenges arise they are usually ones we know how to address. While work can help adults develop friendships, social networks, and a feeling of satisfaction, most of us also find satisfaction and fulfillment in other arenas.

Our jobs are part of our social role and self-image, and not necessarily the major part.

For children, this picture looks very different. In this country, the primary occupational role for children ages five to eighteen is student. Children spend nearly as much time engaged in school and its related activities as adults do at their jobs, and often more. While adults can choose their jobs and find new ones if they're not satisfied, children don't get to choose where they go to school or what they will be taught. They are required to work in multiple disciplines in which they have no prior experience. They are constantly faced with learning novel tasks, confronting unique situations, and dealing with feelings of incompetence. While being asked to learn something new can be exciting, not knowing can be daunting and tiring. For most kids, friends, social networks, and self-image are intimately associated with their role at school. Their feelings of success and competency are strongly influenced by their school performance, both academic and social.

The way our society organizes learning affects all kids, but it has a special impact on kids with disabilities or learning disorders. For children with NLD, a school environment can be terrifying and overwhelming. If you're a child with NLD, every day of school can be like the first day in a new school, over and over again. You don't know where you are. You don't know the rules. You don't know who your friends are and who the bullies are. You don't know which adults and children are safe and could provide support and comfort. You don't know where the bathrooms are, and you don't have any friends to help you, and when you ask a teacher for clarification, she's likely to say, "How many times do I have to tell you that?" Imagine trying to work in such an environment day after day. Few working adults could tolerate it, much less succeed.

Zachary's kindergarten experience taught us a lot about the importance of choosing the right school for children with NLD. As we first learned in kindergarten, a school setting for children with NLD is best when structured, has minimal adult interactions for the child to interpret each day, has schedules and routines, and is organized and predictable. Zachary's kindergarten was exactly the opposite. We had chosen it with the best of intentions, but the very things it was designed to provide left Zac at an utter loss to know what was expected of him. In retrospect, it's obvious that nearly every aspect of that school made it difficult for Zac to succeed. It's no wonder he called the school a "torture chamber."

They told us they were not able to accommodate the learning style of one child whose needs were so different from their philosophy of learning (even though it violated their stated philosophy). We were deeply disappointed.

With six weeks of school left in the year. I didn't want to take my child out of school while he was so aware that he was failing because I didn't want teach him that we run away from failure. Instead, I wanted to show him that we step away from environments that don't support us in our growth and wellness and that we move on to something that will be better.

With great determination and much deep breathing, I found ways to be positive about this change. My husband and I each spent hour after hour thinking about what we wanted for our son. We hired a sitter one night, went out to a restaurant, and made a list of what we wanted for our son's education, our goals for him, and our goals for his life. I had to revisit the losses of my life and make sure they remained mine and didn't expand to color and amplify the current situation. My son was vulnerable and he would believe anything I told him. If I said, "Those people are monsters and we're the good guys and we'll save you," what would happen when the new school wasn't perfect? If I told him the current school was terrible, then I'd be teaching him any school could be terrible.

By the time the team of teachers, principal and specialists met, we had our goals and emotions relatively clear. We wanted our son to love learning again, to be happy, and to feel that he could succeed if the grown-ups around him understood his needs.

I said to the principal and resource teacher, "Clearly, you're not going to teach our child anything between now and the end of the year. You have already lost him. He has no trust here. He has faith left in no one here. Between now and the end of the school year, in the next six weeks, you can do one thing: Help him leave here thinking that maybe a school can be okay when it has its attention on the needs of that child." To the credit of the school and its staff, for the most part they did that. They basically left him alone with occasional checks on his emotional wellness. They let him go to the resource teacher throughout the day as he felt the need as long as he told Erica where he was going. I kept him home if the class went on a field trip because field trips were too over-whelming—if he got scared, no one knew how to comfort him.

The resource specialist at the school worked with Zachary on com-puters, allowed him to read advanced books and play with more com-plicated mathematics. They played strategy games on the computer, and the resource teacher taught Zachary many of the secrets of those games. More important, the teacher gave Zac a safe environment to learn in. Zac felt liked by this teacher and anchored by him.

Parents in the class came to an evening to listen to an occupational therapist, a colleague of mine, explain learning styles and sensory inte-gration. As the evening progressed, many parents began to disclose their struggles with their own children. Awareness, education, acceptance, understanding, and adjustment are all stages that healthy people and healthy communities go through. I felt this group of parents gave us that sense of community more deeply at the end than they had all year. Par-ents arranged play dates with Zachary and his classmates with a new level of compassion and understanding.

If you ask Zachary about the end of that year, he will tell you he was in the wrong school and that when the grown-ups figured him out, they did things that made him feel better. It gave him hope that his new school would be even better. It taught him that the people around him cared; they just hadn't known how to help.

Once I'd gotten Zac set up safely for the remainder of the school year, I began searching for a new school for him to start in September. We hired an educational consultant who gave us a list of schools in our area to consider. I visited seven public schools and a few private ones. Zachary had told me that his number one requirement was a teacher who had a smile. I have since learned that research bears this out as a simple but good indicator to judge a teacher's teaching method (Brooks, 1997). When adults are polled about what they remember about an inspiring teacher, they recall the teacher's smile. Adults still remember the smiles of their special teachers, the calming hand on the back, the secret thumbs-up, or the plus on the report card with a smiley face.

Considering Zac's number one requirement, I prepared a checklist of what else we needed in his new school. I was looking for a school com-munity that seemed open to accommodations, appeared well organized, had no plans for remodeling or restructuring within the next three years, had computers in the classroom and a computer lab, had a resource teacher who smiled and appeared knowledgeable, and had consistency in the quality of teachers for grades one to four. The computers were important because they offered a nonpeople related activity for my son to engage in at recess and gave him the option of typing his assignments. I looked for quality teachers by watching to see if the children in the classroom could ask for clarification, if they were able to follow directions easily, and if they were corrected in a way that built them up instead of cutting them down.

One school I visited had open classrooms; that was a deal breaker because it appeared chaotic and noisy. Another school had punitive teachers—one called a child a "buffoon" with me, a visitor, in the back of the room! A third school required too many worksheets, which would have been difficult and frustrating for Zachary. The last school's teachers were very inconsistent between first and second grade; the second grade teacher was rude and disorganized, while the first grade teacher was warm and supportive. The other schools had an equal number of good things and negative things, resulting in a neutral or uninspiring presentation.

The small school we settled on had a huge computer room and seemed open to accommodations. While I was observing, the teachers were sweet and kind. They came to the back of the room and introduced me to the classes, they asked if I had any questions, and they smiled a lot even at the kids who needed them to come over again and again. In one classroom, the class groaned when a child missed a question on a group activity. I was in tears because the teacher stepped right in and by emitting incredible warmth and presence commanded the class to honor his and all errors as a step toward learning. The resource teacher had a beaming smile. The secretaries chatted with me and remembered my name and Zac's name just from my phone calls.

The principal took time with me, listened to our story, and suggested teachers he thought would be a good fit for Zac. He told me something that I will never forget and always love him for: "We will have to count on you to continue to enrich his mind as you clearly have done so far. What we can do at this school, and do quite well I think, is provide him a social environment in which he can develop friends, learn to belong, and develop a solid sense of self-worth. If you understand that in the beginning, you'll be very satisfied with this school. Otherwise, school will always be a source of disappointment to your family." The sincerity of his words pulled me to him while his lack of pretense about his school gave me a clearing into which I could move our family. It gave me the opening to decide, for us to decide as a family, what we wanted from a school for our son. Given our experience at the last school, what we wanted was for Zachary to love to learn again and to have friends. He was, fortunately, smart enough to acquire all the information he needed; it was his heart and soul we needed to help grow. We couldn't provide that at home. He needed to learn it in a community of other friends and authorities. This was the school for my son.

A few days later, Zac and I visited the new school so he'd have a picture of it in his head over the summer. He was so anxious, he actually hid behind my legs, something he had never done in his life. This showed me how terrified he was of school and how truly devastating his previous experiences had been.

We walked around the school and coincidentally ran into the principal. He looked at Zac's name tag and said, "Are you Zac? Are you thinking about coming to our school next year?" to which Zac mumbled "Maybe." Then this man said, "Have you seen our computer room? We're really proud of it and I know you'll like it. Come on, I'll show it to you."

I stood quietly and still. My son walked away hand in hand with an adult he had never met and had every reason to fear because of his associations with the principal from the other school. I was again touched by this man and his compassion for a child he did not yet know.

Zachary took this initial feeling of welcome with him and held on to it throughout the summer. He told anybody who asked him about his new school that they had a computer room with "over fifty computers and they're getting more this summer! The principal gave me a private tour!"

On the day before school started, the principal arranged for Zachary to come in and meet his teacher. Normally, the class list was posted at four in the afternoon the day before school without exception. He made this accommodation for Zac because of his difficulty with new situations and his negative history with school. When we arrived, we explored the room with the teacher as our guide. She spent about an hour pointing out some of her favorite books and telling Zachary he could read any of them in the upcoming year. His eyes widened at that. She asked Zachary if he'd be the computer monitor for the first week, saying, "It would really help me out if you could do that." She sat with him at the computer and showed him the programs, explained all the rules, and left him to play for a while. When school started, he had a job and a role in the classroom, and a place in which he felt competent.

For the first two weeks, Zac did really well, coming home each day and saying school was great. Then one day when I took him to school, he was so anxious and fearful he didn't want to go. I sat with him outside the school, and we talked as the bells rang and the playground cleared of children. I was late for work, but I knew if I sent him to school feeling so anxious, I'd get a call to come get him within the hour. Zac finally said, "It's been a long time since I got sent to the office and I'm afraid it's going to happen today. I don't know what I do that gets me sent there, so I might do it today." This is typical of the anxiety children with NLD feel because they don't know how to read nonverbal social cues. They can't gather comforting feedback from the individuals in their environment and have no way of knowing how they're doing.

I took Zac to the principal, and he reassured him that only good news from his teacher about how things were going had been received and that there was no reason to see him in the office that day. He told me later that he would look for ways to have Zachary come to the office for positive reasons to help dispel the fear. A week later the second graders went to the office to read to the principal. When Zac told me about it, he stood beside me at the table. His face looked sad. He dropped his chin, looked down at the floor and said, "Mom, I got sent to the principal's office today. Actually, we all did, the whole class of second graders." I was imagining a teacher so angry she marched an entire class to the office. Then Zac broke into a smile and said, "We all read to him!" The school had handled Zac's fear really well.

At the end of the year, some of Zac's fears returned. He was cranky and many of his old, inappropriate coping behaviors returned. I talked with the teacher. She, too, was seeing his relapse and assured me she was still giving him extra time to complete assignments, accepting whatever he got done, and not insisting on completion. She said it made her a little sad to hear him saying he couldn't wait for school to be over when the other kids talked about missing each other or missing parts of school. When I talked with Zachary about it, I started with, "You know, at the end of the school year when the schedules change—"

He burst into tears and said, "Everything's changing! Lots of things are different! They're changing all the rules!" He sobbed for about 20 minutes. I said, "When things end that we've enjoyed, we can have some really big emotions and sometimes they're so big and there's so many of them we don't know what they all are, they're just big."

The rest of the evening was fragile and volatile and full of lots of hugs and soothing. Zachary said, "I haven't been to the office all year. I'll bet I get sent this week!" I reminded him that he could talk with his teacher, and that the antidote for big feelings is a tight hug. We talked about who at school he could go to and ask for a tight hug. It didn't seem like enough, but at least he could have some ownership and control of his feelings.

The next day, he came home with a huge smile. When I asked how the day was, he said, "Great. The feeling I have, Mom, is happy. Did you see my smile? I feel happy." I think that was the first time he identified a feeling on his own. The rest of the week was like that, a happy week.

The teacher talked with me at the end of the school year. She assured me she would see to it that Zachary was placed with a teacher next year who would be structured and open to learning about his unique needs. She made an agreement with Zachary that her room would be available at any time for him to use as a respite. What she told him was, "I will need a lot of help next year and I've learned to count on you as a good helper. I will be looking for you to come by whenever you want next year. Just because you'll be in the third grade doesn't mean you can't come back to my classroom, okay?"

The resource teacher and I met to set new goals on the Individualized Educational Program (IEP). In second grade, Zachary met and surpassed all his IEP goals, but in the third grade the writing requirements would escalate, and the teachers were aware they would need to help him through this change. Additionally, the resource teacher would help Zac learn the rules of four square, the game of choice at recess. That way, he could choose to join a peer game when he wanted and would know the rules of play. I thought that goal was brilliant. It demonstrated for me, again, that this team of teachers really understood his needs and were looking ahead to design a program that would best support him as he developed.

On the last day of school, Zachary made cards and necklaces for some of the staff. He gave them to the principal, the resource teacher, the social studies teacher, and his teacher. One person he didn't want to forget to make a card for was the secretary. When he handed it to her, she asked if she could give him a hug or if he was too big for that now. He said she could give him "a little one." That school, that group of caring, charismatic adults, saved a life in one year.

Assessing the School

While the right school can make a world of positive difference, the wrong school can make the symptoms of NLD more severe, create anxiety and depression, and exacerbate inappropriate coping behaviors. How do you know if your child's school is right for him? There is not a national clearinghouse of information regarding schools that offer a good fit for children with NLD. Contacting an educational consultant or certified educational planner or networking via parent groups can be valuable. Once we discovered Zac's NLD, we realized that he had been telling us for months that he was afraid and anxious at school. In retrospect, we understood that what he'd been trying to communicate was much more serious than just not liking school. If we had known how to listen, we would have understood he was also telling us he didn't know how to behave, how to have a good day, or how to succeed. Our children teach us how to listen, some parents are better students than others.

Listen when your child talks about school. Learn as much as you can about what stresses her at school and is in the way of her success. Children with NLD often don't have the skills to identify or explain their feelings. If you listen closely, you may be able to help your child zero in on the source of her anxiety in the classroom. Does the teacher use clear, logical explanations? Does the teacher explain her rules? Can her teacher help her identify the rules that are invisible?

Does your child grow anxious at night when there is school the next day? Do most of his comments focus on academic failures and fears? This might mean that the teacher's expectations are not explicitly stated, or it might mean that accommodations for your child's learning style need to be put in place. Are his fears about other students who taunt him or about his lack of friends? It may be that the school does not know he is being bullied. They may need to be educated about his vulnerability. Does he talk about friends at school? Does your child seem afraid of the school environment?

If your child is not succeeding in school, it may be that with therapy and appropriate accommodations, his current school can work for him. But this isn't always the case. Many children with NLD do change schools several times. Sometimes a school or an individual teacher is unable to accommodate his needs. Sometimes a child needs to go where he doesn't have a history, where he can have a fresh set of peers who will not judge him by his previous behaviors. When the child is working on improving a behavior, he needs people around him who can forgive him when he accidentally slips up.

Every school, and every classroom, has its own individual culture. Finding one that's right for your child usually requires some intensive research. It's important to visit the schools, talk to the teachers and principals, and sit in on the classroom for a morning to get a clear sense of how that school works on a daily basis. Children with NLD do best in structured classrooms with predictable schedules and routines. But structure does not mean rigidity. The best schools for children with NLD will be warm, caring, and flexible about accommodating your child's learning style.

The bottom line for all kids is a school that meets their needs. Sometimes this will be a public school, sometimes a private one, and sometimes home schooling will be the best choice. Whatever choice you make for your child, remember, you do not have to accept an inadequate situation. If your child's needs are not being met, try to work with the school to make changes. If that doesn't work, go elsewhere. Too often I hear of parents who accept a poor placement because they believe the school authorities when they say, "This is the best we can offer." Parents can say, "Your best is nowhere near good enough."

Appropriate Schools

Appropriate schools are open to accommodations. Talk to the principals and teachers about your child's needs. Although by law every school has to accommodate a child's learning disorder, some schools will happily work with you to come up with creative solutions, while others will resist changes.

Appropriate Teachers

Appropriate teachers appear friendly and welcoming and smile frequently. I was impressed by one school that had posters everywhere that said "Practice Random Acts of Kindness" and then listed concrete examples. Children's names were listed throughout the room with positive remarks alongside them. VIP posters of individual children were everywhere.

Find out whether or not your child would have the same teacher all year. If the school is planning any major changes in either the physical plant or the curriculum within the next three years, that might be a school to avoid. Change is very difficult for children with NLD. Once they have learned the layout of a school and its instructional modes, it can be very stressful for them to have to start over from scratch.

A good way to learn more is to drop in when the teacher isn't expecting your visit. Is she flustered or does she smile, welcome you, and invite you to observe? Is she kind to children who appear to need more of her time? Is the school clean? Can you find your way around easily? (If you can't, chances are your child *really* can't.) What kind of signs and messages decorate the walls?

Do the teachers use a lot of worksheets? Because of their difficulties with handwriting and written expression, if the teacher always expects a child to demonstrate knowledge through writing, a child with NLD will find this very difficult and frustrating. Can a child demonstrate her knowledge orally? Can she tape record her responses or tell them to a teacher?

Classrooms

Look for classrooms that are neat and orderly, but kid-friendly, with things like soft pillows in the reading area, stamps in the writing area, computers in each room. If the desks are positioned to encourage children to help each other, that's a good sign that the school encourages social interaction. When you sit in on a class, notice whether the children appear comfortable. Do they raise their hands easily? Are they all participating?

Does the room have a schedule of the daily events posted for all children to see? That can be very helpful for children with NLD who need structures and routines to help them anticipate what change is coming next.

Do the children have their own desks or cubbies? Will they remain the same throughout the year? Zac used to have meltdowns every time his cubby was moved because he couldn't figure out where to put his coat or find his lunch. Children who have visual-spatial organizational deficits will be baffled and anxious if the classroom is rearranged.

It can be helpful if the school has a room the child can go to for some downtime. Does the school have a library, computer room, or guided learning center where he can go? Are the classroom teachers willing to let your child be excused when he needs a break?

Social

Are social interactions considered a priority? Does the school foster peer relations? Children with NLD need to be able to practice their social skills in a supportive environment. If the classroom discourages social interaction, they won't get a chance to practice. Children with NLD also need consistency. Will your child's classmates and peer group be the same throughout the year, or does the school value changing peers? For example, will your child have the same reading buddy all year or will they change every month? Will she be with the same desk mates or will they change?

Discipline

How does the school handle discipline? Are interventions given in a positive, constructive manner, or are they negative and belittling? It's really important for children with NLD to have rules that are clear, explicitly stated, and fair. If a child is being disciplined, he needs a clear explanation of the rule that was broken. Many of Zac's difficulties in his kindergarten came from his having no idea why he was being punished. "You can come back to the group when you can behave" is vague and confusing. "The rule is we don't interrupt each other," is specific and helpful.

When you visit a school, take time to talk to the resource teacher. How is the resource room utilized? Is there one kid in the room? Are there several? Are kids isolated and left alone working on worksheets and busywork, or are they actively engaged in a learning process? What do their faces look like? Do they look tortured and sad, or busy and engaged? Is the room pleasant and conducive to good work, or is it a dark closet?

Sometimes the search for the right school can be hard. When the neighborhood public school can work for your child, that's ideal, because then his classmates will be neighbors and playmates. But if the local school isn't working, start looking at other public schools. There's a lot to be said for them, but they don't always work, and at that point, you may want to explore what private schools offer.

Consider Home Schooling

Some parents of children with NLD choose to home school their kids. Home schooling for children with NLD has the advantage of built-in accommodations: You know your child's learning style and you can build your instruction around his needs. Some children with NLD really need home schooling. A significant disadvantage is that it provides children with NLD with very little practice in social skills, one of their deficits. If you choose to home school your child, it's important to compensate by setting up other situations where your child can make friends and play with kids outside of the family setting.

Conquer Homework

The elementary school curriculum has changed a great deal over the past thirty years. What used to be a first grade curriculum has been pushed down to kindergarten and even pre-K and preschool classrooms. Even though developmentally kids are not ready to write until the second grade, they're now expected to write their names in kindergarten. Homework is now the norm for elementary school. Schools have suggested standards for how much homework a child should have. In first or second grade, it's usually about ten minutes a night, in third, it's usually no more than 20 minutes a night, and in fourth it's supposed to be 30. However, when teachers assign homework, they often have unrealistic expectations of how much time the assignment will require. This has a special impact on children with NLD, who typically have difficulties with handwriting and with completion. Ten minutes of homework for them can easily become two hours, which for a six- or seven-year-old, is an unreasonable expectation.

When a teacher plans a lesson and homework, of course she'll use teaching methods that work for the majority of children. But children with NLD learn differently from the way most of the kids in their classrooms learn. Once children with NLD learn something, they know it, and repetition doesn't help them remember. Rather, repetition can be a source of frustration, especially if the child is required to use a lot of handwriting.

If your child's teacher is willing, it's very helpful to work with her to restructure homework assignments to make them useful and meaningful for your child. That's why it's so important to have a teacher who is open to accommodations. If you've developed a rapport with the teacher and shown that you're supportive and want to collaborate with her, it can be very successful.

Using the materials provided by the Gifted Association, we've been able to explain to Zac's teachers the unique needs of his learning style and develop alternative programs that help him learn on his level. We worked with Zachary's teacher to accommodate his spelling assignments, using a process called "collapsing the curriculum." On Tuesday, Zac takes the test normally given on Friday. Then, during the week, he may have to find ten words in his reading he is unfamiliar with, look up the definitions, and be able to spell them on Friday.

It's a good idea to include in the child's IEP, "Child will be graded on quality and not quantity of the work produced." Children with NLD can as easily master a math concept by doing five math problems as by doing 25. In fact, the effort put forth in the handwriting required for 25 problems is likely to be so tiring to these kids that the goal of mastering a math concept gets lost in the process of filling out a worksheet.

When Zac has put forth his best effort for 45 minutes and he's not done, I don't see the value in his working past the point of success. If he is tired and ten more problems remain on the math homework, I write an explanatory note to the teacher. To Zac I'll say, "You've done a good job. The goal of homework is for you to understand the concept and to build the habit of working on independent assignments. You've met that goal. The number you got done is secondary. Next time, you'll be able to complete them all, I'll bet." This way, the focus is on the child and his actual learning and not some arbitrary product, like a worksheet.

We came to understand that handwriting is a tool, not a process in itself. If a child is learning to write, then writing is not a tool for them yet. We can't ask a person to both learn a tool and use it. The same is true for reading. Reading is a tool, we use it to get information as well as enjoyment. If we ask a person who is learning how to read to read directions, they will likely be unable to both read and follow the directions within a time constraint. Writing is only a tool when a child has learned to automatically form letters and move a pencil across the page, otherwise, it's a process being learned and not a useful method to communicate ideas.

I'd recommend you insist on a workshop for the school staff to educate them about NLD. Find ways to support the teachers. They're going to need to provide extra time and efforts on behalf of your child. They're your child's best chance for success in the school environment. Look for ways to make their load lighter by volunteering in the classroom or offering to buy extra supplies for the classroom. Your attitude makes a difference both in modeling for your child and allowing the teacher to have the time and energy available to support your child.

Overcome Setbacks

Our story of finding a school for Zac's second grade year was a dream come true. That school continued to be a godsend through the third grade. Zac's third grade teacher, Mrs. Long, was a beautiful, calm and kind woman. She looked and acted like those teachers in storybooks that we all long for. She allowed Zac to stand at his desk to do his work, to take breaks to get a drink when he needed one. She was open to any and all accommodations for him. She went to a workshop on supporting advanced readers and developed a special book-bag program that was available for all children but required for Zac. Mrs. Long also had mornings when the kids could bring in their sleeping bags and breakfasts and read. She made field trips safe and comforting for our Zac. When Zac speaks of her, he always smiles and says, "She is the best teacher in the world."

Eventually we met up with a teacher who was a very bad fit for Zac. My son regressed to being depressed, sick, and begging to stay home from school. She seemed indifferent to our repeated attempts to help

Zac. When he began to tell me his plans for leaving the school, hiding in bushes until I came to get him, and opening the power box to shut down power as a distraction for him to escape, it was obvious that we needed to step in and protect our child.

We had several IEP meetings to try to teach his teacher about NLD and to explain Zac's accommodations. She was righteous and unmoving and refused to accommodate Zac's special needs and learning style. Each time she dug her heels in further and pressured Zac emotionally with more teasing, yelling, and humiliation. We worked with the principal to set up an independent study program to get our son out of this woman's class, but she blocked it. We began the process of moving Zac to another school, this time at mid-year. It was a horrible time for us all. Zac had to leave his friends and his community. He had to endure the trauma of this teacher single-handedly stripping him of much of the positive sense of self the two teachers before her had helped him build. She yelled and belittled and berated him and is, in my opinion, a disgrace to the teaching profession.

Again using my school checklist, I went off in search of a new school for him. I wrote a letter to the district and informed them I had removed my son from his current school due to noncompliance with his IEP and emotional abuse from his teacher.

Some of the parents we were friends with felt we were overreacting, but we knew it was unacceptable to allow our son to feel so tortured by a teacher. I went to several schools, some intolerable, some okay, and a couple that would have been acceptable. Then I found one that made me feel so comfortable that I had to fight back tears. I again saw teachers who were smiling and students who were friendly and comfortable in their classrooms. I observed several classrooms. The teacher the principal recommended was kind and supportive. He clearly did not change anything about his style for the parent in the back of the room. He was open to accommodations. He was interested in a new student. I felt my muscles relax and my eyes well with tears, my physical response to finding safety for my child.

Zac started his new school a couple of weeks later. He and I went to the school at lunchtime to check things out. *Each* one of the students came up in turn and introduced themselves to Zac! I was impressed. The teacher, Mr. Spruce, set Zac up with a buddy to show him around and help him adjust. Mr. Spruce assimilated our son into the class as if he'd been there all along. Zac began to smile, look forward to school, and feel as if he belonged within a couple of weeks. It was a miracle. It was a good fit. Zac feels it was a good and appropriate move and sent him the message that staying in an abusive situation is unacceptable, even when it's familiar and convenient. Moving away from abuse is always better than staying.

Zac has now moved on to fifth grade. His teacher, Mr. Kappa, is a dream. He is quiet, kind, supportive, and organized. He has Happy Dwarf and Grumpy Dwarf dolls in his class, and as Zac says, "Usually Happy's there, but if Mr. Kappa hasn't had enough sleep or has had a bad day, Grumpy is out and we know to calm down or be extra quiet." Mr. Kappa gives out a weekly report on assignments not turned in. This is his classroom standard, not an accommodation for us, and it helps Zac a great deal.

Even if the school is a good fit, your child's life there won't be perfect. Every school has problems. But what makes a school a good fit is that the staff works to solve the problems instead of expecting your child to live with a bad situation.

Trampling the Grass

I heard a story the other day that sums up how *not* to participate in an IEP team meeting.

If two elephants fight over who gets to eat the grass, they stomp around, charge each other, and trample the grass. This goes on for a long time until eventually one of the elephants gets so tired it gives up and goes away. The other elephant is the "winner," but now the grass is inedible.

Sometimes parents and IEP teams can square off and trample the grass. The child may have services written into an IEP, but the team dreads having the child around and provides services only grudgingly, if at all. What gets trampled is the child's social and emotional well-being.

I know of a current case of a child who has NLD. The parent has worked for several years to get services for him. Recently, she brought in an advocate to help her, and the principal took this very personally. He actually screamed at the mother and told her she was making her child crazy and abusing him. He screamed that she was a horrible mother and should be ashamed of herself. He further said this child would never, *ever* get an IEP as long as he, the principal, was in the district. If you ask me, that's a revved-up bull elephant.

Thirteen

The Individual Educational Program (IEP)

MANY books and workshops on IEPs are available. This chapter is an overview to get you started and the resource section of this book will give you access to specific details.

When your child is diagnosed with NLD, his school may set up an Individual Educational Program (IEP). Under the federal Individual Disability Educational Act (IDEA), all public schools are required to implement an IEP for any child with identified special needs. Although the IDEA provides the guidelines for defining a special need, each state interprets the guidelines, so the definition of special need may vary from state to state and district to district and you will need to contact your state's education department. The school decides whether or not your child meets the definition of special need. But this can be a gray area. If the school says your child does not qualify, and you can prove that the federal law would say he does, that's where you will have some leverage. In 1997 the federal government reinterpreted the IDEA, providing broader guidelines for hundreds of issues. Many schools had interpreted the law so narrowly that they excluded a lot of children who needed services.

An IEP is a legal contract between you and the school and is a binding, legal document. Because it falls under federal jurisdiction, it supersedes any local or state law. If an IEP says the school will provide a state-of-the art computerized wheelchair, by law they have to provide it. How and where they get the money is irrelevant. Expenses and legal issues are why schools are very careful about what appears on an IEP, and why parents need to make sure that the IEP effectively addresses their child's needs.

IEP Teams

Each child's IEP includes a team that works together to oversee her progress and consists of the child's classroom teacher, the school's resource teacher, the school principal, the child's parents, and a representative of the school district, usually the program specialist, whose responsibility is to keep in mind the district's resource and budget restrictions. The district representative moderates the meetings.

Though not officially part of the team, the parents may bring other people to IEP meetings such as a friend or family member who helps them stay emotionally grounded. Some bring educational consultants, the child's private therapists, other experts, and lawyers. IEP meetings can get cumbersome and confrontational. I've been to IEP meetings with as many 20 people. In most situations, the IEP team is a core group of people who are directly involved with your child, who give their time and energy solely to support him. The teachers, principals, and the district representatives don't get paid extra to go to IEP meetings, so they all have an incentive to come to a consensus and make meetings work. However, there are some people in the world who enjoy confrontation, and when you are stuck in a meeting with one, it is very frustrating. Others want to use the forum to talk and tell you how great they are, but they aren't helpful to your child. I strongly advise you get those people off your IEP team. With the exception of the principal and the teacher, you can choose the team members, so it doesn't hurt to inquire about people's reputations or to ask the district for alternative representatives.

Often, professionals associated with IEPs will use boilerplates, goals that are generic and removed from day-to-day school life. Parents need to make sure the language on the IEP is clear enough that their child can understand and know what is being worked on for that year. I think it's important to let the team know what you value. Then the team can work more effectively with your child.

The Parts of an IEP

The written IEP consists of three sections, called Form A, Form B, and Form C.

Form A contains basic information—name, address, date of birth, school, team members, a summary ("Zac was diagnosed with NLD, he moved to a new school, an IEP team was called, he has these strengths and these weaknesses"), and the parents' long-term goal for their child. This might be something like "to be independent in all aspects," or "to be prepared for college." The long-term goal is the ideal outcome that drives the annual goals. If your long-term goal is for your child to go to college, then your annual goals will be different than if your long-term goal is for your child to graduate high school and work in a sheltered workshop.

Form B identifies the annual goals for the school year. The annual goals are meant to move the child toward the long-term goal. An IEP will usually address goals in five or six categories, and each category will have its own page, labeled Form B-1, B-2, etc. For example, B-1 will address social skills, B-2 will address written expression, B-3 will address handwriting, B-4 might address mathematical abilities, and B-5 might address behaviors. Then under each category will appear the specific goals.

Any goal on your child's IEP must be relevant, understandable, measurable, behavioral (meaning you can observe the behavior), and achievable. (RUMBA is the acronym used to help remember those criteria.) Too often what often happens is people on the IEP teams write vague goals that are not measurable: "Jordan will improve handwriting by the end of the year." Vague goals do not help your child. "Improve" is far too general a goal. If at the beginning of the year, Jordan can make none of his letters, and at the end of the year, he can make an A, the school can argue his handwriting has improved, his goal has been met, and they're off the hook. A goal for an IEP needs to be measurable: "By the end of the year, Jordan will be able to make all his letters using cursive, both capitals and smalls, and write one legible sentence independently and within a time period similar to his peers."

It's also very helpful if the goal is inclusive. For example, if under handwriting one goal is that the child will be able to form his letters, and another is that the child will be able to write three sentences legibly without assistance, you don't need both of those goals, just the one that measures three sentences as being able to write three sentences requires the appropriate letter formations. This makes the IEP a tight, effective tool.

One of Zac's areas to address was organization. His annual goal stated, "Zac will be able to turn in 80 percent of his assignments on time, independently." Then there were some short-term goals to help him meet the annual goal, such as "Zac will use an organizer or planner, and he will write down his daily assignments with 100 percent accuracy with teacher review daily." His classroom teacher and the resource teacher shared the responsibility for that, so if the teacher was not able to get to it every day, the resource teacher stepped in.

In addition to stating the goal, each Form B will state who is responsible for addressing that goal—teacher, resource teacher, occupational therapist, etc. Whoever is responsible for helping the child meet that goal is free to come up with her own plan, which is not part of the IEP document. If a therapist is going to work on fine motor skills, she can do it by having the child play with marbles or by having him hold a pencil in his hand. It's up to the therapist's professional discretion how she chooses to treat the child to meet the goal.

Because the IEP is a contract, the school must make sure the child meets his annual goals. If he doesn't, there had better be a darn good reason, such as the family moved, or the child was sick so much, or the child was removed from school. Other than these obvious disruptions in the child's school life, there is no reason why the goals should not be met. If a child moves from school to school, the IEP and its annual goals move with him. By law, parents of children with special needs must be given an update against the IEP whenever the school does its regular evaluations for all children. My son's school has a trimester system for grade cards to come out, so I get notified three times a year. (Not all schools are aware of this change, but by law, they are supposed to be.)

Form C, the third part of the IEP, lists accommodations for the child. Accommodations differ from the IEP goals and are supports that assist the child in meeting her goals. Accommodations might be "There will be computers available in the classroom for the child to use," or "She will be able to get a drink of water when she needs to," or "She will be

allowed to do her work standing up." Accommodations listed on the
IEP are legally binding. If the school promises the child a computer, it
has to provide the computer. If one of the child's accommodations is that
she will never be denied recess, no teacher in the school may ever keep
the child in at recess.

Some IEPs also include an addendum, a list of suggestions that the
parents and the child's previous teachers have found helpful. On
Zachary's IEP, his addendum reads, "If my son falls, even if he just says
'ouch,' please send him to the school nurse because 'ouch' for him
means he's bleeding." The addendum's suggestions are not legally binding agreements. You need enough people on the team to agree that the
accommodation would be reasonable and useful and something the
team can actually implement. "My child will be able to chew gum," will
not make it onto the Form C, because the team knows that some teachers will absolutely refuse to allow that. But perhaps, "my child can have
something for his mouth during seated work" would be allowed.

Annual Evaluations occur each year when the team meets to evaluate
the child's progress against his goals for the previous year, and to identify which areas would be helpful to address the next year. Then they
identify who on the team will be in charge of that goal.

The classroom teacher might say, "I think it's reasonable of us to start
expecting Zac to complete his work. Right now, none of it is complete,
so by the end of next year, I think he would be able to complete it about
half the time." Then everyone on the team will agree that that's a reasonable goal, or that it's not.

Guidelines for Effective IEPs

An effective IEP will have a manageable number of goals that are specific, inclusive, and measurable. I see IEPs that are up to 50 pages, which
is absurd. No teacher or therapist can meet that many goals in a year,
making the IEP unenforceable and useless. I can understand why parents
would be tempted to do that, but it's not effective. The real purpose and
value of an IEP is to make sure a child is progressing toward her long-
term goal. That's what you want to know. The more concise her IEP, the

better you can monitor her progress. That's why it's better to have smaller IEPs and more concrete goals.

When choosing your annual goals, I think it's important to keep in mind your child's feelings of competency, confidence, and optimism. This will help keep the goals, strategies, and interventions in perspective. The goals you choose need to be ones that help your child grow without undermining his sense of confidence. Goals that are too easy or too difficult are equally inappropriate.

It's easy and seductive to make meeting the annual goal your focus. But your child's happiness and optimism are more important. Keep your focus on your child as a person rather than on the goal as a product. For example, at the beginning of the school year, Zac never, ever remembered to turn in his homework. While this is something I would like to change and absolutely could drive the school to accomplish this, I won't because that's not the style I want for my son's learning. Instead, I'd like him to turn in his homework most of the time and own the progress he's made. I'd like to help him understand why it's important to turn in his homework and to have him internalize the motivation and responsibility. From there, he'll have the skill and a greater sense of self-worth. That's more important, I think, than always getting a check in the teacher's grade book for completing an assignment. I think it's unreasonable if a parent or a teacher expects 100 percent success. I'm a successful person by my own standards, but I don't do anything 100 percent perfectly 100 percent of the time. Turning in assignments 80 percent of the time and having a 24-hour grace period for when he doesn't was a reasonable goal that we all felt Zac could achieve within one year.

Using an Educational Consultant

How the IEP is written can make a big difference in how it is established and enforced, and many parents will hire an educational consultant to advocate for them. Paying for a consultant to make sure that the child gets services, that the goals on the IEP are relevant, understandable, measurable, behavioral, and achievable, and that the accommodations meet the child's needs, is money well spent. If the educational consultant can make sure the IEP does what it's supposed to do, it can make a huge difference to your child—emotionally as well as academically. Program specialists, who are usually special ed teachers who have moved into administration, sometimes can fulfill that role if they're really good at their jobs. Otherwise, you may need to check with local parent support groups, resource teachers, or your yellow pages to hire a consultant.

Explaining the IEP to Your Child

We explained Zac's IEP to him by saying, "A group of people who understand your learning style get together once a year and talk about what will help you develop your brain and your body. That's called the IEP team. Not all kids have an IEP, but you have one. We have come up with a list of things for you to work on and a list of things that will help you learn, like if you have extra time, or you can turn in your homework late, or doing your work standing up, or helping yourself to a drink from the fountain at the back of the class without asking permission."

Zachary is really empowered by his IEP. He knows what's on his IEP; he understands that's what he's working on, and he understands who is helping him with each piece. When a substitute teacher is not adhering to his IEP, he knows it. When I see what my child and other kids have accomplished with their IEPs, it confirms the importance of telling your child about his diagnosis.

I recommend explaining the IEP to your child and making sure he knows what's on it. You can explain, "This is what your accommodations are, and if they are not happening at school, let me know." It is helpful and empowering for these kids to understand their learning style and their needs.

When the IEP team decides the child is old enough, he or she is eligible to come to the IEP meeting. Many middle school or high school students will come to their IEP meetings and make suggestions, such as "This year I want to work on being able to write five pages without help. I can do two now, but the rest of my class can write five and that really bugs me. Is that something you all can help me with this year?" That's a child who is really using the power of the team and a team that's really working.

Enforcement of the IEP

The parent's role is to make sure the IEP is enforced. If your child's report says "no progress," you have the right to call a meeting and ask, "Why is there no progress on this goal?" If there is a problem with a therapist, an accommodation, or any other issue, your child needs it to be solved immediately, so be persistent. At the end of the year, you have to verify whether or not your child's annual goals were met. I've seen people on an IEP team write "goal met" when the parents and I would agree it hadn't been met. In one case, the goal was "Jane will identify two to three friends in her classroom." Jane had no friends—no one to play with, no one to come to her birthday party—but the resource teacher wrote "goal met." She justified this with, "I asked her if she could identify anyone, and she named three kids in the class that she knew." If this happens, you need to be vigilant.

On the other hand, when those working with your child are not good people, or when they are not doing their best, that's when you have the power of the law behind you to insist, "You *will* meet this goal. Hire a new teacher if you have to. Bring in an outside therapist if you have to, because your therapist is inadequate or quit. Do whatever it takes because you are obligated to meet this goal."

Resolving Conflicts

When there is outright disagreement about any aspect of the IEP, the negotiation process can go on and on with dozens of meetings until a consensus can be reached. If a consensus can't be reached at the school level, the parents can ask for the school district's program specialist to step in. If she can't resolve the issue, then it will go to the district's director of special education and become a much more complicated process, depending on the size of the school district.

To find out who these people are in your area, call your school district's office and ask to speak to the special education department. Explain your problem and ask who can help you with it. You can be directed to your district's program specialist or a person with a similar job description. That's the person who mediates between you and the school. Then if that mediation is not effective, you go to your state's department of education, ask for the special education division, and present your problem. They will have someone whose role is to help you. That's how you can demand services from a school that's not supporting your child. These are the people who are fair and objective and can mediate to get your child services.

When parents are obnoxious, no one wants to help them. Some parents get a reputation for being whiners or for fighting everything to the detriment of their child. Then the school system pulls in its lawyers and it can get ugly. But when parents are genuinely concerned and persistent, there will be people on the team who support them all the way. Most of the time a program specialist or a special ed director will say, "Look, this is a reasonable parent who just insists that her child needs support, so let's get an occupational therapist to do an evaluation, and let me know if she sees something that we've missed." Sometimes you get a program specialist who's been told, "You will spend no more money on occupational therapy in our district." Then her hands are tied. But those people tend to have ways of helping parents get around the system. She might say, "I'm not the final say," meaning you can go over her head and call the state education department.

If no agreement can be made, the case goes to a *Fair Hearing*, a trial where a judge steps in and makes a legally binding decision. The judge will hear evidence from the parents and from the school district and will say, "This is a reasonable request by the parents, and you need to provide it," or, "You're asking the school for unreasonable accommodations, and they are not legally obligated to provide them." When the process goes as far as that, it can get rather ugly.

The truth is, if you make a big enough stink, you'll probably get results. It's easier for a school to provide $500 of services for your child than it is for them to pay for Fair Hearing Court, which may cost them $4,000. So go all the way to the state, and if you don't get satisfaction, get a lawyer who knows the IDEA, because federal law trumps everything else.

The reverse doesn't happen very often, but some schools are starting to take the parents to Fair Hearing Court because they are tired of the parents' demands or resistance. For example, the school might argue to the judge, "We said the child should be in the special ed classroom, and the parents refused," or "We said we'd provide our school-based therapist, but the parent has refused that and has demanded services from an outside therapist." If the judge ruled against the parents, they would have to repay the school for the services provided.

The IEP is a contract, and whatever is written on it must, by law, be provided for by the school through its own resources. If the school does not provide what it said it would, it must reimburse the parents for providing it out of their own pockets when they secure services on their own. That's another issue that gets taken to Fair Hearing Court: "You said you would provide OT services, but the OT never came, so we provided private OT services. We provided the services ourselves, and now you need to reimburse us."

For example, I know of someone who had speech therapy every year, and he never met his annual goals. I went over his IEP with the mom and explained, "These three goals are all saying the same thing: 'At the end of the year he will understand how to hold his mouth to make the L sound.' Will you be happy if at the end of next year that's all he can do?"

She said, "No, he can do that right now."

"That's right. So you have three goals here and they all say that's what he'll achieve by next year. He's in third grade and he's been in speech therapy for three years. Is that good enough for your child?" She was furious. She'd never understood that his annual goals were useless because they were unmeasurable and vague.

I helped her write a goal that met the RUMBA criteria. Midway through the year, the child still was making no progress, so she took him to a private therapist. Then the school therapist said, "Well, if he's seeing a private therapist, then he really doesn't need to see me, so I'll just follow his progress." The parent said, "Okay," thinking to herself, "You're not helping anyway." The child made good progress with the private therapist, the school-based therapist stopped working with him at all (not the agreement), and then she quit midyear. The parent continued with the private therapist, and the child met his goals by the end of the year.

Then the parent was sent a form by the district that said, "Please sign here saying that you chose to do private therapy and that you understand that the school-based therapist was not available." I told her, "Don't sign it. Instead write to them and say 'I had to provide private therapy because the school-based therapist was not made available to us through the school as per the IEP and where do I go to ask for reimbursement?' " She did that, and they wrote her a check, reimbursing her in full for the therapy she had paid for. Sometimes it's that simple; other times you have to go all the way to a Fair Hearing.

Special Issues for Children with NLD

Most of the time, IEPs work well to support the child. However, my experience has been that every time I go to a meeting with a new group of people, I have to convince them that Zachary really does need special services and accommodations. That understanding doesn't carry over from year to year, especially now that Zac has made such great progress.

Many kids with NLD are very smart and do their academic work pretty well, if not really well. Their needs tend to be subtle. If you're looking from the wrong perspective, their deficits are invisible because they are things like doing the work but not turning it in, not joining in on the playground, or not finishing papers. Teachers typically are trained to see these as behavioral problems. It's hard to convince them that these are in fact neurological deficits. Finishing a paper is not something Zac won't do; it is something he can't do. The law says if a child can't, we put in an accommodation. If the child won't, we put in a consequence.

Ironically, it can be especially difficult to get this point across to the best teachers. I have learned to say, "With you, my child doesn't need any of those accommodations, because you automatically incorporate them as part of your classroom. But we need to have them in writing for the teacher who won't do them automatically." I've also found that having the accommodations in writing has helped guide the teachers to know how to interpret Zac's behavior. Zac's second grade teacher said,

"You know, at the beginning of the year when I first read all that stuff you wrote down for me, I thought, 'Oh my gosh, this is just impossible.' But it turned out to be really helpful. I would encourage you to make sure every teacher reads that every year. Because when I told Zac something like, 'Please copy the sentences off the board,' and he would get frustrated and start kicking the chair, I knew I had asked him to do something he couldn't do. Without the information you gave me, I would have assumed that he was just being a little brat. It really helped me to understand him better." That teacher is a saint.

Every year when I have to explain this all over again, most teachers will say, "Okay, you've got some documentation here. I believe the experts, and I've talked with his teacher last year. I understand that with these accommodations Zachary is a successful child and without them he really struggles. So okay, no problem, let's put in the accommodations." All the great teachers Zac's had have said that. These were the teachers who made a huge difference in Zac's experience in the classroom because they were so accommodating. They allowed him to do his work standing up, to sharpen his pencils when he needed a break, to get a drink at any time, and they didn't hold it against him when he got frustrated if they asked him to do something he couldn't.

But it sometimes happens that we get a teacher who refuses to accept Zac's need for accommodations. Since then, I've learned to say in IEP meetings, "The reality is my son won't qualify for special services as long as you're providing these accommodations. But if you don't provide them, he does qualify, and let's look back at what happened in his primary classroom as an example of that. We need an IEP written for a teacher in the future that doesn't understand NLD or Zac to assure his continued success."

Zac looks pretty good in school because of his accommodations. He is allowed extra time, he can circle the right answer when the worksheet says, "Write the correct response using the choices in the above box," and things like that. But, if he has to go through a class without the accommodations in place, he starts looking more and more impaired.

When the child starts looking "typical," and then the teacher wants to remove the accommodations, that's equivalent to saying, "Well, we've given Mary glasses and she can see the board fine. So now we're going to take those glasses away because she obviously doesn't need them anymore to do math. See? Her math scores have risen to an A level, so it wouldn't be fair to let her use the glasses." We use this example each year when we have to explain why the accommodations are still needed, why a teacher who is a good fit is essential, and why a safe environment is so critical for our son.

The point of accommodations is to level the playing field and to support a child to perform at her level of ability, instead of constantly slogging through a disability.

It can be hard to hold this duality in mind: Here you have your really brilliant, precocious child who is doing well in school, but you also have a child who *can't* do well in school without all the things you do for him, like helping him with his homework, structuring his day, and taking him to therapy. Then you have a teacher tell you, "You're making this up. You're really endangering your child by taking him to all these therapies. He's going to think you think something is wrong with him." Then parents begin to wonder if maybe they *are* crazy. They decide to drop the accommodations, and the child crashes and burns. Then the parents have to get really tenacious and go through the whole cycle again.

Some teachers will tell you, "It's not neurological, it's just spoiled behavior." Or they will tell you, "Some parents want to call it a learning disorder when their kids are just lazy." Or, "I've never heard of NLD. It's just one more thing parents have come up with to excuse the child who won't do the work."

That's what they used to say about dyslexia, ADHD, and all other learning disabilities. The parents of those kids had to fight tooth and nail to get people to wake up, just as parents of children with NLD are fighting now. I tell parents all the time, "Whether you like it or not, you are a pioneer. There is no path to follow. There will be a lot of parents behind you walking the path you're making, but you are in the forefront, blazing the trail for others to follow. So keep going. Don't let the turkeys discourage you."

If Einstein Could Have

When Zac first started language therapy, it was summer. That made it pretty hard. I'd say, "Zac, it's time to get out of the pool and go to speech therapy," and he did not want to go. One day the speech therapist was trying to explain to Zac (without much success) that his therapy was important because he has really big, advanced information and he needs to learn to talk to other people. He didn't care, "Let them learn to talk to me. If they're dumb, I'll just talk to smart people. What's the problem here? I'm going swimming."

Zac likes Albert Einstein. While Einstein gets displayed as the poster boy for every new disorder from ADHD to Asperger's to NLD, he probably didn't have any of those and had aspects of many atypical learning styles. In Einstein's biography, there's a story about his teaching. This brilliant man was not a very effective teacher because no one knew what he was talking about. He'd walk in, he'd draw all these figures on the board, and sometimes he'd forget that there were a bunch of students sitting there. He'd keep going when the bell rang, he'd walk out before class was over, and he never could answer a question. His students said it was an honor to be around him, but they never knew what he was talking about.

So we were driving home after the speech therapist had tried to explain to Zac why he needed therapy, how he needed to build a bridge to others. I said to Zac, "Okay, you know Einstein was brilliant."

"Oh yeah, he was the smartest man in the world. He came up with the theory of relativity and changed our world."

"That's right," I said, "but you know what? He never could talk to people about it."

"Well, that's okay, he wrote it down."

"Well, actually, he had help writing it down, and when he tried to express the theory of relativity in mathematics, he couldn't do it. He found an old professor who helped him express it mathematically."

"Really?"

"Yeah, really. And when he was a teacher, no one knew what he was talking about. He probably taught for about twenty years, Zac, and how many students do you think he had in those twenty years?"

Zac said, "I don't know, thirty a year?"

"Okay, that's reasonable." We did the math for how many people that would be. "Those people who were in Einstein's class, do you think they were really smart, or were they just people off the street?"

"Oh, they would have been the really smart physicists. They'd have to be really good to be in the room with Einstein."

"Well, what do you think our world would be like if those 600 people who were the most brilliant people in physics had understood Einstein's theory enough that they built on it?"

Zac thought about it for a minute. "Oh my God! We could probably time-travel! We could teleport!"

"You know, I bet we could. But Einstein couldn't built the bridge."

"Okay," Zac said. "Okay, I see. I get it."

That was a turning point for Zac. Something came together for him that day that made him *want* to learn to talk to us mere mortals, and he took up the challenge.

Fourteen

Traveling the Maze of Professional Interventions

PROVIDING appropriate interventions for your child with NLD can be like a journey through a maze. You may have to start again and again. You make progress, then discover you have to backtrack. You may put in a lot of time exploring a path only to meet with a dead end. The journey requires determination and effort, and you can expect to feel some frustration along the way.

Get Professional Help

The child with NLD has a neurological dysfunction. Something in the brain is not working the way we typically expect it to, and that "something" causes observable behavioral deficits that affect the child's performance. We know that children with NLD lack connections among the various association sites of the brain. The growth of new neuronal connections can be stimulated by exposing the brain to tasks and activities in an ordered, sequential process. This is what various therapies provide to children with NLD.

Intervention will make it possible for the child to benefit from his everyday learning environment. Most parents and teachers are not able to identify the subtleties of visual-motor deficits, tactile defensiveness, decreased inferential ability, or problems with pragmatic speech.

The therapist provides targeted activities that facilitate a more normalized response to learning. This new learning is marked by the formation of new neuronal connections in the brain and results in more integrated or automatic behavior. To give an example from the realm of motor activities, when you learn to knit, at first you have to watch every little movement, and still you'll drop some of the stitches. But a person who has been knitting most of her life can knit a complicated sweater pattern, watch television, and do a crossword puzzle all at the same time. The neuronal connections from her brain to her muscles are so ingrained, or deeply grooved, that they are accessible with minimal attention. A child just learning to write her name will use tremendous mental concentration to perform the task, but most adults can sign their name in the dark, upside down, or in any other challenging situation. The task has become automatic or "integrated." Neurologically, the tracks have been etched into the brain. Therapy builds skills and teaches techniques that allow the child to develop these automatic responses to the demands of the environment.

Use Therapy As an On-Ramp to Life, Not As a Lifestyle

Therapy is an important aid to learning for children with NLD, but anytime a child is in a clinic or with a therapist, she is not in her role of child in a child's social setting. A good therapist will try to make therapy as child friendly as possible, but it is not the same as the time a child spends in school or playing with peers. Typical children do most of their learning in these natural settings, not in therapy clinics. If a child is not typical and is unable to learn in these environments, then we have to take her out and put her into a specialized environment—therapy—that will make learning possible and enable her to benefit from the natural setting when she reenters it. The goal of therapy, however, should be to get the child back into her natural role of child as soon as possible. Parents must remember that therapy is an adjunct, not a substitute, to learning in a natural setting.

Find and Evaluate Therapists

For a variety of reasons, you may choose to have private therapists to work with your child. Sometimes the therapists connected with the schools are not yet properly educated about NLD or may not be a good match for your child. They may not have the skills or time to identify symptoms and develop a plan of intervention, and ultimately a therapist is only as good as their interpretation of assessments and performance. In our case, the school occupational therapist thought the way to deal with children was using a strict behavioral model. Knowing our child, we went to the special education department and said, "This therapist is not a fit for our son and here's why." We made a clear and unemotional presentation of our case to the special education department, asked for a reasonable substitute, and the district representative agreed to have Zac work with one of the district's alternative therapists.

Fortunately, if you need to find a therapist outside the schools, professionals are easier to locate than they were five years ago. To start, you need to get on the telephone and start networking. When I learned about Zac's NLD, I called everyone I knew, went to the library, searched the Web, went to bookstores, and eventually found my way to professionals who knew something about NLD and were able to help me. Parents can start by contacting a local hospital. All hospitals employ speech therapists and occupational therapists (OTs) to do rehabilitative therapy with patients. These professionals may not have training in pediatric therapy, but they will know other people in the profession and can refer you to someone who can help. You may have to follow a trail of referrals before you find a qualified therapist. Your pediatrician may or may not be aware of your community's resources, but it's worth asking. Your county health service may have listings. You could call your state's department of education, explain your situation, and ask what resources they have. You can call the American Occupational Therapy Association or the National Association of Speech Therapists. They have lists of therapists throughout the country as well as their own Web sites. And there are the resources in Appendix A of this book.

In nearly every community, there will be some kind of parent support network. Once you locate it, you're on your way. You may discover it through the schools, through your pediatrician, or by asking other parents, especially parents of special needs children.

Choose a Therapist

Therapists are just like other professionals: There are good ones, bad ones, trained ones, untrained ones, those that are a good match for your child, and those who aren't, and everything in-between. When you first contact a therapist, you will want to ask some initial questions to verify and assess this person's qualifications. Questions might include:

- Has she ever heard of NLD? How much does she know about it? Where did she get her information? As she explains her thoughts on NLD, see if you agree. If the therapist says, "Oh, NLD? The child just needs to be taught some manners," that's a good indication that the therapist is not accurately informed about the disorder.

- If she has not heard of it, go down the list of symptoms for NLD. (Criteria for Identifying NLD.) Ask how she treats those symptoms. NLD is a relatively new term used to explain children who have been succeeding in therapy for years. Therapists who have not heard of the disorder may still have excellent skills in treating its symptoms (which is all any of us can do for these children anyway). Just because she hasn't heard of NLD doesn't necessarily mean she can't work with your child.

- Ask about her training and certification. This will give you some indication of her specialties and experience.

- Ask her what frame of reference she uses to diagnose and treat. Therapists who work with children with NLD should have a sensory integration frame of reference, meaning they have some training in treating the sensory processing piece of this disorder, which research indicates is a key element of treatment. They must know how to listen and relate to the needs of your child. Speech therapists should be able to demonstrate to you that they're competent in pragmatics and language, receptive language skills, and speed of processing of language and not just speech articulation. Psychotherapists need a proficiency in understanding nonverbal language, too, and use various methods, not just medication or behavioral theory.

- Ask her how long she typically sees a child and the diagnoses on her caseload. If she says two years, this may indicate that she is someone who will drive the therapy independently of you. If she says six months, she is more likely to be someone who likes to work with a child while teaching the parents how to integrate therapeutic activities into family and community life. Either approach can work and be appropriate.

Beyond the initial assessment, it's important for you to know what kind of person the therapist is. I think good professionals approach a child as a good coach would—they really fall in love with the kid. Great coaches like Red Auerbach, George Allen, John Wooden, and Tim Galway, when asked what's the number one piece that made them the most effective coaches of all times, say, "You have to love your players." Great coaches and great therapists feel touched by their players, taught by the children, and feel honored to get to work with those they mentor.

Not only should the therapist be a loving and kind person, he or she must value the parents' love and knowledge about their own child. The therapist has expertise in a specific form of intervention. Parents' main resource is their intuitive knowledge of the little person who came into their lives, and the depth of their love for their child. Parents are the ones who provide care and "treatment" when the child spills, falls, vomits, breaks a family heirloom, steals money for ice cream, wakes up at night, or runs away from school. If you meet a professional who doesn't value that, who doesn't incorporate that into treatment, that's probably not a good professional to work with your child. Speaking both as a parent and a professional, this piece should never be discounted.

I would encourage you to insist that all professionals working with your child must:

- be kind, patient and loving

- have unconditional positive regard

- behave respectfully to you and your child

- listen to you

- demonstrate that they hear what you tell them by incorporating your observations into your child's treatment, or explain their reasons for not doing so

- make progress with your child

- have a good sense of humor—these kids are *funny!*

Another critical issue is the therapist's attitude. Does he or she consider the goal of therapy to be the child or a specific product (such as shoe-tying, handwriting, or sequencing)? I cannot emphasize enough that the child—not the particular skill to be mastered—must be the focus of therapy. If the therapist says, "He didn't get all of the assignment done on the worksheet," when the child is screaming and crying, that's not a good working situation. You need a therapist who can help the child stay calm and focused even if that means getting only a fifth of the worksheet done. That's a much more useful learning experience. Given that so many people are product driven, and given that we live in a product driven society, it may be up to you as the parent to change your therapist's focus. You will need to articulate your goals for your child and invite therapists to help you with them. This can help them focus on the person rather than a product.

For example, one therapist I know, Wendy, is a great therapist. I have seen her work with children and help them make progress when no one else could. One girl she worked with, Manny, was eight years old and couldn't write her name. She would avoid it in any way possible—running to the center of the room and twirling, blowing on whistles, bouncing on a trampoline. Wendy made up a song for Manny, "Let's bounce, one two three four then twirl five six seven eight and blow n-i-n-e and t-e-n then sit down and make M for Manny, then A for Manny" and so on. Within a short period of time, this girl was writing beautifully. Sure, the child didn't finish the alphabet in the first week or two, but Wendy was able to build a relationship of trust with the child, rather than struggle with her, and within a relatively short time Manny was writing. After years of attending to the product without success with other professionals, Wendy attended to Manny, and then Manny was successful. That's a great therapist doing great work.

A good therapist will work with you to help you integrate therapy into your child's daily life. Anything that the child is working on in therapy should be applicable in a natural setting—at home, school, or in the child's social life. A good therapist will be able to give you five to ten cost-free ways to practice a skill. For example, for speech homework, Zac was told to bring a game to a social function and teach one other child to play the game. This helped him practice social skills, communication skills, sequencing, organization of thought, and to make friends. That's functional, realistic homework. Once, Zac arrived at OT therapy and announced, "School sucked. I was in trouble the whole day." The therapist had Zac calculate the number of minutes in his day, and the number of minutes he had been in trouble. She used the opportunity to tease out the black-and-white, absolute thinking he was prone to by having him calculate that in reality he was in trouble for two minutes. This was a revelation for him and an insight that has remained with him to this day, years later.

Finally, part of the therapist's role is treating the family. It's important not only for your child to be cared for, but for you also to feel cared for by the therapist. That means finding a therapist who understands the reality of your daily life. If you are like most parents of a child with NLD, adding one more activity to your day, even if it takes only five minutes, can be a challenge. You want a therapist who understands that when he gives you an activity to do at home with your child, finding time for it may mean you have to give up something else, sometimes something as basic as brushing *your* teeth so your child can have five more minutes of your time.

When to Move On

Once your child begins working with a therapist, you will want to observe his or her progress. If you don't see improvement after four to eight sessions with the therapist, the therapy is probably not working. You may want to speak with the current therapist and express your concerns or look for another therapist. You're paying for the treatment; you need to see results. If the treatment is provided by the school, you're ulti-mately paying for that, too, as a taxpayer and your child is paying directly and dearly by taking his time away from receiving therapy that *will* make a difference. Even if the therapist is someone you personally like very much, he or she might not have the necessary skills or insights to help your child.

Parents can get very attached to therapists. Sometimes therapists will want to discharge before the parent will let them. Parents may need the support system the therapist provides. They may feel that therapy is one piece that's working for the child, and they do not want to disrupt it. However, it's important to remember that therapy is an adjunct to, not a replacement for, the child's natural setting.

Get the Most Out of Therapy: The Parent's Role

Therapists can provide their expert insight into learning styles, and they can give children with NLD specific activities to build the neurons in the brain. However, to be effective, therapy cannot be a one-hour-a-week event. The brain does not work that way; the muscles do not work that way. Children with NLD will benefit only if the therapeutic activities are incorporated into their daily lives.

For therapy to be truly effective, parents must be shown how to incor-porate the information and activities into every aspect of the child's life. Parents must use therapy as a direction for daily movement, thinking, and relating. Most therapists see a child one to three times a week for 30 to 50 minutes. That's not enough to bring about significant change. But if the therapist trains the family to follow through with the therapy at home, then the child is getting "therapy" many times a week. This enables the learning to become etched into the brain faster and to be integrated with daily experiences more efficiently, thus causing a more significant change.

Therapists can guide you and give you good ideas, but you have to follow through. You also need to know what to follow through with, or you'll be wasting your child's time (and yours) with activities that are not going to help. Ultimately, making this effort—and, yes, it is hard work—will not only benefit your child; in the long run it will also save you time and money.

If you can't afford to pay for ten therapy sessions, there are ways to make one or two of them helpful. Attend the therapy session without your child, ask a lot of questions, and ask the therapist to train you in ways to apply activities at home. After a few months, when you've seen some progress, you can go back for another session and more activities. We did this for Zac's vision therapy, and that was sufficient. We also did this with tutoring. We hired a tutor for a limited time, learned how to help Zac learn, and then incorporated this into our way of helping him with homework. The key here is to follow through—if you don't do that, you've wasted your money and your child's time.

Often parents don't realize the importance of being involved during therapy. If a therapist doesn't allow you to be present or have some way of giving you therapeutic tools for your child, find someone else.

There are some children who fall apart when their parents are around, and the therapist really can't provide therapy for them when the parents are in the room. If your presence interferes with the child's ability to work, the therapist should explain to you, in a way that you agree and feel comfortable with, why she needs to see the child privately. You will have to trust your therapist to tell you the difference. This is another reason it's important to find a therapist with whom you can establish good communication.

If you stay involved with a session, you get more out of it and get more value for your money. Your participation can range from sitting and observing, having monthly meetings with your child not present, getting ideas and asking questions, to being another therapist. An involved parent can apply therapeutic information in activities at home, which ultimately means that I can expand the child's therapy sessions to include other skills and activities. It's okay for you to ask the therapist questions during therapy or to ask for training you can apply at home. I consider it part of my professional role to let the parent know how much her participation is beneficial to her child or whether it is interfering with the child's treatment.

The reality, however, is that not every parent is up to that level of involvement. Some parents need to use therapy as a break to sit in the waiting room and read or take a nap. As the parent of a child with NLD, I understand that sometimes parents need time to take care of themselves. I have often used Zac's treatment time to catch up on paperwork, balance my checkbook, have lunch (at 4 P.M.), or to take a nap. I think that helped me be more present for Zac and able to attend to his needs. Many therapies I sat in with him to learn how to bring home the concepts and the activities, but sometimes I just needed the time for myself, and that is okay.

In order to integrate information and therapies into daily life, therapy sessions can teach you the rationale behind these activities and why they're important for your child. The child will likely have some kind of homework, an activity you can do together. You can ask the therapist for reading or classes to take in the community.

If the speech therapist says to practice categories, driving home we start categories. I'll say, "Name four kinds of cars before we pass that exit sign." I always try to make it a game, but therapy is part of every minute of Zac's life. When we watch *The Simpsons*, we discuss the social language and inferences Bart makes and the invisible rules that his family continually breaks. We turn the sound off on movies and play "Guess the Emotion" by observing the characters' facial cues and body language. Before or during homework, Zac bounces on balls to get proprioceptive input, which has an organizing effect on the brain. If he wants to be sedentary and play video games, he has to sit on a ball or take "movement breaks." We practice money skills at the bagel store. A bagel costs less than a dollar, so Zac has to count change, make appropriate eye contact, and practice all the other social skills involved in that transaction. Cooking uses sequencing and math. Dinner is an opportunity to practice humor. Sunday breakfasts, Dad reads and explains each comic strip to teach inference, social language, and humor. Because Zac won't pick these up on his own, we have to consciously teach and teach and teach. Snuggling with Dad for Sunday comics and singing or dancing silly, made-up songs for multiplication tables is not a chore. This isn't work at our home: We make it fun and exciting and a part of our family life that we all enjoy and look forward to.

Another method we use to help Zac integrate therapy into daily life is the homework jar. In it I put coupons for karate homework, math homework, vision therapy homework, and occupational therapy homework. We draw out two a day and do assignments, totaling 30 minutes. Sometimes he asks for more OT time or vision therapy time, but that's optional. This helps us keep therapy homework in balance. Whenever the therapist gives Zac a tedious assignment, we try to fit it into family life. For example, we do a lot of his speech homework at dinner, making it part of our conversation, so we are both modeling examples for him and providing a way to integrate his homework into ordinary family life. We also take activities and together we make them into card games or board games Zac can then play with us or his friends.

Another approach I take is to look for things Zac is already doing that I can label "homework." Once Zac bought a pack of Magic cards with allowance money he'd saved up. He wanted me to play Magic with him, and he was teaching me the rules. His homework from speech was to learn how to teach a game to another person. The rationale for the exercise was to have a way of entering a group of children he doesn't know and to always have a game or activity with him as a conversation starter. So as we were playing Magic, in which he was very absorbed, I said, "How clever of you to do your speech homework with me," and then he realized the connection. I try to label activities in his life all the time and activities in *my* life, too.

Use Any Therapist As an Educator

To get more out of therapy, you might pay the therapist to meet with you and your spouse or family. He or she can make sure you all understand what to do, how to do it, and why it's important, so that you can proceed with confidence. You can also use the therapist to educate you about your child's diagnosis. Parents of children with NLD get mountains of paperwork from professionals. These are often thousand-dollar reports that are totally useless to the parents because no one has taken the time to interpret them. It's not that the parents are stupid, but the reports tend to be written using clinical terms and jargon for specialists. A service I offer in my clinic is meeting with parents and interpreting reports for them. Parents are usually hugely relieved to have this information made accessible and can finally take advantage of that information.

Your child's therapist can also train the staff at your child's school. If the therapist goes to the school and trains the teacher and the child's aide in integrating these treatments, then you have a therapist, a teacher, and an aide (as well as you) all working toward the same goals. This means your child is getting a consistent, clear therapeutic message throughout his day. This would cost you perhaps a hundred dollars, but as a result, your child gets the equivalent of 30 hours of therapy a week, and that's good value for the money.

Schools are generally accommodating about bringing in outside professionals to train the school staff. On an IEP team this theoretically happens anyway. But if your child is seeing a private clinician, or if your child is doing different kinds of therapies, you may need to facilitate this communication. Or, as often happens, if you're the parent of a child with this "weird" diagnosis called NLD that no one in the schools has heard of yet, you really do need to facilitate some kind of education for the school. You, the parent, must be proactive and make the communication happen.

Motor Skills

Children with NLD tend to be sedentary, have low energy, and low endurance. They often prefer to sit on the couch and read, sit in front of the computer and absorb information, or sit and play video games. We all need to work a little, play a little, and rest a little. Children with NLD will likely need support in finding this balance, or the scale will tip toward lethargy. Children with NLD need to develop their gross motor skills, but they won't develop them while they are sitting on the couch reading. As a parent of a child with NLD, you need to provide abundant opportunities for your child to develop motor skills in balance with all the other aspects of life. Your therapist can help you design a program that is reasonable given your child's current level of ability, and she can help you choose toys and activities to add to your child's play area to promote specific learning through selected activities. That way therapy is woven into everyday life, but it's also invisible to the child.

Gross motor skills are developed by using muscles to run, jump, kick, push, and pull—all the types of play that used to be part of childhood before our lives became overscheduled and overstructured. Often when parents start to work on motor skills, they think they need to buy a lot of big, expensive toys. But kids do really well with 20 feet of rope. They can play tug of war. You can park your car so that the tire is on the rope and see if your kid can pull it out from under the tire. You can put knots in the rope and have her pull things through the house, or you can hold one end and have her pull herself to you along the rope. Milk cartons are great for stacking and crashing into or throwing things at. Empty two-liter bottles are great bowling pins. Digging holes in the dirt builds endurance and strength (and insects are fascinating to collect and observe).

Keep your child moving, and she'll be developing motor skills. If you need ideas, any book on motor skills development or on physical education for kids will help you. Carol Kranowitz's book *The Out-of-Sync Child Has Fun* is a bonanza of activities.

Life Skills

Occupational therapy often focuses on Activities of Daily Living (ADLs), also known as life skills. These include tasks such as buttoning clothes, brushing teeth, tying shoes, making a snack, sharpening a pencil, or doing homework. ADLs are the minutia of life, things you don't pay attention to unless you can't do them. Children with NLD have a lot of trouble with these skills. All of their symptoms manifest in difficulty performing the necessary skills of daily life.

Children with NLD absolutely have to be taught life skills. They're not going to pick them up on their own. So if you want to make the most of your child's therapy, make practicing life skills part of your child's daily life. These are kids who should be in charge of cooking a family meal once a week, for example. Cooking builds skills these children need: sequencing, planning, organizing, and thinking something through. Children with NLD often don't cook or do other household chores because they tend to be messy and take a very long time and their efforts are not helpful. Often parents don't have the patience or tolerance for mess to allow their child these opportunities. But if you don't do it now, soon you will have a teenager who is totally dependent on you for every small household task. This is the principle of early intervention: You need to build the skills now and teach the child the importance of being helpful to the family, of contributing in ways they are able, and that your family values their contribution. Mistakes are part of the learning process.

Parent Groups

Parent groups are another way to get more out of your child's therapy. If your town lacks a parent group, you can start one through NLDA (see Resources). If you know of any other parents of children with NLD, ask them over for tea. Ask them who else they know, and then you'll have four or five parents to meet and share experiences. Each of you can describe what your therapist did with your child, so you can learn about different activities to try. This exchange of information will also help you evaluate therapists for their effectiveness and communication.

Workshops

You can educate yourself about NLD and your child's needs by attending workshops. The professionals who work with your child are on the mailing lists for the scores of workshops all over the country. You can say to them, "I'm interested in attending workshops. Will you let me know if something appropriate comes up?" Or you may come across a useful book that includes an advertisement for the author's workshops. You can also look for workshops on the Web.

At a workshop you will likely have the opportunity to learn about the latest research in NLD. You may hear about successful techniques that haven't shown up yet in the literature. You will hear of relevant books and other publications. You'll learn who the experts are and which ones are offering good advice. You will hear about some children who are improving and some who are not. You'll be able to talk to other parents about what things they've done that either worked or didn't work.

Workshops cost money, and you can find ways to reduce your expenses. Almost every workshop will have scholarships for volunteers. It is always worth asking. Rest assured that someone else is asking also.

The Therapies

Children with NLD will likely need professional therapy in a number of different areas. As a parent, it can be hard to make sense of all the treatment options. Not every therapy—including some frequently recommended in schools—will be appropriate to the child with NLD. You need to know what each therapy addresses and how it will or will not benefit your child.

Occupational Therapy

Occupational therapy addresses the child's performance of self-help skills, adaptive behavior and play, and sensory, motor, and postural development. OT is designed to improve the child's ability to perform tasks in home, school, and community settings.

Children with NLD often have trouble paying attention because of the problems that arise from poor sensory processing. If a child is preoccupied with too much sensory input, such as the feel of his clothes and the pressure of the chair against his legs, he will have trouble listening to a teacher. Because of their poor attention to the body in space, poor postural muscle control, a hyporeactive system (i.e., the body doesn't perceive falling until it's too late to recover), and a tendency for weakness on the left side, these children also frequently fall out of their chairs. A child who is falling, or a child who is trying to cope with too much sensory input, is not going to be able to sit with a speech therapist for 30 to 45 minutes of cognitive thinking. She'll get tired and frustrated and most likely have a meltdown. Under those conditions, she won't be able to benefit from the therapy. Starting with occupational therapy helped Zac develop better muscle control and endurance and decreased his anxiety and frustration. He was able to have better control when he moved, was less clumsy, and felt better about himself overall.

Sensory Integration

We learn through our senses. What we see, what we hear, what we touch, and what we experience through the perception of movement from our joints and muscles are our foundations for learning. *Sensory integration* theory is a way of looking at how the brain and the body work together to process sensory stimulation. Each person has a different level of sensitivity to sensory stimulation. Every once in a while I will hear someone say, "Oh, research doesn't show sensory integration is effective." That cracks me up. On the one hand, there's a large body of research supporting sensory integration, on the other hand, there's little research supporting language therapy, behavioral modification techniques, psychotherapy or even any of the curriculum your child is studying. Every written text on nonverbal learning disorder, ADD, ADHD, Asperger's, and autism cites sensorimotor deficits—who else is going to work on those but a sensory integration therapist? You may be interested to know only 30 percent of medical procedures are backed by research. For example, while many believe estrogen is important to prevent bone fractures and heart disease in older women, and women were given this remedy for over 20 years, the research, finally in, shows that not only does estrogen NOT prevent bone fractures and heart disease but it may, in fact, prevent women from taking medications that HAVE been demonstrated to prevent fractures and heart disease. In fact, the side effect of taking estrogen, increased risk of breast cancer, is a real threat. What has been shown, in research to prevent fractures? Exercise that creates bone impact such as walking and running and weight lifting—all forms of proprioceptive input or heavy work, the same kind of input we teach in sensory integration therapy. So next time you try to get sensory integration for your child and you are told you can only have behavior modification and medication, ask for researched documentation that behavior modification will help your child and studies that demonstrate that Ritalin will enhance academic performance in your child. You'll start an interesting discussion.

Children with sensory processing difficulties respond to the world as they experience it. Unfortunately, to the people around them, their responses can seem like deliberate misbehavior. In Zac's first years of school, his teachers noted that he didn't like music. This surprised us because Zac has loved music from an early age. When he was three, he listened to the Moody Blues night after night. He could identify instruments played on tape, and he liked to sing and play his toy guitar and drums. How could he not like music? Eventually we learned he was auditorally hypersensitive. Noises that don't bother most of us sent him screaming through the house holding his ears. In school, when there was singing during circle time, he would cover his ears and rock back and forth, and if that didn't work, he would stick his feet straight up in the air. This often had the effect of getting him "excused" from the group. This way he was able to get his immediate need met (he got away from the offensive sensory input), but his action was labeled as a "behavior problem." His coping skills were functional, but not very successful. Once we found out about this, we were able, with the help of his OT, to develop coping strategies that both were successful socially and met his sensory needs.

Sensory integration therapy begins by examining the child's pattern of perception. An occupational therapist will explore how the child perceives her environment through the sensory channels. If the response is not typical and not functional (a person can be atypical but be able to function and therefore not need treatment), then the therapist can begin to normalize that perception.

Activities of Daily Living (ADLs)

The only way to learn ADLs is by doing them. But because these kids are physically slow and clumsy, often their parents will do tasks for them. Thus, these children tend not to develop needed skills because they don't get the necessary practice. Sometimes, doing for another who is unable to do for herself is an act of compassion, but sometimes we need to allow her to fail, to try and learn to be independent. Classroom teachers, even though they are trained to teach children to do for themselves, also often step in when they can hold back. If a teacher has 30 kids who need to get their coats on, he lines them up and buttons their coats and sends them out the door. Occupational therapists, however, are trained to let the child learn to do for herself and in activity analysis (*why* can't she do it on her own?). I worked with a teenager who was unable to carry a tray of drinks, couldn't cut an apple herself, and didn't know how to take off a dress or shirt if it didn't have buttons. After showing her how to don and doff an overhead garment, she said to me, "Why didn't anyone ever teach me that before?"

The answer, I think, is that no one knew to teach her. Most kids figure out this "simple" act themselves. Yet it's not a simple act. It takes many skills to put clothes on or to take them off. Additionally, children with NLD tend to avoid ADLs out of frustration or embarrassment, and they are very good avoiders. For years, Zac avoided wearing jeans that had buttons. I didn't know this. All I knew was if I bought GAP jeans, he wore them every day, and if I bought jeans at Sears he wouldn't wear them. I thought maybe it was the way the seams were sewn, maybe one was flatter and more comfortable. Then, in second grade, I took him to Sears for back-to-school clothes. In the dressing room he was unbearably slow in trying on the clothes. He goofed around, laughed, acted silly, sang into the mirror. When he finally put the pants on, I asked him, "Do you like them?"

"Yes," he said.

"Are they comfortable?"

"Yes."

And then with a stroke of divine common sense, I said, "Will you wear them?"

That's when he told me, "No, because they have buttons, and I can't get them off in time to go to the bathroom. Can't we just go to the GAP?"

Parents can help by selecting one or two tasks that the child can work on to develop independence in and let the child know this is the lesson, saying something like, "I'll help you tie your shoes, but you're working on getting your socks and shoes on all by yourself."

Children with NLD need to be enabled to use their abilities. They need increased exposure to ADLs, opportunities to succeed, and chances to fail in a supportive environment. They will need many more repetitions than the average child in order to build the neural pathways in the brain that will allow them to master the tasks and apply their skills in other areas.

Speech and Language Therapy

Speech and language therapists, also called speech and language pathologists (SLP), train simultaneously in two disciplines: speech therapy, how to make the mouth articulate sounds properly, and language therapy, how to organize the words in the mind for functional communication. Children with NLD can usually articulate as well as most adults—and better than some!—but they need help accessing their knowledge, organizing it, and communicating it. This is the realm of language therapy and is often referred to as *cognitive processing* and language retrieval.

Although children with NLD have a vocabulary that sounds like a college professor's, they can't always access it. When the teacher says name three animals, they may be able to say "cat," but then they freeze, and they feel stupid. They know a hundred animals, but they have problems with retrieval, especially in a confrontational setting like a classroom. A language therapist, or language pathologist, helps these children develop language retrieval and the ability to categorize language.

The language therapist will observe and test your child's language and thought processes. For example, he might check to see if the child can talk to him in a sequential, coherent way while he asks her to get a piece of paper out of her notebook. That's called *parallel processing*. As the language therapist watches a child process information, he can identify the gaps in the child's processes, and then he selects activities that help a child in that area. Can she explain the steps of washing a car? That might seem simple, especially if your child tests at the twelfth grade level for language skills on an IQ test, but those tests focus on vocabulary rather than the social uses of language. The child with NLD may be able to cite dictionary definitions for very difficult words, but still be unable to have a conversation. When she's asked to talk about washing the car, she may say something like, "You put water all over it. Then you dry it. You have to get some soap." Then she'll freeze and won't be able to retrieve anything else. She knows that something comes next, but she can't find the words for it. The therapist will say, "Think about the steps during the soaping process," which in the therapist's terms is called a *cue*. The therapist gives the child a cue to restart her thought process or to help the child organize the process of prioritizing all the thoughts in his head in order to retrieve the relevant ones. Over time, the therapist works on decreasing the number of cues a child needs and increasing the cognitive demands. Instead of describing washing a car, the therapist might ask her to describe the steps of a science experiment.

The language therapist will probably help the child see the implied information, perhaps by using pictures or through logical explanations. She might say, "I really put my foot in my mouth that time, didn't I?" and then ask the child what that means and the therapist will then teach about figurative speech.

A good speech therapist will take the time to explain the hidden meanings logically and sequentially. One of the strengths of these children is that you can explain to them on a very rational level how things work, and they will understand. A child with NLD may understand a concept only in that one situation, but need help to apply that concept in other situations.

Language therapists also work on the pragmatics of speech, that is, the social aspects of communication. Pragmatic language therapy may include learning to take turns, learning the difference between questions, comments, compliments, and rhythms of conversation, or learning about different tones of voice, inflections, and other nonverbal cues.

Vision Therapy

We tend to think of vision as a function of the eyes, but the eyes are only part of a process. The eyes bring in information that the brain then sorts, filters for relevance, interprets, comments on, and, if appropriate, tells the body how to react.

Children with NLD tend to have typical eyesight—their eyes work properly—but their perception of what they see is often impaired because their brains do not properly process the information their eyes take in. A child looking at vertical instructions for a pattern to make with Legos may not be able to duplicate the pattern in the horizontal plane of a table. If you put this same child in front of a chalkboard and say, "Copy this information into your notebook," she can't do it because she hasn't developed that part of her brain.

A vision therapist, or an OT who has special training in vision therapy, will give the child activities that build the brain's ability to interpret what the eyes see. While an occupational therapist would do exercises with the child that use the whole body, including vision, a vision therapist focuses specifically on vision and perception difficulties. If your child's visual deficits are significant enough, a vision therapist may be brought in to supply specific activities and exercises. Often a vision therapist is also trained in occupational therapy, or the two therapists work together to provide the service to the family. This allows the vestibular piece and the visual piece to be combined and children are often more successful in a shorter period of time.

Zac's vision therapist suggested two activities that became favorites: I drew letters on his back, and he would have to write them on the blackboard. This is actually a very complex process. The brain has to register the letter tactually, remap it visually, and execute it on the blackboard motorically. In the process, the brain builds those neural connections. In another activity, we set out carpet squares in a particular design and then drew that design on a piece of paper. On the paper diagram, I marked the squares that we pretended were stockpiling weapons for the Evil Empire. The rest of the squares were rebel bases. Zac's job was to run around the squares on the floor and bomb the Evil Empire bases with bean bags without destroying the rebel fleets. To do this, he had to hold the vertically presented visual image from the paper in his mind, remember the sequence, and then motorically execute the command. We sometimes changed the activity by having him bounce on a large therapy ball while he did the bombing or even lie on the ball on his stomach, arch his back, and throw to target enemy sites.

Occupational therapists usually work on visual perception through ADLs. The child might be asked to look in the silverware drawer and find all the forks. This gives the child practice in visual-spatial organization, visual closure, and depth perception. As she gets better at this, the drawer can be messier and the item to locate more complex. It can be the child's job to set the table with silverware each dinner. Parents can make it more challenging by asking for specific pieces of silverware.

This area of weakness for children with NLD will need continual intervention, and daily chores are rich opportunities. Sorting laundry, sorting socks, categorizing canned goods when it's time to put away groceries are all tasks that are visually rich opportunities. When cleaning up his room, we would say to Zac, "Pick up three things that are square, then come give me a kiss," or "Pick up all the white things on the floor, and when you're done we'll jump up and down and pretend we're broccoli getting dressed in lemon butter." It was silly, fun, and effective vision therapy in small, daily doses.

Psychotherapy

Psychotherapy, also known as "talk" or "play" therapy, helps many people. The theory behind it is that talking over issues that bother you with a counselor, a psychologist, or a psychoanalyst will help you gain some insight. That insight will then reframe how you see your problems and will eventually also change your behavior. This process is helpful for many people. However, this theory does not hold true for children with NLD. These are children who can talk forever, yet they lack the capacity for insight into their words and behavior because they are unable to make inferences or to anticipate consequences. For these children talk therapy is often useless and extremely irritating, especially if they have been told that they are supposed to have insights and changes in behavior, which subsequently don't happen. This therapy can become another arena in which they are set up to fail.

With that said, a psychotherapist with an understanding of the subtle but pervasive language deficits associated with NLD can be invaluable. The therapist will convey to the child, "It's my job to understand you, not your job to be clear. If I don't understand, then I need to figure out what you mean." The focus of psychotherapy should never be how you are feeling, but how are you perceiving your world. That's an important distinction for children with NLD who really do not have a good emotional vocabulary in a world that assumes that they do. Problems with perception and cognition can cause deficits in social relations, as we see in the child with NLD. This can lead to feelings of poor self-esteem and hopelessness. Understanding where the problems lie in the brain, or in the perceptual cognitive process, the therapist can then devise a plan that zeros in on the true source of the patient's feelings of unhappiness. Therapists need to be trained to understand how to recognize the sources of dysfunction and treat that, not overrelying on one tool to attend to all problems. Medication will never be the answer for everyone, nor will talk therapy that seeks to find and assign blame for social impairment.

When Zac was seven, he went through a phase of using language in a way that would put most psychologists on red alert. Zac used to say, "I really love violence. I love violent movies. I love violent books. *I love violence.*" You can imagine I was disturbed (and my in-laws were horrified). The therapist we worked with helped us understand that Zac was not a violent child and that he was misusing the word *violence*. It turned out that when he said *violence*, he really meant action and the art behind special effects.

Despite their large vocabularies, children with NLD have language deficits in pragmatics, functional language, and interpretation. That said, psychotherapy can be helpful for families of children with Nonverbal Learning Disorder. The people who are helpful in this field are those who help the family understand how to love their child even when he or she is different, and who can help them cope with the inevitable stress of parenting a child with NLD. Parents or siblings may benefit from talk therapy with a therapist who understands the diagnosis and what the child is capable of, as opposed to what you might expect a child with a high IQ and verbal skills to be capable of. I also think play therapy can be helpful for the child with NLD if the therapist understands that the meaning of play is different for children with NLD and that it is not directly projective. It the therapist understands *that*, they get the child and they get NLD. It can help the therapist understand the workings of the child in order to communicate that information to the parents and help them adapt their parenting style to their child's needs.

Behavior Therapy

Behavior modification is generally not helpful for children with NLD unless it addresses a behavior that they can control. I tried to use behavior modification techniques with Zac countless times. I would set up charts and give him stars if he didn't fall out of his chair at dinner. He *never* achieved the reward because he was failing as a result of his inability to not fall. Once we provided appropriate therapy, he stopped falling.

We have discovered in clinical work a truth that doesn't seem to have transferred into the schools: You *cannot* change a behavior through behavior modification techniques if the behavior is the result of a cognitive dysfunction. These behaviors do not relate to a child's willingness to comply but rather his ability to do so. To change the behavior, you have to increase the environmental supports, or you have to increase the person's ability to overcome the dysfunction and use rewards that are meaningful to the child. If a child with a sensory deficit does not feel hot water, you can't change his behavior by giving him a reward for not sticking his hand in hot water. If you think a cookie is a good reward or a sticker because it works with other children, you can't use it as a reward if it isn't something this child feels inspired to achieve.

When working with a child with NLD, a behavior therapist first has to examine the cause of the child's inappropriate behavior. This is true for all children, but for children with NLD, it's critical not to assume that the child's intention is to manipulate, get attention, or control others. Behavior therapists, more often than not, are not aware of NLD. They are trained to look at the behavioral goal, such as staying in a chair. They are not trained to examine the underlying cause of the child's actions. The focus of this therapy is the product and not the child.

Therefore, for this particular therapy, it is terribly important for the parents to be vigilant. If she tries a behavior plan for a week and the child makes no progress, the therapist needs to reexamine the situation for its underlying causes and work with the team to determine if there is a sensory processing piece driving the behavior. Within the context of behavioral therapy, a reward is something that increases behavior so it is either offered or withheld. If a reward is not increasing behavior, it is not a reward, *even if* it has been a reward for someone else in the past. A behavior plan can fail a child if it does not provide rewards that change a child's behavior, but a child cannot fail a behavior plan. Just because the plan typically works for most children does not mean the child fails when it doesn't work for him. Too often, those administering the plan then resort to punishment in an attempt to change the child's behavior. This is not good behavioral treatment, it's age-old punishment, consistently found to be ineffective.

Too often, parents put professionals up on a pedestal and never think to interrogate their methods. Especially with behavior therapists, it's important to ask about their training and their frame of reference. Ask what they do when a child doesn't meet the behavior plan. Ask them what they think is happening. Although school teachers and administrators, who are themselves trained in behavior modification, tend to think very highly of these therapists, parents need to be very cautious and very active in monitoring the therapy.

Ultimately, most behavior problems in children with NLD can be corrected through other means. Once the deficits of the child with NLD are addressed by other therapies, inappropriate behaviors tend to diminish or disappear. When we tried to get Zac to get ready for school in the morning, it used to be a constant battle. We tried the star charts, we tried withholding privileges. But when we implemented a routine and posted a sequence of the tasks he needed to achieve in the morning, within two weeks he was able to be independent with his morning routines without the negative behaviors. We used a compensation for his cognitive deficits, not a behavior reward system for achieving a behavior result.

Other Interventions

Beyond professional therapy, a number of other interventions can be valuable for the child with NLD.

Tutoring

Tutoring is a useful intervention, especially when it's used to prepare the child for material that will be presented later in the classroom. Children with NLD don't function well in novel situations. So when a teacher opens a book and says, "Now we're going to start geometry," your child may be frozen for a week and be unable to take in the new information. But if the child has already been introduced to geometry in a safe setting, she'll think, "Oh, geometry, that's what my tutor talked about," and will be better prepared to learn. It can be very helpful for you to ask your child's teacher for the school year's curriculum and to hire a tutor to preview that material with the child over the summer or during the school year. Another option is for you to tutor your child yourself.

Like every professional who works with your child, a tutor needs to be patient, kind, and genuinely like children. He or she must also understand mixed abilities, that is, that a child can be gifted in one area but not in another. It's important that the tutor have reasonable expectations of your child's ability, and it's important that you see progress.

It may be a good idea to sit in on the first couple of sessions your child has with her tutor so that you can monitor their interactions and know if it's a good working situation. I did this with Zac's tutor. Once I was sure Zac was comfortable with her, I'd sit in another room nearby doing my own work while still listening to them.

Many teachers tutor to make extra money, so if your child has teachers you like, you can ask them if they tutor on the side. If they don't, they probably can recommend someone who does. In many towns and cities you can find professional tutoring services that are probably good, but check them out carefully to make sure that your child will work with someone who understands her needs and that there will not be a lot of shifting from tutor to tutor.

Team Sports

Sports are a great way for children with NLD to develop motor skills and build endurance. Team sports, however, are not the place to begin. Team sports have such strong visual-perceptual and social components that they can be very challenging for these kids, even overwhelming. In soccer, for instance, you have to know where all the players are on the field, where the ball is, and anticipate where it's heading. Then you have to use motor planning to get yourself to the ball and motor plan how to kick it, and you have to anticipate what the other team will do next. These are all areas of weakness for the child with NLD. It's good to have team sports as a goal to reach later, but they may not be the best place these kids experience their first athletic endeavors. The best sports for these children, like karate, dance, gymnastics, or swimming, allow them to progress individually so they are competing only with themselves while they build coordination, endurance, self-confidence, and frustration tolerance.

Swimming

Swimming is a great activity for children with NLD. It's very safe—they can't fall—and it's very soothing. It builds endurance without taxing the system, so children tend to be successful faster. A common symptom of NLD is difficulty with bilateral reciprocal movement, using both sides of the body together. If a child swims without using both sides together, she'll swim in circles, so she gets instant feedback as to whether or not she's doing it right, and, as a result, improves her bilateral symmetry.

Swimming lessons are especially helpful. The instructor does not need to have any special training in working with children with NLD, but he or she must be a kind person who likes kids and will take time to explain. I recommend private lessons, or lessons with no more than one other child, rather than group lessons. In group lessons, the instructor tends to call out instructions to a group of kids who are hovering at the side of the pool for 30 minutes, whereas in a private lesson your child gets direct instruction and more actual swimming time. You might pay 20 dollars for a group lesson and 50 for a private lesson, but with a private lesson your child actually learns to swim, while with group lessons you may end up having to go back again and again before your child learns.

Karate

Karate is another great activity for these children. (Karate is possibly the most Americanized and accessible of the Asian martial arts, and other martial arts may be valuable for children with NLD.) In karate, the students hear a command, process it mentally, integrate it into their bodies, and execute it. This sequence uses many different parts of the brain together. Karate classes provide immediate, direct feedback about performance. Then the children try again. That's the structure of the class—everyone tries again, even the sensei—the teacher—tries again and again and again. Even though everyone's at a different level, everyone is working on trying again. So there is no stigma attached to failure; it's seen as part of the process.

When choosing an instructor, make sure to find someone who is patient, positive, and focuses on the child's development, not on how successfully the child performed the routine. Find someone who likes kids and who will take the time to explain. My husband and I always had fun watching Zac perform his routines during karate testing for the next belt. The children would be placed in groups of three or four to perform their routines in sync with one another. We could see our son's "delay"—he would be about one or two seconds behind the other three children—but his movements were precise. He had the routine memorized and had obviously practiced. Fortunately, the instructors had taken the time to know Zac. They realized this was his best and would not likely change in the near future, and they passed him to the next level based on his personal mastery of the routine just like the other kids.

Gifted Programs

If you look at the criteria for giftedness and the criteria for NLD, there's quite a lot of overlap. According to the definition, gifted children are not gifted in all areas. They may be gifted visually yet have an auditory learning disability—they're really mixed. Because gifted kids need a multi-sensory approach to learning, the gifted programs teach differently than regular classroom programs, and their style is often helpful to children with NLD.

Many gifted programs are run free through the public schools. Go to the gifted teacher and find out what's available. Others are privately run and may charge a fee. Also, there are many organizations, videos, books, workshops, and Web sites dedicated to gifted children that provide helpful information (see Appendix A, Resources). For example, using materials provided by the Gifted Association, we've explained Zac's learning style to his teachers and developed alternative programs that help him learn on his level. At the Gifted Association's suggestion, we made accommodations to some of Zac's homework assignments using a process called "Collapsing the Curriculum." We reduced the amount of repetitive busywork he was required to do because we found the repetition did not support his learning.

Handwriting

Handwriting is typically taught in the classroom through a series of worksheets children are supposed to copy or fill in. However, that method doesn't work for children with NLD. If a child doesn't know left from right, she is going to have a hard time placing letters in the correct manner and may reverse them. If the child has problems with visual-spatial organization, it will be difficult for her to space letters and words on a sheet of paper. *Dysgraphia*, problems with handwriting, is often part of the NLD syndrome. Dysgraphia is related to lack of muscle strength and endurance (low tone), poor motor planning (praxis), and the inability to think and write at the same time (problems with parallel processing). These children use cognitive thought to form letters—it isn't an automatic action for them. To experience this, take a simple paragraph from any magazine. Write the paragraph (either print or cursive) and capitalize all the vowels. This will force you to concentrate on your letter formation in a way similar to the way children with NLD have to concentrate. To make it a third grade level task, compose a paragraph on, say, washing a car, and again capitalize all the vowels. You'll see why these kids get so fatigued during writing tasks. What manifests as poor handwriting is not really the writing itself, but the result of the true problem: inability to perform multiple novel tasks simultaneously, such as composing, recalling the shape of letters, recalling the placement of the pencil when starting and stopping letter formation, visually organizing spacing of letters/words on a page. For most of us, using writing is a tool of expression. When we are facile with tool use, it becomes helpful. However, if we're still working on the process of learning HOW to use the tool (such as a saw or in this case, a pencil) then it's not a tool and we shouldn't attempt to use it as such. Children who use reading as a tool can be given written directions and use those directions as a tool to accomplish a task. Children who use handwriting as a tool can move on to the process of using a pencil to express a thought. But a child who cannot read (dyslexia) cannot move on to performance with written directions and a child with dysgraphia cannot move on to written expression using a pencil. Teachers get this mixed up all the time with handwriting in spite of years of training and good understanding in the area of dyslexia.

Handwriting Without Tears, a program that has been adopted in schools across the country, is very helpful for children with NLD. It was developed by an occupational therapist whose child wasn't succeeding in handwriting. She did an activity analysis of handwriting and found where her child was struggling. She discovered that she could make handwriting manageable if she made the letters without the loops or curlicues that caused her child difficulty. These modifications also helped other children improve their speed and letter formation. Another helpful program is *Loops and Groups* by Mary Benbow, an OT who has specialized in the kinesthetic aspects of handwriting and provides creative materials to develop hand skills and perceptual skills of handwriting. Mary also leads terrific courses on handwriting and NLD she calls *Readin's Fine But Handwritin's a Disaster!*

While the child is acquiring the skills underlying handwriting, it's important to decrease the demand for handwriting in the classroom. Children with NLD should be allowed to demonstrate their knowledge orally, through a presentation, drawing a picture, or tape recording their answers, so they have an opportunity equal to their classmates to demonstrate their knowledge using methods that don't require a pencil. Remember, handwriting is not a process, it's meant to be a tool, and if it's not fluent, it can't be used as a tool.

Use Every Lesson along the Way

Getting the right help for your child can be very challenging, but as your child begins to blossom, it will all be worth it. It is important that you find some professionals on whom you can rely and use the knowledge and guidance they offer to help you best facilitate your child's success. It is as equally valuable to eliminate those professions who are not a fit for your child as it is to find those who are. It's a journey and along the way you and your child are learning about relationships, expressing your needs, and getting what you need from others. Use the journey, successes and failures, to build a stronger understanding of what works for your child and help your child learn this lesson as well. Eventually, your son or daughter will follow your lead and begin to self-advocate and navigate through mazes to find a community that is supportive and nurturing.

Cracking the Egg

We have used eggs to learn about gravity and falling and why we wear safety helmets. We've learned how to pad an egg sufficiently to withstand a fall of over 15 feet without harm. We have used eggs for lessons of addition, subtraction, division, and fractions, and then eaten the resulting cookies, cakes, and pies. We have explained idioms to Zac, talked about him being a good egg, of how we sometimes lay an egg, and the feelings we have when we fail so completely. But my favorite discovery about eggs came when we were struggling for yet another hour on how to write a descriptive paragraph for school.

At this point, Zac enjoys creative writing and hopes to some day be the next Stephen King or Isaac Asimov. When he's motivated and the idea is his, he can write pages and pages of funny, brilliant text. He won an award for his story "Wrong School" and is currently compiling a book on NLD all by himself. Despite his talents, when it comes to writing a mere paragraph describing a Wisconsin Fast-Growing Plant, he stares at blank paper, eventually writes three or four tangential phrases, and turns it in for a C or even an F. Something in his brain just doesn't connect.

Zac's teacher, Mr. Kuhns, has given me the outline that the teachers use to grade a paper, mapping out what elements they look for in a descriptive paragraph for a science observation. We are looking at his two-inch drawing of his plant. It looks like a stick with two sets of testicles (those are, apparently, the leaves) and a blob of pencil lead (reported to be emerging buds). There are three random thoughts scribbled at the bottom of the page: veins are white; flowers starting to come out; a leaf is falling off. That's it. That's his plant observation for fifth grade, worth 100 points.

Using the guide that the teacher provided, I began to prod him, trying to tease out what else he observed. I tried encouraging him to think about the senses: What did he see, what did it smell like, what did it feel like? Zac's repeated response: "There was a stem and leaves! What more do you want from me!"

"Oh, there was a huge stem going out of your classroom's roof, and the leaves were purple and gold."

"No, it was four inches tall and green."

"Oh, it was this tall and green like my shirt"—a washed-out, barely pale green shirt.

"No, it was dark green like—like the grass."

"Oh, it was this tall and dark green, like grass. Let's write that down." Then I remembered those eggs that have served us so well in so many of our teaching moments.

"Zac, I have an egg in my head called 'plant.' When you say 'plant,' I go into my brain and get out my plant egg. I crack it open and see the plant from *Jack and the Beanstalk*. Or I see the irises Uncle Jimmy sent us from Kentucky that bloom right there, outside our kitchen window. But I have never seen a Wisconsin Fast-Growing Plant, and I don't have an egg in my brain for that, so I have to use an egg I know. You have an egg in your brain you call plant. You know exactly what is in there, right? It's four inches tall, it bent over and had to be propped up, it was green like grass. But you have to crack that egg for me so it can then be in my head. Otherwise I don't have the same picture in my brain as you do."

I waited. His eggs were cracking open. I could see it on his face and in his eyes. He began to describe the plant for me, going through each of the senses. He wrote about five green leaves with white veins, green like grass, a fresh-smelling plant that smelled like Fruit Loops, about three buds, and roots so wild they were growing out of the container and into the watering system beneath, anchoring it well.

All that day we talked about other eggs in our heads, cracking them open for each other.

Epilogue

WHEN we learned about Zac's NLD, I thought we had to give up the child we had imagined living in a future we had created for him. My husband and I swallowed many bitter pills about our son and his "diagnosis" and "prognosis." We choked down information about social deficits, about not learning math beyond a fourth grade level, and how Zac would never be able to live independently because of his 40-point split between his verbal and performance IQ scores. Eventually I realized I had *this* child, not one of Rourke's children, but my special Zac, a mystery to watch unfold. That day was the day I felt a warm compassion pour into me. It was a feeling of wonderment and acceptance and blessedness.

I had been quick to believe the "experts" telling me with complete certainty who my child would become in 20 years. I would see who my child really was and help him the best I could.

Zac once met Byron Rourke at an NLD conference. Rourke is a tall and imposing man with blue, sparkling eyes. When he speaks at conferences, he brings with him many books he's written to be sold there. Zac had been invited to bring his book, too. He had brought 35 and had one left to sell. He earned a dollar for each one, the rest of the sales were donated to NLDA. He had his eye on buying a video game with his accumulated dollars. So he walked up to Dr. Rourke and asked if he'd like to buy his last book. Dr. Rourke bent down and had a beautiful, kind, peer-to-peer conversation with my son, which left Zac feeling pretty special. Rourke agreed to buy the book if Zac would sign it, which he did.

Zac's "deficits" are virtually invisible now. Even if you were a therapist who specializes in children with NLD, you would not identify my son now. He's gone from the first percentile in motor skills to the ninety-ninth. He's considered a jock—he's the second-fastest runner in his grade, and he loves soccer and plays well. He's also the vice president of his school.

Zac's differences—those things I was once told to be frightened about—are now the very things that make him wonderful. His view of the world is often upside down or backward, or from a perspective that I imagine is from underneath an edge the rest of us cannot see. He's funny and very sophisticated in his world view. He is never impressed by pretense or distracted by convention. He doesn't ever want to compete for anything because it would be cool or prestigious, only because it would be fun or interesting or practical. He wanted to run for vice president at his school because it got him out of class once a week and would let him control the kind of "spirit days" the school had. He joined a theater class because it seemed fun. Zac isn't motivated by greed or power or looking good, but goes straight for comfort and happiness and enjoyment of life. He's a lot like his father in that way. It's his own version of nonconformity, and it's one of my jobs to allow Zac the choice to have this difference.

Zac is currently learning how to insult others. It is the language of most ten-year-old males and a language Zac doesn't understand. Bill remembers having to learn the rules of insulting in fifth grade, when insulting became a way of greeting others. We've begun teaching that to Zac. The rules are, the insult has to be completely and obviously untrue, otherwise it's mean. But children who are learning anything often accidentally break those rules as they experiment. That's why sometimes those insults hurt even though they are from a friend. So you can call a friend an eight-eyed, lily-livered, poor excuse for pond scum, but you can't make fun of a short kid for being short or a chubby kid for being fat. We're practicing this by playing "The Insult Me Game." In this game, you have to keep insults going back and forth. If you hesitate for three seconds, you lose the round. If you say something hurtful, you lose the game. It's a bit like watching Robin Williams and Billy Crystal playing comedy together. When we presented all this to our son, he said, "Great, I had to become bilingual and learn all the social language codes and stuff, and now I have to become trilingual and learn the codes of fifth grade boys. When will it ever end? Next I'm going to study Japanese. How hard could it be after this? And would I then be quadrilingual or just move straight into multilingual?"

Zac is right, of course. His first language is one of stating the truth, the obvious, and the concrete. In his language, there really are no shades of truth, no frills, no protective euphemisms. I always know where I stand with Zac around. I know, for example, when my breath stinks, or when my clothes make me look fat, and how my underwear compared to my husband's looks huge. I know when my son wants a hug or kiss and when he doesn't. I know when he is full of appreciation and love for me. I know when he likes something and when he does not. Life is easy with his precise and accurate language. He points out stupidity in my world that I washed my hands of many years ago, like accepting "fun size" candy bars. As Zac says, there's nothing fun about one bite of your favorite candy bar. A "fun size" should be a foot long.

Now that I've learned to speak Zac-ese, being around such straight honesty feels like coming home, not to a native language but to a place I always knew, a place of clarity and security. Zac carries with him the kernel of sweetness from whatever alien place he has come from, and he plants it all around us. When he wakes up in the mornings and smiles, the sun warms up and gets brighter in our home. We would be lost without the magic and beauty my son brings to our lives. If he hadn't come to us, I know we wouldn't know what our lives were missing, but I know this: It would be gray more often in that life and the sun not as brilliantly orange and red and yellow and the trees nowhere near as green.

Once, we left a restaurant at night and I was freezing—I mean so cold my jaws hurt from chattering. I have lived in Boston and walked through snow up to my waist, but sometimes in California, it gets bone cold at night. This night I was having a miscarriage, though I didn't know it at the time. All I knew was I felt miserable and afraid and overwhelmingly cold. Zac came up behind me and started kind of pushing me, not roughly, but a strong, persistent push. My teeth stopped chattering, and I had a sense of warmth come through me. It was an odd feeling.

Then Zac said, "Did you feel that?"

"Yeah, I felt you pushing me."

"I was giving you some of my warmth, did it work?"

"Yeah, it did, I feel a lot better."

"Good, because I'm cold now. I guess it went where I wanted it to."

He may not always remember to turn in assignments, and he may say something in a rude voice when he doesn't mean to, but watch him move around in this world and touch others, and you will see him light up life. You know, this child of ours—perhaps like your child—is filled with magic.

Acknowledgments

Books, like children, need a community to grow.

Many people shared their time generously to support me and I thank them. First, to my husband, Bill, who stepped over laundry and moved piles of papers off the kitchen table and who loves us both when we spill and when we break through to our personal victories, and who creates a place of serenity in our home that allows me to have a place of calm in my heart and head. To my son, Zac, who taught me that angels exist on this earth in many forms, who is an inspiration to me and many others, and who is truly "the wonder boy." I hope he does become president and change the educational system, financial system, take care of all the children, and write gripping fantasies in all the ways he raves about, and I hope he never forgets to hug me. I love you, Zac.

I have had the honor of being taught by many of our nation's finest teachers: Mrs. Cecil loved me unconditionally in the second grade and taught me kindness, Mrs. Ross nurtured my love of science in the 5th grade, Mrs. Kleinstiver urged me to write in the 7th grade, Dr. McNearney taught me to think in college, Marti Southam reminded me to feel deeply and laugh deep in my belly in graduate school, and Evelyn Jaffe believed in me, always. Bless them.

My gratitude also to those who made this book a reality: to Carol Kranowitz, whose friendship made the book possible and whose whimsical edits made the story better, for Paula Jacobson, whose deep thoughts and clear perspective told me what the book was about, and for Kevin Sullivan, who found time amidst his gaggle of girls to read and comment and encourage. My gratitude for my editor, Sheila Curry Oakes, who calmly walked me through rewrites and page trimmings. Kitsey Canaan, writing coach extraordinaire, read every tangential thought and moved this book from chaos to completion, offered graceful, unique insights, and knew what to trim and what to insist I find the courage to leave in. Thank you, Kitsey, I don't know why anyone would try to write without you. And to Carolyn Baum, who is my role model in occupational therapy.

My deep thanks to those who knew and loved me before I knew myself: To my mom, Maggie, for always reminding me I have a great kid and who loved me when I wasn't one; my only sister, Lora, who taught me what unconditional love is; my grandma Hilda, who taught me how to love with simple, caring gestures and my spirit sister; Cathyann, my wise, best friend, who lets me borrow her most snuggly sweatshirts for months at a time and floats orange maple leaves on New England's rocky ocean for me each fall. To Dawn Wheeler, my high school writing buddy who expected me to grow up and be a writer (I forgot until you reminded me at the class reunion). To my dad, Jim, who let me crawl on his back and rest when I was a kid and believed I was an angel. To John and Linda for caring enough and showing it—we are so lucky to have you as parents.

To those who have helped Zac with his IEPs, his social struggles, and his problems with inference and movement—thank you. To Marcia Rubinstein, Judy Lewis, and Kathy Allen, my fellow board members of NLDA who work as tireless champions for those with NLD, and Meryl Lipton who is my role model for caring for children with NLD. And last but not least, to Sue Thompson, whose pioneering work on NLD saved my son's life and the lives of many others. I pray she is amply rewarded for all she's done; and Steve Nowicki, whose books allowed us to understand nonverbal language with depth and clarity while developing compassion for our child. Thank you to our wonderful neighbors, Jennifer for mowing my grass because she could see I was busy with the book, to Eric for being a 6 foot, 5-inch-tall peer for Zac, both of them: thanks for taking Zac so lovingly into your hearts.

And I am thankful for those that worked behind the scenes to help this book happen—to Diane Lamkin and Yoonok Shin for taking Zac to amusement parks and sleepovers so I could write, to Jin-Uk Shin for typing chapters in the middle of studying calculus and then making a special delivery to me on a Saturday and learning the value of completion.

Thanks to Debbie and Carrie, their partnership in making The Lighthouse Project a place that parents and children can rest, grow, and explore, fulfilling the purpose of many bright lights coming together to create safety in a storm. Bless you.

Appendix A:

Resources

Recommended Books

Sensory Integration:

Sensory Integration and the Child, 11th printing. Jean Ayres. An overview of sensory integration for parents

Playground Politics: Understanding the Emotional Life of your School Aged Child. Stanley Greenspan, MD

The Importance of Early Identification and Early Intervention with NLD: Strategies that Work. Audiotape of presentation at 1997 NLD Symposium, Rondalyn V. Whitney, MOT, OTR, available on Amazon.com

The Out of Sync Child: Recognizing and Coping with Sensory Integration Dysfunction. Carol Kranowitz

Social Skills:

Good Friends Are Hard to Find: Help Your Child Find, Make and Keep Friends. Fred Frankel *Raising a Thinking Child Workbook* by Myrna Shure (social skills treatment in a book)

Helping the Child Who Doesn't Fit In. Steve Nowicki and Marshall Duke. Brilliant book to support children with NLD—the guidebook for understanding and treating nonverbal learning disorders

Teaching Your Child the Language of Social Success. Steve Nowicki and Marshall Duke. Brilliant book to support children with NLD—the guidebook for understanding and treating the nonverbal cues lost in nonverbal learning disorders

Guides:

Crossover Children: A Sourcebook for Helping Children Who Are Gifted and Learning Disabled. From Council for Exceptional Children by M. Bireley

Emotional Intelligence: Why It Can Matter More Than IQ. E. Goleman. This book will empower you as you ask for social training at the school

Left Brain, Right Brain: Perspectives from Cognitive Neuroscience. Sally Springer

Molecules of Emotion: Why You Feel the Way You Feel. Candace Pert. Explains the neurology and chemistry of feelings and behavior. Good to help parents understand how the anxiety of NLD compounds the learning disability

No Easy Answers: The Learning Disabled Child at Home and at School. Sally Smith. A very practical and positive book that will give you ideas and hope about children who learn differently

Playground Politics: Understanding the Emotional Life of the School Age Child. Stanley Greenspan, MD

Star Shaped Pegs, Square Holes: Nonverbal Learning Disorders and the Growing Up Years. Kathy Allen. Order through the NLDline.com

Succeeding Against the Odds: How the Learning Disabled Can Realize their Promise. Sally Smith

Syndrome of Nonverbal Learning Disabilities: Neurodevelopmental Manifestations. Byron Rourke. This is the book for psychologists to use in identifying NLD. Helpful criteria from "one of their own"

The Nonverbal Learning Disorder Guide for Teachers, Parents, Employers, and Therapists. Rondalyn Varney Whitney, MOT, OTR. Order through ThelighthouseProject.com. Includes checklists for choosing a school, destressing the environment, criteria for the identification of NLD, developing an IEP for children with NLD, accommodations for home and school, and more

The Source for Nonverbal Learning Disorders. Sue Thompson. This is the book that saved my son's life. It explains NLD and gives information from the educational perspective to get you started. Other books have come out since that provide a more comprehensive approach and give a more hopeful prognosis, but Sue's book is still the bible of NLD

Why Zebras Don't Get Ulcers: A Guide to Stress, Stress-Related Diseases, and Coping. R. Sapolsky. Tells the importance of destressing your child

Math Help:
Math for Smarty Pants. Marilyn Burns

Math Wizardry for Kids. M. Kenda and P. Williams

Beyond Facts and Flashcards: Exploring Math with Your Kids. Janice Mokros

Games for Math. Peggy Kaye. Peggy Kaye is a tutor. Her books provide short lessons to build fundamental math concepts using fun games and activities. Kids love the games and they learn math skills they had previously struggled to integrate. The book also helps to identify the foundational skills missing so a more targeted approach can be applied.

Mathematical Power: Lessons from a Classroom. Ruth Parker. This is a great book on the importance of teaching "numeracy" or a basic intuitive understanding of mathematical information rather than rote learning. Very helpful, very instructive, based in research rather than opinion, and more important, it works.

Treatment Strategies:
Teaching the Tiger: A Handbook for Individuals Involved in the Education of Students with Attention Deficit Disorder, Tourette Syndrome or Obsessive Compulsive Disorder. M. P. Dornbush and S. K. Pruitt. Full of ideas, treatments, and accommodations

Games for Reading. Peggy Kaye

Games for Learning. Peggy Kaye

Games for Writing. Peggy Kaye

Inside Out: What Makes A Person with Social-Cognitive Deficits Tick? A Manual and Workbook. Michelle Garcia Winner. SLP order through Michelle at 4871 Trent Drive, San Jose, California 95124

Parenting:
Helping the Child Who Doesn't Fit In. Sal Severe

Raising a Thinking Preteen. Myrna Shure

Stress and Your Child: Helping Kids Cope with the Strains and Pressures of

Life. Betty Youngs. Tells you how to see if your child is stressed and what to do if they are. Gives practical advice for parents

Bringing Out the Best: A Resource Guide for Parents of Young Gifted Children. J. Saunders (This is one mailing list to get on—Free Spirit Press is an amazing resource. Their phone number is 612-338-2068)

The Optimistic Child: A Proven Program to Safeguard Children Against Depression and Build Lifelong Resilience. Martin Seligman. This book lives up to the promise in its title

Books That Provide Teaching Moments:

The King Who Rained by Fred Gwynne, Pub: Aladdin. A book that illustrates the nonverbal errors many of our children have by showing the humor behind raining kings and other oddities

Hands Are Not for Hitting by Martine Agassi, Pub: Free Spirit. Explains why we don't hit others and what we can do instead

The Honest Book About Lies by Jonni Kincher, Pub: Free Spirit. Explains many of the nonverbal rules of "fibbing"

How Rude!: The Teenagers' Guide to Good Manners, Proper Behavior, and Not Grossing People Out by Alex Pacher Pub: Free Spirit. Uses anecdotes and "teen-talk" to get the points across

Web Sites

NLDline.com
The original and most comprehensive Web site on NLD

NLDA.org
The official Web site of the Nonverbal Learning Disorder Association

The LighthouseProject.com
Web site with practical information, articles, and activities for NLD as well as information on therapeutic intensives for out-of-state clients.

www.kidpower.org
Kidpower International
PO Box 1212, Santa Cruz, CA 95061. 831-426-6997 Provides effective safety training for kids

www.theideabox.com
Great activity ideas to promote learning from teachers and therapists

www.nagc.org
The National Association for Gifted Children
Provides information and resources on addressing the giftedness of children

www.therapyshoppe.com
Therapy supplies for sensorimotor strategies (whistles, slant boards, seat cushions, and more)

www.ldonline.org
Rich site with *many* resources. Especially helpful are the pages and pages of accommodations and additional resources

- **www.ldonline.org/ld-indepth/special_education/peer-accommodations.html** (for general accommodations)

- **www.ldontine.org/ld-indepth/teaching-techniques/teaching-2.html** (for accommodations for teachers to use)

- **www.ldonline.org/ld-indepth/teaching-techniques/504-plans.html** (accommodations for 504 plans)

- **www.ldonline.org/ld-indepth/writing/dysgraphia.html** (accommodations for problems with handwriting)

- **www.idonline.org/ld-indepth/technology/nalldc-guide.html** (accommodations for adults)

www.sinetwork.org
Sensory Integration Resource Center
A wealth of research material on sensory integration issues

www.cde.ca.gov
keyword: Accommodations
This is the California Web site of our state educational department. It refers to the national law and provides a concise definition that distinguishes accommodations and modifications

www.puzzlemarker.com
For those homework assignments "make a crossword of your spelling homework . . ." This is a site designed by a student and it's great for kids to use for homework, gifts, etc.

www.neuropsychologycentral.com
Explains the details associated with neuropsychological testing, how to find a tester and questions to ask

www.ideapractice.org
Information on special education law, questions, and answers, links to other sources. Sponsored by the Council for Exceptional Children Leadership Initiative

Organizations

Nonverbal Learning Disorders Association
PO Box 220 Canton CT 06019-0220
email *NLDA@nlda.org*
fax: 860-693-3738
Annual symposium in April said to be the most comprehensive training opportunity and the most hopeful message sent regarding NLD. Symposia tapes available on the Web site

National Association for the Gifted
NAGC Membership
1707 L Street, NW, Suite 550
Washington, DC 20036

Appendix B:

Sensory Strategies

Sensory Strategies for Teachers

1. Help rearrange desks in the classroom

2. Fill egg crates (small ones that kids can carry) with books to take to other classrooms. Teachers could ask kids to move these crates back and forth as needed

3. Help the gym teacher move mats, hang them up, etc.

4. Chewy candy breaks (this addresses the janitor's "no gum rule"). There are lots of chewy candy that take a while to chomp and don't get stuck on other surfaces

5. Sharpen pencils with a manual sharpener

6. Have students carry heavy notebooks to the office or from class to class or wear a weighted backpack when walking from class to class. The rule of thumb is only add 5 percent of the child's body weight

7. Carry books with both hands, hugging the book to yourself

8. Tie Thera-Band around the front legs of a chair that a child can kick his legs against or wrap their legs around or push on

9. Have child pass out papers/objects to class members

10. If there is a garden project at the school, have child dig the dirt

11. Push against a wall

12. Open doors for people

13. Use blowing toys such as kazoos to soothe transitions. Children follow the teacher's rhythm to "get in sync" as a group

These ideas are a compilation from many therapists, collected to give teachers ideas for heavy-work activities. Heavy work can be very organizing for children.

Sensory Strategies for Parents

1. Carry heavy items (baskets with cardboard blocks, groceries for Mom, etc.)

2. Allow child to chew gum, eat chewy or crunchy foods, or sip water from a water bottle with a straw while doing homework

3. Yard work, including mowing the lawn, raking grass/leaves, pushing wheelbarrow

4. Housework, including vacuuming and mopping, carrying buckets of water to clean with, or to water flowers/plants/trees

5. Push a friend in a wheelbarrow

6. Milk shake or smoothie rewards sipped through a narrow straw (Smoothies: Add fruit juice to a blender, then frozen fruit such as strawberries, bananas, or peaches, and blend until smooth.) Milk shakes can be made from low-fat milk, fruit, and ice

7. Suck applesauce or yogurt through a straw

8. Have the child "help" by pushing in chairs to a table or push chairs into table after a meal

9. After a bath, parents can squeeze child and rub him/her briskly with a towel

10. Use heavy quilts at night and tight, flannel pajamas

11. Activities such as gymnastics, horseback riding, wrestling, karate

12. Carry the laundry basket

13. Go "camping" with a heavy blanket pulled across a few chairs. Child can help set up and take down the blanket

14. Push against a wall

15. Have the child color a "rainbow" with large paper on the floor or with sidewalk chalk outside while child is on her hands and knees

16. "Hot dog" game where child lies across end of a blanket and is rolled (ends up inside the rolled-up blanket with head outside)

17. "Sandwich" games (child is place between beanbags, sofa cushions, mattresses, and light pressure is applied to top layer)

18. Animal walks (crab walk, bear walk, army crawl)

19. Play "row, row, row your boat" both sitting on the floor, pushing and pulling each other

20. Two children can play "tug of war" with jump rope

21. Hide small toys in a large container of uncooked rice and let the child find them with their hands, guess what they've found but without looking.

22. Let your child carry in the groceries

23. Let your child water the garden by carrying gallon milk cartons full of water

24. Pile up every pillow you have in your home. Let your child run and jump into the pillows. Once they land, bury them in the pillows and give a squeeze—ask your child if they want more squeezing or are ready to run and jump again

25. Morning showers are very helpful for most children. It provides deep pressure, which can be very organizing in the mornings for children who have trouble with transitions

Strategies for Sensory Diet: The Older Child and Teen

Bean bag chairs (provides deep pressure)

Tight leotards or biker shorts (provides deep pressure)

Thera-Band (large rubber bands for exercise—provides proprioception)

Chair push-ups/wall push-ups (proprioception)

Tight hugs (self-delivered—provides deep pressure)

Oral strategies (pretzels, gum, gummy worms, etc.)

Chores (carry groceries, rake leaves, chop wood, push mower)

Sleep in sleeping bags

Use punching bags/bop dolls

Squeeze balls for the hands

Sew weights in the pockets of clothing for deep pressure

Shower/baths/swimming (provides deep pressure)

Wrestling/karate/fencing

Large trampoline

Hiking

It is important to train yourself, as the caregiver, to recognize "sensory homework" that is organizing and helps your child (of any age).

Glossary

504 plan—Over the past several years, educators have focused much effort on the role of classroom accommodations in addressing the special needs of students with learning difficulties. Section 504 of the Rehabilitation Act of 1973, an antidiscrimination law, obliges public schools to provide accommodations to students who have learning difficulties even if they do not qualify for special services under the Individuals with Disabilities Education Act (IDEA). Under Section 504, the meaning of "disability" is broader. A child is protected if he has any physical or mental condition that seriously limits a "major life activity." This means taking care of yourself, walking, seeing, hearing, or speaking. It also means breathing, learning, and working.

Although both **504** and **IDEA** legislation address students with attention, learning, and other difficulties, **504** has become the more global vehicle for accommodating children with unique needs, including ADHD or other health impairments. Only children who are also covered by IDEA are entitled to have one.

Accommodation—The Rehabilitation Act of 1973 provides certain education remedies (504 plans) for students with disabilities, but who are not part of the special education system. The concept and practice of "inclusion" has resulted in new challenges for teachers, administration, and parents to provide effective educational experiences for students. A building consensus supports the idea that the curriculum (what is intended that students learn) is not to be altered or modified for students who otherwise qualify for 504 plans.

What this means, in a practical sense, is that teachers and administrators must provide instructional and environmental accommodations for these students, **but that the curriculum is the same for all students (a modification).**

Activities of Daily Living (ADLs)—Self-maintenance tasks to include grooming, oral hygiene, bathing/showering, toilet hygiene, personal device care (glasses, contact lenses, contraception, etc.), dressing, feeding and eating, medication routine, health maintenance, socialization, functional communication, functional mobility, community mobility, emergency response, and sexual expression.

ADA—Americans with Disabilities Act of 1990. This law follows the principles established under Section 504. It provides for the protection from discrimination of persons with disabilities and allows claims for compensatory and punitive damages.

ADHD—Attention Deficit Hyperactive Disorder. A condition identified as a medical diagnosis by the American Psychiatric Association's Diagnostic and Statistical Manual III-Revised (DSM III-R). This condition is also often called Attention Deficit Disorder (ADD) because of that usage in a previous edition of DSM. Although it is not a service category under IDEA, children with this condition may be eligible for service under other categories or under Section 504.

Advocate—An individual who is not an attorney, but who assists parents and children in their dealings with school districts regarding the children's special education programs.

Annual Goals—A required component of an IEP. Goals are written for the individual student and can be for a maximum of one year.

Bilateral Integration—Coordinating both sides of the body during activity. See **Bilateral Psychomotor Coordination**

Bilateral Psychomotor Coordination—Coordinating both sides of the body during activity. See **Bilateral Integration**

Body Scheme—Acquiring an internal awareness of the body and the relationship of the body parts to each other.

Categorization—Identifying similarities of and differences among pieces of environmental information.

Cognitive—A term that refers to reasoning or intellectual capacity.

Cognitive Integration—The ability to use higher brain functions.

Concept Formation—Organizing a variety of information to form thoughts and ideas

Conduct Disorder—A psychological disorder defined by a pattern of behaviors beginning before age twelve marked by a defiance of authority, destruction of property, and disregard of others' needs. Observed cruelty to animals or bullying behaviors at an early age.

Disability—A physical, sensory, cognitive or affective impairment that causes the student to need special education. NOTE: *There are significant differences in the definitions of disability in IDEA and Section 504.*

Dyspraxia—The inability to conceive and plan a new motor act in response to an environmental demand.

Fine Motor Coordination/Dexterity—Using small muscle groups for controlling movements, particularly in object manipulation.

Form Constancy—Recognizing forms and objections as the same in various environments, positions, and space.

Generalization—Applying previously learned concepts and behaviors to a variety of new situations.

Gross Motor—Using large muscle groups for controlled, goal-directed movements.

Hyposensitive—A dysfunction of sensory integration in which sensations (auditory, tactile, olfactory, vestibular, proprioception, taste, vision) fail to create a response in a timely or typical manner.

IDEA—Individuals with Disabilities Education Act (IDEA—Act [Pub. L. 101-476]) enacted by Congress in 1975 The main premise of the IDEA requires states to provide each eligible child from 5–21 years of age, with a disability, a "free, appropriate public education" that is designed to meet their unique needs and prepare them for employment and independent living. In 1997, IDEA 97 (Pub. L. 105-117) made many changes to the law to strengthen it and help assure better compliance and understanding for both parents and schools.

IEP—Individual Educational Program. The IEP emphasizes an educational approach to meeting the student's needs through the provision of special education relation services The IEP is a federal, written document, developed and implemented at the school site by a team of individuals to include the parents, regular classroom teacher, special education teacher, special education administrator, and possibly other professions working on behalf of the child. Can also refer to the document developed at an IEP meeting that sets the standard by which subsequent special education services are usually determined appropriate.

IEP Meeting—A gathering required at least annually under IDEA in which an IEP is developed for a student receiving special education.

Initiation of Activity—Starting a physical or mental activity.

Laterality—Using a preferred unilateral body part for activities requiring a high level of skill.

Learning Disability—A difference in learning to read, write, compute, or do schoolwork that cannot be attributed to mental retardation or impairments of hearing or sight. An eligibility category under IDEA and described in detail within the statute.

Level of Arousal—Demonstrating alertness and responsiveness to environmental stimuli.

Level I Due Process Hearing—An administrative remedy for alleged violation of the rights of children with disabilities, which is created under the Illinois School Code. *Note: New procedures became effective July 1, 1997.*

Level II Due Process Hearing—An administrative remedy provided under the school code, which provides for appeal from Level I decisions. This remedy must normally be exhausted in order for a court to consider a special education matter. *Note: New procedures became effective July 1, 1997.*

Mainstreaming—This term does not actually appear in law. It refers to IDEA's preference for the education of every child in the least restrictive environment for each student and has been most widely used to refer to the return of children with mild disabilities to a regular classroom for a portion of each school day

Modification—A change of the curriculum to allow a child to perform work at his or her level but at a level below the class. A modification changes the assignment (do addition rather than multiplication), whereas an accommodation enables (do the multiplication tables orally rather than written) a child to demonstrate knowledge commensurate with peers.

Muscle Tone—Demonstrating a degree of tension or resistance in a muscle at rest and in response to stretch.

Nonverbal Cue—Information delivered via gesture, tone of voice, inflection, inference, proximity, objectics, touch, or other unspoken methods of communication.

Occupational Therapy—A special education related service that is usually focused upon the development of a student's fine motor skills and/or the identification of adapted ways of accomplishing activities of daily living when a student's disabilities preclude doing those tasks in typical ways (e.g., modifying clothing so a person without arms can dress himself/herself).

Postural Control—Using righting and equilibrium adjustments to maintain balance during functional movements.

Praxis—Conceiving and planning a new motor act in response to an environmental demand. Praxis includes the subcategories of ideation (coming up with an idea), motor planning (making a plan to move the body), and execution (acting). Children with NLD have difficulty with the execution stage of praxis.

Problem Solving—Recognizing a problem, defining a problem, identifying alternative plans, selecting a plan, organizing steps in a plan, implementing a plan, and evaluating the outcome.

Psychosocial Skills—The ability to interact in society and to process emotions. Includes psychological skills such as identifying ideas or beliefs that are important to self and others (value), identifying mental or physical activities that create pleasure and maintain attention (interests), and developing the value of the physical, emotional, and sexual self (self-concept). Social skills include identifying, maintaining, and balancing functions one assumes or acquires in society—worker, student, friend—(role performance) and interacting by using manners, personal space, eye contact, gestures, active listening, and self-expression (social conduct), using verbal and nonverbal communication to interact in a variety of settings (interpersonal skills) and using a variety of styles and skills to express thoughts, feeings, and needs (self-expression). Psychsocial skills also includes self-management such as identifying and managing stress and related factors (coping skills), planning and participating in a balance of self-care, work, leisure, and rest activities to promote satisfaction and health (time management) and modifying one's own behavior in response to environmental needs, demands, constraints, personal aspirations, and feedback from others (self-control).

Sensory Defensiveness—A sensory integrative dysfunction in which sensation (auditory, tactile, vestibular, proprioception, visual, olfactory, and taste) cause excessive emotional reactions, hyperactivity, or other behavioral problems.

Sensory Integration (SI)—The organization of sensory input for use. The "use" may be a perception of the body or the world, an adaptive response, a learning process, or the development of some neural function. Through sensory integration, the many parts of the nervous system work together so that a person can interact with the environment effectively and experience appropriate satisfaction. Field of study developed by Jean Ayres, PhD, OTR.

Sensory Modulation—According to Jean Ayres, PhD, OTR, sensory modulation describes the brain's ability to monitor its own activity. Modulation involves facilitating some neural messages to produce more of a perception or response and inhibit other messages to reduces excess or extraneous activity.

Sensory Processing—Interpreting sensory stimuli to include tactile, proprioceptive, vestibular, visual, auditory, gustatory, and olfactory aspects.

Short-Term Objectives—A required component of an IEP. Each annual goal must have at least one short-term objective.

Social-Cognition—Term popularized by Michelle Garcia Winner, SLP, to refer to the inability to take the perspective of another and organize thought (cognition) for good social interactions and social success.

Social-Cognitive Deficit—Refers to individuals who have difficulty with social cognition. Includes diagnoses such as NLD, Asperger's, autism, ADD, and ADHD.

Spatial Relations—Determining the position of objects relative to each other.

Stereognosis—Identifying objects through proprioception, cognition, and the sense of touch.

Strength—Demonstrating a degree of muscle power when movement is resisted, as with objects or gravity.

Syndrome—a group of signs and symptoms that collectively characterize a disorder.

Tactile Discrimination—Being able to discriminate the differences between objects and attributes of objects via the tactile (skin) system.

Tactile Memory—The ability to receive, store, and retrieve information gathered via the tactile system.

Tactile Perception—The ability to receive and understand information gathered via the tactile system, commonly referred to as "skin."

Termination of Activity—Stopping an activity at an appropriate time.

Topographical Orientation—Determining the location of objects and settings and the route to the location.

Transition Planning—At a minimum, this is planning for adolescents' post-school lives and must begin by age 14½. This involves preparation of a document called an Individual Transition Program (ITP). Good practice may involve planning for earlier transitions as well as incorporating such plans into the child's IEP.

Visual-Motor Integration—Coordinating the interaction of information from the eyes with body movement during activity. Coordination of what is seen with an action. For example, one uses visual-motor coordination when catching a ball.

Visual-Spatial-Organization—the ability to use the visual system to understand the relationships between objects in the environment (distance between chair and table, book and glass of milk) and organize movement so as to navigate among those objects. Also includes ability to then organize the items in the environment for proper use (such as papers and pencils organized for initiation of homework).

Work and Productive Activities—Purposeful activities for self-development, social contribution, and livelihood to include home management (clothing care, cleaning, meal preparation, and clean-up, shopping, money management, household management, household maintenance, and safety procedures), care of others, and educational activities.

Vocational Activities, and Play or Leisure Activities—Including exploration of play and leisure activities and performance of play and leisure activities.

Bibliography

Allen, K. (1995). *Star-Shaped Pegs, Square Holes: Non Verbal Learning Disorders and the Growing Up Years* NLDline.com.

Armstrong, Thomas (1987). In Their Own Way: Discovering and Encouraging Your Child's Personal Learning Style. G. P. Putman's Sons, NY.

Ayres, A. J. (1978). Learning disabilities and the vestibular system. *Journal of Learning Disabilities, 11 (1)*, 30–41.

—— (1979). *Sensory integration and the child*. Western Psychological Services. LA, CA.

—— (1994). *Sensory Integration and the Child*, 11th printing. Western Psychological Services. LA, CA.

—— (1969). Deficits in sensory integration in educationally handicapped children. *Journal of Learning Disabilities*, 2, 160–168.

Bader, B. W. (1975). *Social perception and learning disabilities*. Moon Lithographing & Engraving. Des Moines, IA.

Beck, J. (1986) How to Raise a Brighter Child: The Case for Early Learning. Pocket Books. NY.

Benowitz, L. I., D. M. Bear, R. Rosenthal, M. M. Mesulam, E. Zaidel, and Sperry (1983). Hemispheric specialization in nonverbal communication. *Cortex, 19*, 5–11.

Bireley, M. (1995) *Crossover Children: A Sourcebook for Helping Children Who Are Gifted and Learning Disabled*. Council for Exceptional Children. Reston, VA.

Brazelton, T. B. (1992). *Touchpoints: Your Child's Emotional and Behavioral Development*. Addison Wesley Publishing Company, New York.

Brumback, R. A., C. R. Harper, and W. A. Weinber (1996). Nonverbal learning disabilities, Asperger's syndrome, pervasive developmental disorder—should we care? *Journal of Child Neurology, 11 (6)*, 427–429.

Burns, M. (1982) *Math for Smarty Pants*. Little, Brown, and Co. Canada

Chandler, B. (1997). *The Essence of Play: A Child's Occupation*. American Occupational Therapy Association. Bethesda, MD.

Davis, C. (1997). *Complementary Therapies in Rehabilitation: Holistic Approaches for Prevention and Wellness*. Slack Incorporated. Thorofare, NJ.

Dornbush, M. P. and S. K. Pruitt (1995). *Teaching the Tiger: A Handbook for Individuals Involved in the Education of Students with Attention Deficit Disorder, Tourette Syndrome or Obsessive Compulsive Disorder*. Hope Press. Duarte, CA.

Duke, M., S. Norwici (1996). *Teaching Your Child the Language of Social Success*. Peachtree. Atlanta, GA.

Efferson, L. (1995). *Neurological Rehabilitation*, 3rd Edition. Umphred, D. A. Editor. Mosby-Year Book, Inc. St. Louis, MO.

Fink, G. R., J. C. Marshall, P. W. Halligan, C. D. Frith, R. S. Frackowiak, and R. J. Dolan. (April 22, 1997). Hemispheric specialization for global and local processing: the effect of stimulus category. *Biological Science, 264 (1381)*, 487–497.

Fisher, A. G. (1991). Vestibular-proprioceptive processing and bilateral integration and sequencing deficits. In Fisher A. G., E. A. Murray, & A. C. Bundy (Eds.), *Sensory Integration Theory and Practice* (pp. 69–107). Philadelphia: FA Davis.

Frankel, F. (1996). *Good Friends Are Hard to Find: Help Your Child Find, Make and Keep Friends*. Perspective Publishing. LA, CA.

Frick, S., R. Frick, P. Oetter, E. Richter. (1996). *Out of the Mouth of Babes: Discovering the Developmental Significance of the Mouth*. PDP Press. Hugo, MN.

Galbraith, J. (1984) *The Gifted Kids Survival Guide: For Ages 10 and Under*. Free Spirit Press. Minneoapolis, MN.

Geschwind, N., and A. M. Galaburda, (1985). Cerebral Lateralization: Biologic mechanisms, associations, and pathology. *Archives of Neurology, 42,* 428–459, 521–552, 634–654.

Gillberg, C., S. Steffenburg, G. Jakobsson. (1987). Neurobiological Findings in 20 Relatively Gifted Children with Kanner-type Autism or Asperger's Syndrome. *Developmental Medical Child Neurology* Oct. 29 (5). 641–9.

Glasser, W. (1986). Control Theory in the Classroom. Harper. NY.

Goleman, E. (1995). *Emotional Intelligence: Why It Can Matter More Than IQ*. Bantam Books. NY.

Gozdz, K. (1995). *Community Building: Renewing Spirit & Learning in Business*. New Leader Press. San Francisco.

Grandin, T. (1995). *Thinking in Pictures: and Other Reports from My Life with Autism*. Doubleday. NY.

Greene, Lawrence (1987). *Learning Disabilities and Your Child: A Survival Handbook*. Fawcett Columbine Books. NY.

Greenspan, S. (1993). *Playground Politics: Understanding the Emotional Life of your School Aged Child*. Addison Wesley. Reading, MA.

Healy, J. (1990). *Endangered Minds: Why Children Don't Think and What We Can Do About It*. Simon and Schuster. NY.

Izard, C. (1991). *The Face of Emotion*. Appleton-Century Crofts. NY.

Kaye, P. (1987). *Games for Math*. Pantheon Books. NY.

—— (1984). *Games for Reading*. Pantheon Books. NY.

—— (1991). *Games for Learning*. Pantheon Books. NY.

—— (1995). *Games for Writing*. Pantheon Books. NY.

Kenda, M and P. Williams, (1995). *Math Wizardry for Kids*. Scholastic Books. NY.

Klin, A., F. Folkmar, S. Sparrow, Eds. (2000). *Asperger Syndrome*. Guilford Press. NY.

Klin, A., S. S. Sparrow, F. R. Volkmar, D. V. Cicchetti, and B. P. Rourke. (1995). Asperger's syndrome. In B. P. Rourke (Ed.), *Syndrome of nonverbal learning disabilities; neurodevelopmental manifestations* (pp. 93–118). Guilford Press. NY.

Klin, A., F. R. Volkmar, S. S. Sparrow, D. V. Cicchetti, and B. P. Rourke. (1995). Validity and neuropsychological characterization of Asperger's syndrome: convergence with nonverbal learning disabilities syndrome. *Journal of Child Psychiatry, 36(7)*, 1127–1140.

Kranowitz, C. (1998). *The Out of Sync Child: Recognizing and Coping with Sensory Integration Dysfunction*. Penguin Putnam. NY.

Kurcinka, M. S. (1991). *Raising Your Spirited Child: A Guide for Parents Whose Child Is More Intense, Sensitive, Perceptive, Persistent, Energetic*. HarperCollins. NY.

Love, E. B., S. Nowicki Jr., and M. P. Duke (1994). The Emory Dyssemia Index: a brief screening instrument for the identification of nonverbal language deficits in elementary school children. *The Journal of Psychology, 128 (6)*, 703–705.

Minskoff, E. H. (1980). Teaching approach for developing nonverbal communication skills in students with social perception deficits. *Journal of Learning Disabilities, 13 (3)*, 118–124.

Mokros, J. (1996). *Beyond Facts and Flashcards: Exploring Math with Your Kids*. Heinemann. Portsmouth, NH.

Myklebust, H. R. (1975). Nonverbal learning disabilities: assessment and intervention. In H. R. Myklebust (Ed.), *Progress in learning disabilities* 3, 85–121. Grune & Stratton. NY.

Nowicki, S., and M. P. Duke (1992). *Helping the Child Who Doesn't Fit In.* Peachtree Publishers. Atlanta, GA.

Nowicki, S., and M. P. Duke (1992). The association of children's nonverbal decoding abilities with their popularity, locus of control, and academic achievement. *Journal of Genetic Psychology, 153 (4),* 385–393.

Nowicki, S., M. P. Duke, and E. A. Martin (1996). *Teaching Your Child the Language of Social Success.* Peachtree Publishers. Atlanta, GA.

Parham, D. L., and Z. Mailloux (1996). Sensory Integration. In J. Case-Smith, A. S. Allen, and P. N. Pratt (Eds.), *Occupational Therapy for Children* (3rd ed., pp. 307–356). Mosby. St. Louis, MO.

Parker, R. (1997). *Mathematical Power: Lessons from a Classroom.*

Pert, Candace (1997). *Molecules of Emotion: Why You Feel the Way You Feel.* Simon & Schuster. NY.

Ratey, J. (1997). *Shadow Syndromes: Recognizing and Coping with the Hidden Psychological Disorders That Can Influence Your Behavior and Silently Determine the Course of Your Life.* Pantheon Books. NY.

——— (2000). *User's Guide to the Brain: Perception, Attention, and the Four Theaters of the Brain.* Pantheon Books. NY.

Rein, R. (1994). *How To Develop Your Child's Gifts and Talents During the Elementary Years.* Contemporary Books. Chicago.

Rosen, Mark (1998). *Thank You for Being Such a Pain!* Random Three Rivers Press. NY.

Ross, E. D. (1993). Nonverbal aspects of Language. *Neurologic Clinics, 11 (1),* 9–23.

Rourke, B. (1988) The syndrome of nonverbal learning disabilities: developmental manifestations in neurological disease, disorder, and dysfunction. *The Clinical Neuropsychologist* 2:4, 293–330.

——— (1988). Socioemotional disturbances of learning disabled children. *Journal of Consulting and Clinical Psychology, 56,* 801–810.

——— (1989). A childhood learning disability that predisposes those afflicted to adolescent and adult depression and suicide risk. *Journal of Learning Disabilities, 22 (3),* 169–175.

——— (1989). *Nonverbal Learning Disabilities: the Syndrome and the Model.* Guilford Press. NY.

——— (1995). *Syndrome of Nonverbal Learning Disabilities: Neurodevelopmental Manifestations.* Guilford Press. NY.

Sapolsky, R. (1994). *Why Zebras Don't Get Ulcers: A Guide to Stress, Stress-Related Diseases, and Coping.* W. H. Freeman and Company. NY.

Saunders, J. (1991). *Bringing Out the Best.* Free Spirit Publishing. Minneapolis, MN.

Saunders, J., P. Esperland. (1991). *Bringing Out the Best: A Resource Guide for Parents of Young Gifted Children.* Free Spirit Press. Minneapolis, MN.

Seligman, M. (1995) *The Optimistic Child: A Proven Program to Safeguard Children Against Depression and Build Lifelong Resilience.* Harper Collins. NY.

Semrud-Clikeman, M., G. Hynd (1999). Right Hemispheric Dysfunction in Nonverbal Learning Disabilities: Social, Academic, and Adaptive Functioning in Adults and Children. Web site: Nonverbal Learning Disorder, NLDline.com.

Severe, S. (1999). *How to Behave So Your Children Will Too!* Greentree Publishing. Tempe, AZ.

Shapiro, L. (1998). *How to Raise a Child with a High EQ: A Parents' Guide to Emotional Intelligence.* Harper Perennial. NY.

Shoemaker, A. (March 31, 1997). Speech-language disorders impact quality of gestures. *Advance for Occupational Therapists,* 20.

Shure, Myrna. (1999). *Raising a Thinking Child Workbook: Teaching Young Children How to Resolve Everyday Conflicts and Get Along with Others.* Research Press.

———— (1997). *Raising a Thinking Child: Help Your Young Child to Resolve Everyday Conflicts and Get Along With Others: The "I Can Problem Solve" Program.* Henry Holt & Company. NY.

———— (1998). *Raising a Thinking Preteen: The "I Can Problem Solve" Program for 8–12 Year Olds.* Henry Holt & Company. NY.

Smith, S. (1991). *Succeeding Against the Odds: How the Learning Disabled Can Realize Their Promise.* Tarcher & Putnam. NY.

———— (1991). *Succeeding Against the Odds: How the Learning Disabled Can Realize Their Promise.* Tarcher Putnam. NY.

———— (1995). *No Easy Answers: The Learning Disabled Child at Home and At School.* Bantam Books. NY.

Springer, S. P. and G. Deutsch (1981). *Left Brain, Right Brain.* W. H. Freeman and Company. San Francisco.

Stancliff, B. (1997). *Smart, Honest, Trusting, Loving—What's the Problem?* OT Practice. August, 15–17.

Thompson, S. T. (1997). *The Source for Nonverbal Learning Disorders* LinguiSystems, Inc. East Moline, IL.

Tuttle, C. G. (1995, 1996). *Challenging Voices: Writings by, for and about People with Learning Disabilities.* Lowell House, LA, CA.

VanCleave, J. (1994). *Geometry for Every Kid.* John Wiley and Sons. NY.

Vaughn, S., N. Zaragoza, A. Hogan, and J. Walker (1993). A four-year longitudinal investigation of the social skills and behavior problems of students with learning disabilities. *Journal of Learning Disabilities,* 26 *(6),* 404–412.

Walker, S. Y. (1991). *The Survival Guide for Parents of Gifted Kids.* Free Spirit Press. Minneapolis, MN.

Whitney, R. (1997). *The Importance of Early Identification and Early Intervention with NLD: Strategies That Work.* Audiotape of presentation at NLD Symposium, Contemporary Medical Education. Danville, CA. www.NLDA.org.

—— (1999). *The NLD Guide for Parents, Teachers, Therapists, and Employers.* The Lighthouse Project. San Jose, CA.

—— (2000). *Strategies for Today: Hope for the Future.* Audiotape of presentation at 4th annual NLDA Symposium. Available through NLDA. Canton, CT. www.NLDA.org.

Whitney, Z. (1998). "Wrong School," in *Kids Write Through It!: Essays from Kids Who Have Triumphed Over Trouble.* Fairview Press, MN.

Winner, M. (2000). *Inside Out: What Makes a Person with Social-Cognitive Deficits Tick? A Manual and Workbook*

Youngs, B. B. (1985). *Stress and Your Child: Helping Kids Cope with the Strains and Pressures of Life.* Fawcett Columbine Books, NY.

Index

504 plan
  and Adam, 61–61
  description of, 271

Academic performance, and NLD, 22–23
Academic settings, and play, xi
Accidents, NLD child, 26, 31–32, 135–136, 139, 145–146, 148–149
Accommodations
  description of, 271–272
  IEP, 211–212
  NLD-friendly schools, 199–200
  purpose of, 219–220
"Acting out," NLD, 11
Activities of daily living (ADLs)
  complexity of, 41
  description of, 272
  teaching, 121–122, 235–236, 239–240
  and vision therapy, 243–244
Activity. See Termination of activity
Adam, NLD diagnosis, 59–62
Addendum, IEP, 212
Adults, with NLD, 175
Advocate
  description of, 272
  NLD child, 160–161
  of parents, 159
  school system, 156
Allen, George, 227

Allen, Kathy, 122
American Occupational Therapy Association, NLD referrals, 225
Americans with Disabilities Act of 1990, 272
Amusement parks, NLD child, 119–120
Annual evaluation, IEP, 212
Annual goals, IEP, 210–211, 213, 272
Anti-anxiety medication, 56, 71
Anxiety
  function of, 151–152
  and NLD, 11, 70–71
  and NLD child, 151, 152
Apology
  NLD child, 117
  of parents, 105
Appearance, and NLD child, 124, 173–174
Arousal. See Level of arousal
Asimov, Isaac, 143
Asperger's syndrome (AS), vii, 71, 72–73, 74
Attention Deficit Disorder (ADD), vii, 15, 69–70
Attention Deficit-Hyperactivity Disorder (ADHD)
  description of, 272
  and NLD, vii, 15, 56, 69–70
Auditory perception, 15, 239
Auerbach, Red, 227
Autism, 72–73

Avoidance behavior, 27–28, 110
Ayres, Jean, 275

"Bad behavior," 33, 52, 62
Balance, and NLD, 26
Bedtime, and NLD child, 41–43
Bedtime stories, 42, 116
Behavior modification, 101–102
  and NLD, 4, 7, 9, 11, 103, 245–247
"Behavior problems," 11, 12, 239
Behaviorism, 101
Benbow, Mary, 252
Bilateral Integration, 272
Bilateral psychomotor coordination,
  description of, 272
Birthday parties, and NLD child, 177–178
Blazing Saddles, 165
Board games, 130
Body, right to one's own, 162
Body scheme, description of, 272
Boundaries, 121
Brain
  development of, 75–76
  NLD development, 9, 223, 224
Bribes, 5, 6
Bullies, and NLD child, 35–36, 142–143,
  150–151, 153–155

Categorization, description of, 272
Charlotte's Web, 131
Children
  explain NLD diagnosis, 80–83
  sensory strategies, 269–270
Children's Health Council, diagnosis, 8, 13
Classrooms, NLD accommodations, 200–201
Clinical depression, description of, 152
Cocoon, 126
Cognitive integration, 272
Cognitive processing, 241
"Collapsing the curriculum," 203, 250
Communication, nonverbal, 15. *See also*
  Nonverbal communication
Community
  depression prevention, 150
  and NLD child, 92, 99–100
Compliance, and NLD child, 47, 102, 144
Concept formation
  description of, 273
  and NLD, 17
Conduct disorder, 273
Connections, and NLD, 18
Contingency plans, 162
"Controlling" behavior, 28, 109–111
Cooking, 186, 235

Correcting adults, 45–46, 104
"Correction chips," 46
Creative thinking, and play, xi
Cue, 241
Curious, NLD child, 116

Daniel, NLD diagnosis, 56–59
Denial, parental response, 77, 79, 81
Depression
  and NLD, 5, 11, 12
  of parents, 77
  prevention of, 149–150, 151
Developmental delays, and NLD, 24
*Diagnostic and Statistical Manual of Mental
  Disorders, 4th edition (DSM-IV)*, 68, 72
Dialogue, and NLD, 18
Dilbert Newsletter, 48
Disability, description of, 273
Discipline
  and NLD child, 97, 101–103
  in school, 201–202
"Down-time," 24, 96
Driving, and NLD child, 119
Dysgraphia, 251
Dyslexia, ix, 34
Dyspraxia, 273

Educational consultant, IEP, 213–214
Ego development, 99
Einstein, Albert, 221–222
Emergencies, practice for, 161–162
Emotional injuries, NLD child, 144
Emotional safety, 149–153
Estrogen, 238
Evil, recognition of, 158–159
Expectations, appropriate, 106
Explanations
  IEP provisions, 214–215
  NLD diagnosis, 107–108
"Explanatory style," 149
Exploratory behavior, and NLD, 25, 171–172
Eye contact, NLD child, 171–172

Facial expressions, 23, 167
  and NLD child, 171
Fair Hearing Court, IEP, 216–217, 218, 274
Falling, 3, 31–32, 148–149, 237. *See also*
  Accidents
Farting, rules of, 164–165
Feedback, and NLD, 17
Fine motor coordination, 273
Following directions, 28–29
Form A, IEP, 210
Form B, IEP, 210–211

Form C, IEP, 210, 211–212
Form constancy, description of, 273
Friendships, NLD child, 176–181

Galway, Tim, 227
Generalization, 273
  and NLD, 24, 106, 182
Gestures, 23, 167
Gifted Association. *See* National Association
  for the Gifted
Gifted programs, and NLD child, 250
Good parent, and responsible parent, 98, 132
Graphomotor skills, and NLD, 26, 27. *See*
  also Handwriting
Greenspan, Stanley, 179
Grief, parental response, 9, 10, 13, 77, 78
Grooming
  and NLD child, 23, 34–35, 173–174
  as self-care, 78
  "teaching moments," 124–125
Gross motor function, description of, 273
Gross motor skills, development of, 234–235
"Guess the Emotion," 232

Handwriting (graphomotor skills), and NLD,
  26, 27, 55, 62, 204, 250–252
Handwriting Without Tears, 251–252
Harry Potter, 187
Head injuries, and NLD, 15, 146–147
Helping the Child Who Doesn't Fit In, 168
High sensory threshold, 19–21
Hobbit, The, 132
Home
  child-friendly, 186–187
  safety risks, 146, 147
Home schooling, 157, 202
Homework
  label of, 233
  and NLD child, 39–41, 202–203
  and therapy, 232
Homework jar, 232
Hospitals, NLD referrals, 225
Humor, NLD child, 48–49
Hygiene, 23, 173–174
Hyposensitive, definition of, 273
Hypothesis testing, and NLD, 17

Idioms, 21
Idiosyncracies, 126–127, 141
Independent diagnosis, 66–67
Individualized Educational Program (IEP),
  and bullies, 155
  conflict resolution, 215–218
  for Daniel, 59

description of, 208–209, 273–274
enforcement, 215
explain to child, 214–215
grading, 203
guidelines for, 212–213
for Jennifer, 55
parts of, 210–212
play skills, 178–179
for Zachary, 141, 148, 149, 160
Individualized Educational Program (IEP)
  meetings, 274, 207, 214–215
  team, selection of, 209–210
Individuals with Disabilities Education Act
  (IDEA), 67, 208, 273
Information, on NLD, x, 92–93
Initiation of activity, 274
"Insult Me Game, The," 256
Integrity, NLD child, 48
Intellectual lives, fostering, 127–130
Interdisciplinary social skills group,
  184–185
Interests, developing, 179–180
Interpersonal distance
  NLD child, 169–170
  rules of, 121, 167
Interventions
  NLD, 10–11, 223–224
  therapies, 237–247
Invisible rules, 154, 187–188

Jack and the Beanstalk, 254
Jennifer, NLD diagnosis, 53–56

Karate, 163, 248, 249–250
Kidpower, 163

Language, and NLD, 16, 49, 103–105,
  245
Language retrieval, and NLD child, 241–
  242
Language therapy, value of, 241–242
Laterality, 274
Learning, and NLD child, 128–130
Learning disability, viii, 14, 274
Learning disorder, viii, 14
Left brain hemisphere, 9
Level I/II due process hearing, 274
Level of arousal, 274
Life skills. *See* Activities of Daily Living
  (ADLs)
Literal speech, and NLD child, 43–45
Logic, and NLD child, 83, 103–105
Loops and Groups, 252
Low sensory threshold, 19, 20, 25

Mainstreaming, 274
Manny, NLD child, 228–229
Math skills, teaching, 91, 129–130
McVeigh, Timothy, 158
Measurement, and NLD, 23
Mechanical arithmetic, and NLD, 19
Medication, and NLD child, 71, 152–153, 245
Meltdowns
  clothing, 174
  at home, 5, 39, 42, 91, 112, 139
  at school, 4
  sensory modulation, 138
  shopping, 136
  social occasions, 109
Memory, and NLD, 15, 22
Mental retardation, and NLD, 15, 69
Metaphors, 21
Miami Vice, 174
Modification, 274
"Mommy's boy," 4, 6
Money
  and NLD, 23
  and treatment plan, 88–89
"Monkey brain," 100–101
Monologues, NLD child, 46
Mortal Combat, 137
Motor skill
  development of, x–xi
  and NLD, ix–x, 15, 22, 26
Movement, and NDL, xii, 38
"Movement breaks," 232
Muscle tone, 26, 274

National Association for the Gifted, 203, 250, 266
National Association of Speech Therapists, NLD referrals, 225
Neurological deficit, viii
Neurological development, xi
Nonverbal communication
  deficit types, 167–168
  and NLD, 15, 23, 166–167
Nonverbal cues, 9, 15
Nonverbal Learning Disabilities, 10
Nonverbal Learning Disorder (NLD)
  adult insensitivity to, 159–161
  assets/strengths, 15–16
  causation, ix–x
  diagnosis, 10, 11–12, 52–68
    Adam, 59–62
    Jennifer, 53–56
    John, 56–59
    Zachary, 8, 9, 13

functional description, 21–29
genetic component, ix
as gift, 83–84, 91
misdiagnosis of, 68–74
personal definition, 29–30
prevalence of, ix
prognosis, 10, 76
resources, 261–266
syndrome of, ix, 14–16
technical definition, 16–19
treatment plan, 88–94
Nonverbal Learning Disorder Association (NLDA), 62, 266
Novelty, and NLD, 17, 24, 37, 247
Nowicki, Steve, 166, 173

Objectics
  description of, 167
  and NLD child, 173–174
Obsessive-compulsive behaviors, and NLD, 11
Obsessive-Compulsive Disorder (OCD), and NLD, 15, 69, 70
Occupational therapist
  and ADLs, 239–240
  description of, 274–275
  NLD referrals, 225
  school assessment, 64
  value of, 237
  vision training, 242–243
Occupational therapy social skills group, 181, 183
Oppositional Defiance Disorder (ODD), 44, 56, 70
Optimism, 150
Optimistic Child, The, 149–150
Organizational capacity, and NLD, 17
Organizational skills, teaching, 122–123
Originality, and NLD, 24

Paralanguage, description of, 167
Parallel processing, 241
Parent Effectiveness Training, 98
Parent groups, 236
Parenting
  criticism of NLD, 113–114
  an NLD child, 97–98, 114–116
  therapeutic activity, 230–233
Parents
  and child injuries, 146
  and psychotherapy, 245
  response to NLD, 9–10, 33, 49, 76, 77
  sensory strategies, 268–269

Paul, NLD adult, 175
Persistence, NLD child, 114–115
Pervasive Development Disorder (PDD), 73
Physical safety, NLD child, 144, 145–149
Pinky and the Brain, 84
Play
  and NLD, 28
  role of, xi, 179
Play skills, NLD child, 178–179, 181
Playdates, NLD child, 176–177
Playgrounds, safety risks, 147–148
Polite requests, 44–45
Postural control
  Britt, 118–119
  definition, 275
Posture, 23, 167
"Practice Random Acts of Kindness," 200
Pragmatic language therapy, 242
Praxis, description of, 275
Previews, and NLD child, 108–109, 177
"Problem child," 112
Problem solving, 275
  and NLD, 17, 23
"Psychological immunization," 149–150
Psychology social skills group, 181, 182
Psychomotor coordination, and NLD, 17, 27
Psychosocial skills, description of, 275
Psychotherapy, use of, 182, 244–245
Punishment, 97, 102

Ratey, John, 75–76
Ravi, interpersonal distance deficit, 169–170, 172
Readin's Fine But Handwritin's a Disaster!, 252
Reading
  appropriate material, 131–132
  pleasure of, 49
Reading comprehension, and NLD, 19, 23
Reasoning, and NLD, 23
Rehabilitation Act of 1973, 271
Rehearsals, and NLD child, 108–109
Repetition, 106–107
Reports, reviewing diagnostic, 65–66
Resources, treatment plan, 88–93
Responsible parent, 98
Responsibility, and NLD child, 139
Rest times, 137
Rewards, behavioral modification, 5–6, 11
Rhythm, 23, 167
Right brain hemisphere, 9, 22
Ritalin, 56, 158, 238
Robotics, laws of, 143

Role acquisition, and play, xi
Rote behavior, and NLD, 17
Rote learning, and NLD, 23
Rourke, Byron, 10
  meeting with, 255–256
  NLD criteria, 16–17, 18–19
  NLD dynamics, 15
Routine, and NLD, 15
Rules
  adult behavior, 159
  on bullies, 154–155
  invisible, 157, 187–188
  "NLD," viii, 86
  and NLD child, 47, 103–104, 115, 140
  playdates, 177
RUMBA, IEP goals, 210, 217
Running away, in kindergarten, 5, 8

Safety
  awareness, 26, 144–145
  emotional, 149–153
  judgments, 161
  physical, 145–149
Schools. (*See also* Teachers)
  as changing environments, 191
  and IEP, 208–209, 217
  and NLD accommodations, 198–204
  and NLD diagnosis, 62–66, 67–68
  reducing stress of, 141
  safety risks, 147–149
  unsafe, 156–157
Schoolwork, and NLD child, 37–39
Schreier, Herbert, 74
Segues, and NLD, 18
Self, NLD child's view of, 29
Self-advocacy, NLD child, 160–161
Self-care, parental, 77–78, 231–232
Self-deprivation, NLD child, 25
Self-esteem, 150
"Self-talk," 23, 39, 123
Seligman, Martin, 149–150
Sensorimotor skills
  and NLD, 16
  and play, xi
Sensory defensiveness, description of, 275
Sensory integration (SI), 238, 275–276
  dysfunction, and NLD, 15, 19, 24, 69, 238–239
  therapy, 239
Sensory modulation
  description of, 276
  and NLD child, 137–138
Sensory processing, description of, 276

Sensory registration, and NLD, 19–20
Sensory strategies, 267–270
Sesame Street, x
Setbacks, 180–181, 204–206
Sexual abuse, NLD child, 144, 145
Sexuality
  and NLD child, 120–121
  "teaching moments," 125
Short-term objectives, 276
Siblings
  of NLD child, 111, 112
  and psychotherapy, 245
Simpsons, The, 89, 130–131, 232
Skinner, B. F., 101
Sleeping, NLD child, 42
Social distance, and NLD, 23
Social relationships, and NLD, xii, 201
Social skills
  assessment of, 64
  development of, x, xi, 161
  and neurological deficits, 168–172
  and NLD, ix–x, 23, 166–167, 201
  and NLD child, 170–171
Social skills group
  limitations of, 185–186
  types of, 181–185
Social-cognition, 276
Social-cognitive deficit
  description, 276
  NLD child, 175
Socialization, and play, xi
Source for Nonverbal Learning Disorders, The, 10, 144
Space, nonverbal rules of, 121, 167, 169–170
Spanking, 102
Spatial orientation, and NLD, 16, 28
Spatial relations, 276
Special needs, 208
Speech prosody, and NLD, 18, 23–24
Speech therapists, NLD referrals, 225
Speech therapy, 241–242
  social skills group, 181, 182
Spouse, educating one's, 79–80
"Standby assist," 147, 148
Star-Shaped Pegs in Round Holes, 122
Star Wars, 132
Stereognosis, 276
Strength, 276
Stress
  description of, 140–141
  and NLD, 11, 24, 35
  and NLD child, 152
Stress reduction strategies, 135–141

Stuart Little, 132
Student Study Team, school diagnosis, 63–64
Suicidal ideation
  NLD, 10, 12
  NLD child, 7, 155
Superman, 125
Support system
  parental, 78
  treatment plan, 90–92
Survival skills, and NLD, 23. _See also_ Activities of Daily Living (ADLs)
Swimming, 248, 249
Syndrome, description of, 276

Tactile deficits, NLD, 16
Tactile discrimination, 276
Tactile imperceptions, and NLD, 25–26, 37–39, 71–72
Tactile memory, 276
Tactile perception, 276
Talk therapy, use of, 244–245
Teacher social skills group, 181, 183–184
Teachers
  abusive, 155–156
  injury recognition, 148–149
  and NLD accommodations, 200
  sensory strategies, 267–268
"Teaching moments," 124–126
Team sports, use of, 248
Television, use of, 130–131
Termination of activity, 276
Testosterone, 160
Therapist
  educator role, 233–234
  selection of, 225–230
Therapy
  role of, 224
  types of, 237–247
Thompson, Sue, 10, 11, 144
Thresholds, sensory, 19–21
Time
  and NLD, 18, 23, 167
  and NLD child, 44, 135–140
  treatment plan, 89–90
Tom Sawyer, 19
Tomo, social skills deficit, 170, 171, 172
Tone, 23
Tony, theatrical interests, 180
Tooth brushing, 41
Topographical orientation, 276
Touching, rules of, 121
Tourette's Syndrome, and NLD, 15, 69, 70
"Train Ride to Hogwarts parties, A," 187
Transition planning, 276

Travel, and NLD child, 140
Treatment plan, NLD, 88–94
Tutoring, 247–248
Twain, Mark, 164, 165

Unconditional love, ego development, 99
User's Guide to the Brain, The, 75–76

Verbal capacity, and NLD, 18, 53
Victims, NLD children, 36
Vision therapy, 242–244
Visual attention, and NLD, 28
Visual memory, and NLD, 55
Visual-motor integration, description of, 277
Visual-perceptual development, and NLD, xii, 28–29
Visual-spatial integration, NLD child, 170
Visual-spatial organization, 277
Visual-spatial skills, NLD, ix–x, 17
Vocational activities, 277
Voice tone, 15, 167
  NLD child, 168–169

Websites, NLD resources, 264–266
Weschler intelligence test (WISC), 64
Withdrawal, NLD, 10, 12
Wooden, John, 227
Work, adult roles, 190–191
Work/productive activities, 277
Workshops, NLD, 236
Written expression, and NLD, 23, 39–40
"Wrong School," 253

Zachary
  animal balloons, 180
  apology of, 117
  auditory sensitivity, 239
  on being late, 2
  and the bully, 142–143
  car wash, 43–44
  on clumsiness, 50–51
  compliance of, 47
  concept formation deficit, 17–18
  correcting adults, 45–46
  first grade experience, 193–197
  fourth grade experience, 204–206
  fifth grade experience, 206
  hide-and-seek, 133–134
  homework, 39–40
  honesty of, 48
  kindergarten experiences, 3–8, 33, 37, 191–193
  lawn mowing, 85–86
  learning a script, 189
  math problem, 95–96
  monkey bars, 31–32, 148–149
  NLD diagnosis, 8–9, 13
  Popsicle purchases, 36, 153–154, 155
  science writing project, 253–254
  second/third grade experience, 197–198, 204
  sense of humor, 48–49, 74
  speech therapy, 221–222
  trash removal, 44
  voice tone deficit, 168